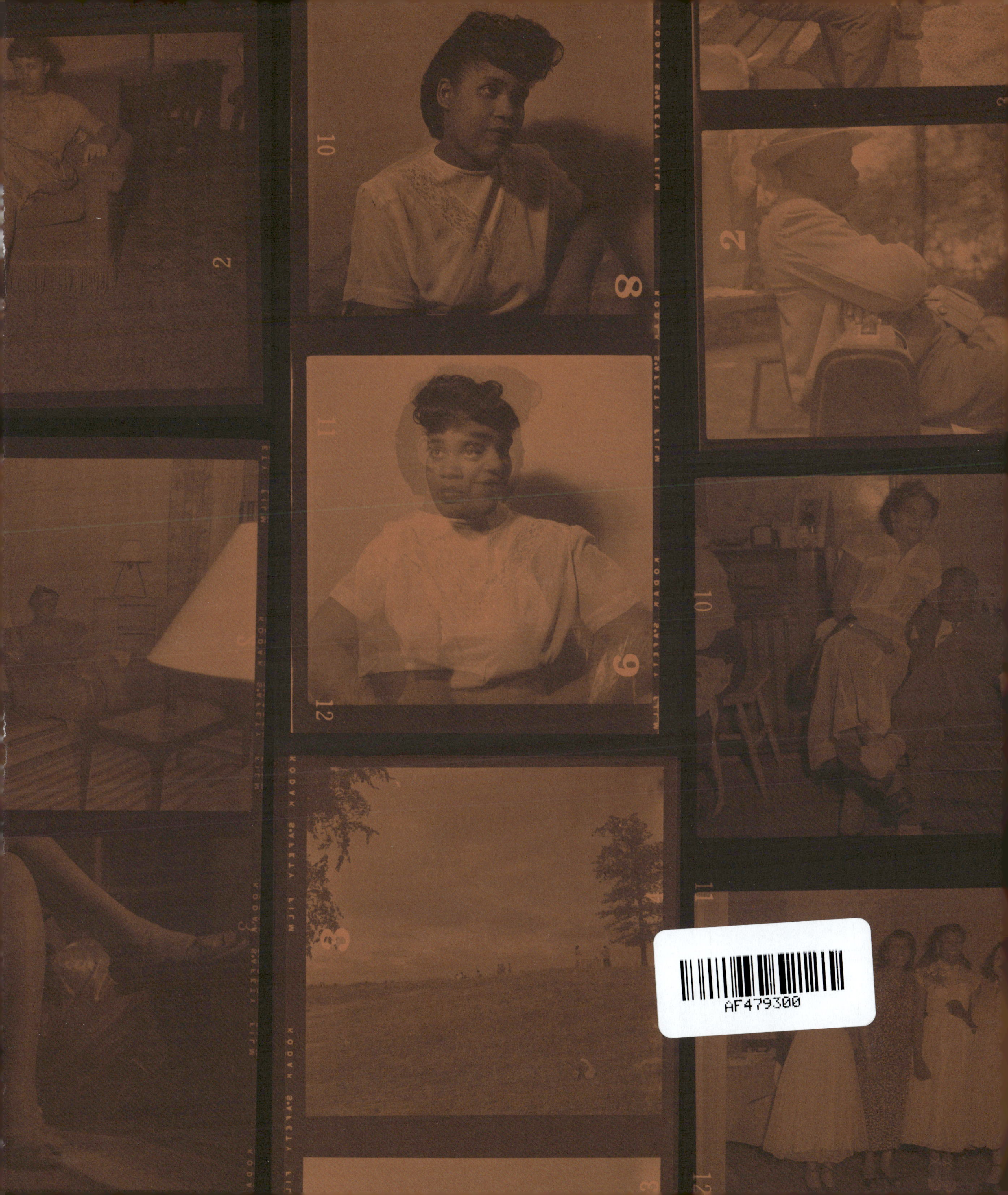
AF479300

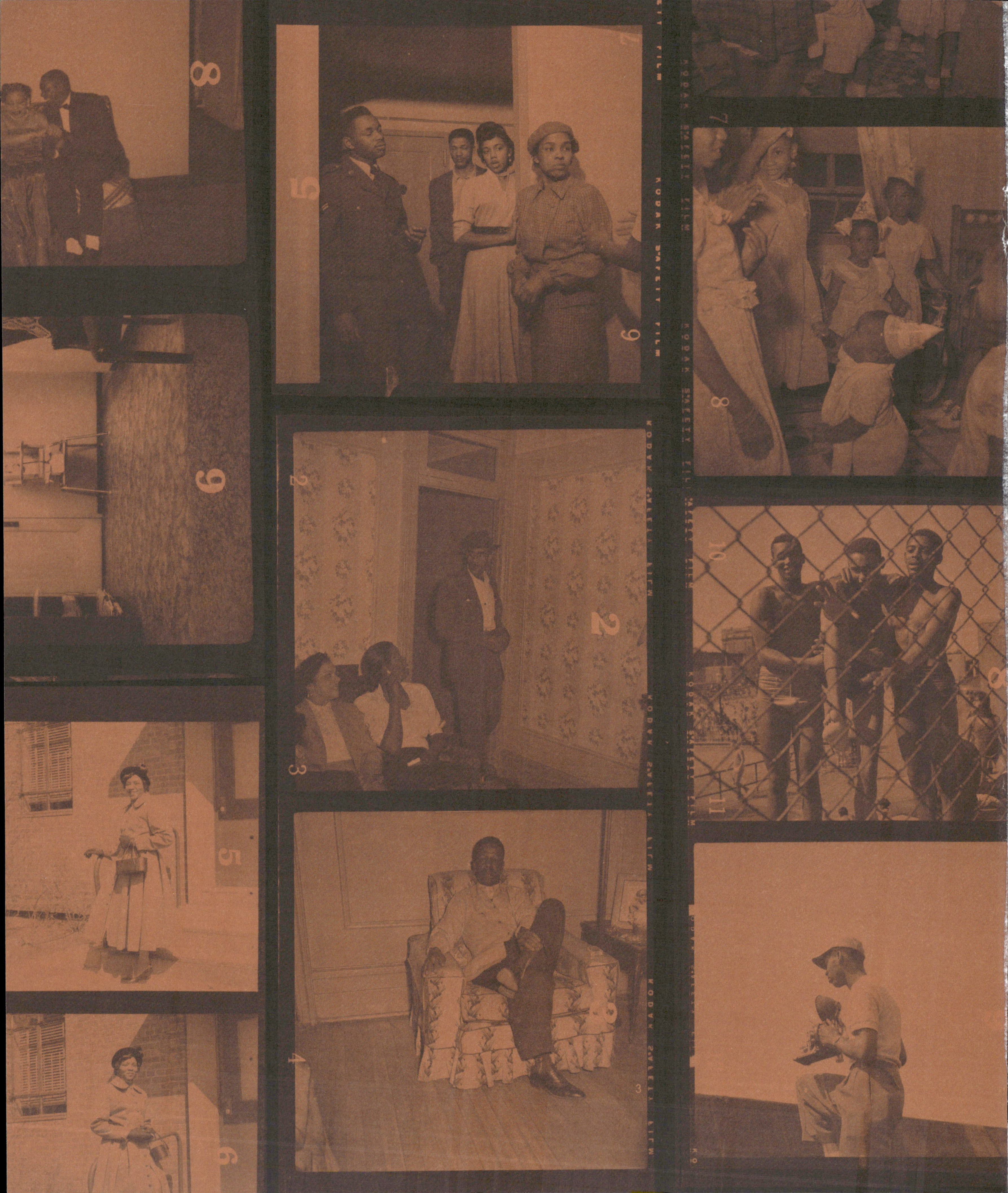

# Darrel Ellis

# Darrel Ellis

Derek Conrad Murray

Tiana Reid

Sadie Barnette

Alanna Fields

S*an D. Henry-Smith

Paul Mpagi Sepuya

Ariel Goldberg

Steven G. Fullwood

Visual AIDS, New York

# Contents

# Foreword

At the heart of Visual AIDS' mission is the charge to "preserve a legacy," but this isn't just one clear directive. For a small nonprofit with a deep sense of care and thirty-plus years of experience invested in this work, preserving an artist's cultural contribution is a unique project each time. We provide a support system and a platform for a network of family, friends, lovers, curators, art galleries, advocates, collectors, scholars, and many others— a group that forms organically over time and is different for each individual artist. Visual AIDS is also an archival resource for artists living with HIV and estates of artists who have been lost to AIDS; often, we are the only available resource in our ambitions to preserve images of artworks, biographic information, and ephemera with the hopes of sharing these with a wider audience through our website, exhibitions, commissioned videos, activist broadsheets, public events, and publications like this one.

In the case of an artist such as Darrel Ellis, who died at the height of the AIDS crisis at only thirty-three years old, on the verge of success but without gallery representation or financial means to support his work, the preservation of his legacy fell initially to family and friends. In consultation with Ellis's family, artist, curator, and writer Allen Frame took the extraordinary step of archiving and preserving hundreds of Ellis's artworks along with notebooks and ephemera in a storage space in the Bronx for nearly thirty years, not knowing when or where this body of work might find its place in the world. Throughout the history of the AIDS pandemic, woven between the stories of incalculable loss, we encounter many narratives like this, of family and friends going the extra mile to ensure that a loved one is not forgotten. This book, and the current rediscovery of Ellis by the art world—including gallery shows and a slate of museum exhibitions—would not have been possible without Allen's multi-decade dedication to this project. We are indebted to his commitment, and the vision he put forward in his 1996 retrospective of Ellis's work at Art in General and its accompanying catalog, which provided an important source of inspiration and scholarship for many of our contributors.

In 1994, two years after Ellis's death, artist Frank Moore and writer David Hirsh created the Archive Project, soon after housed at Visual AIDS, with the goal of preserving images of artworks created by artists living with HIV and AIDS, so that their work would not be lost to history. Allen Frame, who was already involved with Visual AIDS through his role in the Visual AIDS Artist Caucus and the creation of the Red Ribbon, provided a selection of Ellis's work to be archived in slide form when the Archive Project began. The work made a lasting impression on all who saw it, and the idea to create a monograph was discussed over many years. A 2018 grant from the Andy Warhol Foundation for the Visual Arts finally made it possible.

We are excited to share this publication, which provides the most comprehensive account of Ellis's work to date, including eighty plates, new critical essays by scholars Derek Conrad Murray, Tiana Reid, and Steven G. Fullwood, an illustrated chronology featuring never-before-seen excerpts from the artist's journals, an examination of Ellis's unique photographic process, and a roundtable discussion with artists Sadie Barnette, Alanna Fields, S*an D. Henry-Smith, and Paul Mpagi Sepuya, moderated by Ariel Goldberg, providing new insights into Ellis's legacy and the impact of his work today.

Ellis's work is complicated in many ways, both in its multiplicity of mediums (drawing, painting, experimental photography) and in its subject matter and relationship to identity and loss. His fascination with reclaiming a family history lost to him through the tragic death of his father, along with his desire to wrest his own image from the hands of successful white artists, has always contributed to the power of his work. However, it took on even greater resonance in 2020, as we were finalizing the writing for this book and planning its shape and form. Not only was the world reeling from the effects of the COVID-19 pandemic, but the United States was ignited by a powerful activist reckoning against racism and white supremacy. Revisited in the context of the Black Lives Matter movement, Ellis's story underscores the long history and lasting impact of police violence against communities of color, and the essential work that still needs to be done to address the whitewashing of AIDS cultural histories.

While our work often focuses on illness and death, one of the joys in Visual AIDS work is building relationships with the families of artists who have passed away, providing them with a platform to remember, share their loved ones' lives, and create community. We have greatly enjoyed getting to know Darrel's brother, Thomas, and his sisters, Katrina and Laure. In relation to Darrel's legacy, his family plays several key roles—as stewards and siblings, but also as subjects depicted in his artwork. The family's insights and anecdotes have been invaluable in helping us understand the essential family images at the core of Ellis's work.

In addition to the Ellis family, there are many people to thank for bringing this book to life. We are grateful to Allen Frame, James Wentzy, Susan Crowe, Whitfield Lovell, John Ahearn, Joe Lewis, and Peter Galassi, who generously shared their reflections and memories of Darrel with us, and to David Hirsh, who shared his 1991 interview with Ellis, making it possible for us to center Darrel's voice in this book. For their insights and deep engagement with Ellis's work, we thank the contributors, as well as editor Lara Mimosa Montes and Visual AIDS Programs Director Kyle Croft, who have guided this project with great care.

Special thanks to Christopher Burke Studio for its generosity and detailed photography of Ellis's artwork. We also thank Candice Madey, Cay Sophie Rabinowitz of OSMOS, Leslie Cozzi, Cecilia Wichmann, Linda Owen, and Scott Homolka of the Baltimore Museum of Art, Giorgia Von Albertini of Fundaziun Not Vital, Andrés Kapor Prije of Galerie Crone, the Peter Hujar Archive, Laurence Miller Gallery, Sebastian Daub, Ron Clark, Francie Lyshak, Steven Harvey, and George Steinberg for their assistance in gathering images and information for this book, as well as Brandon Eng, who has diligently cataloged and researched Ellis's oeuvre and compiled the illustrated chronology.

For their help in bringing this book from concept to reality, we thank Todd Bradway, Robert Reicher, and Miles Champion, as well as Alex Fialho and Tiona Nekkia McClodden for their advice along the way. We are also incredibly grateful to the design team of Polymode— Silas Munro and Brian Johnson—for their creativity, heartfelt passion for the material, deep understanding of the importance of the preservation of legacy, and commitment to excellence.

Finally, we thank the Andy Warhol Foundation for the Visual Arts and Furthermore: a program of the J. M. Kaplan Fund for providing the funding that made this book possible.

Esther McGowan
*Executive Director*, Visual AIDS

*Untitled* (Self-Portrait after Allen Frame Photograph)
ca. 1990
Ink and wash on paper
23 × 15 inches
Private collection

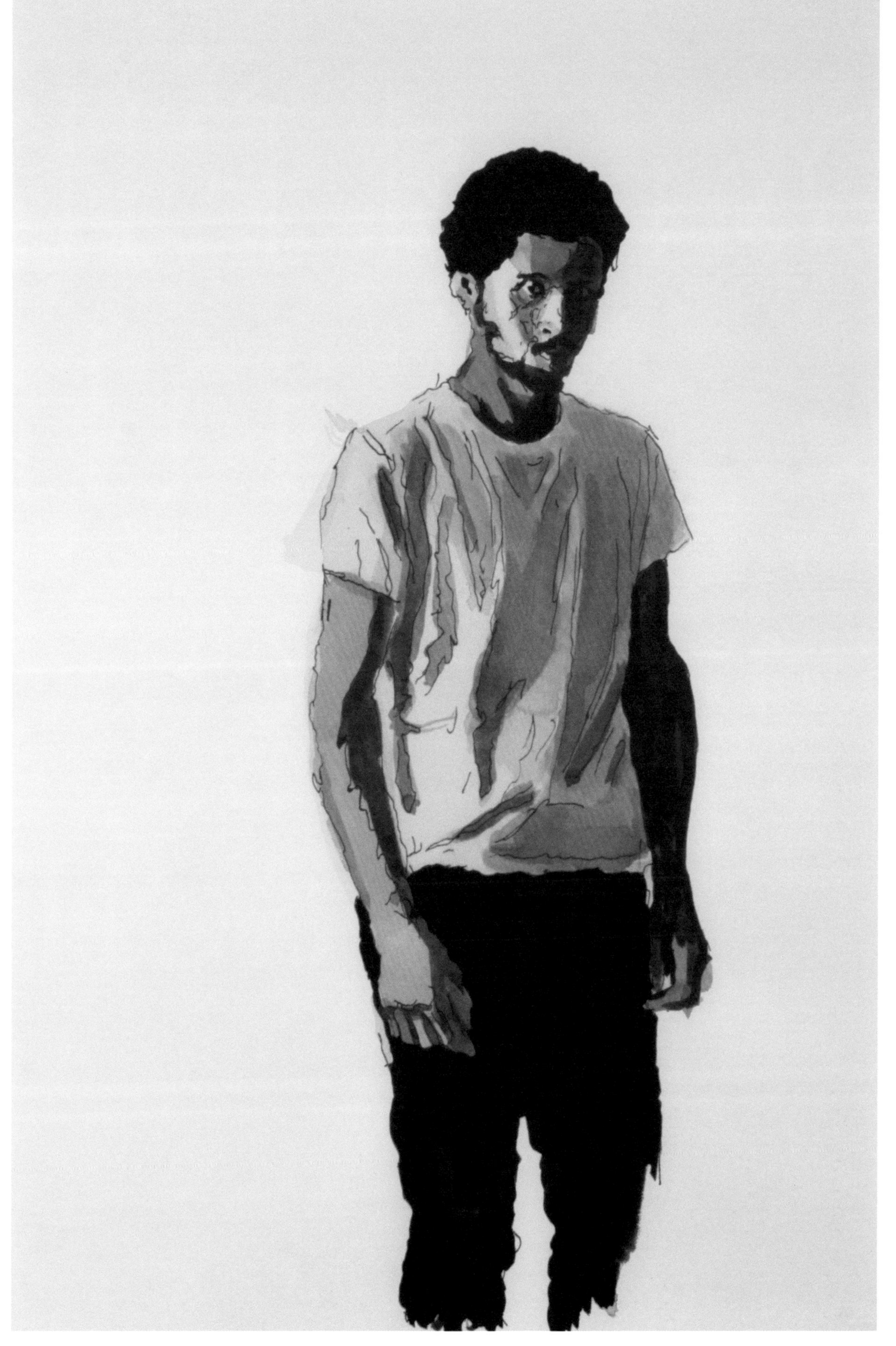

# Darrel Ellis and the Poetics of Opacity

# Derek Conrad Murray

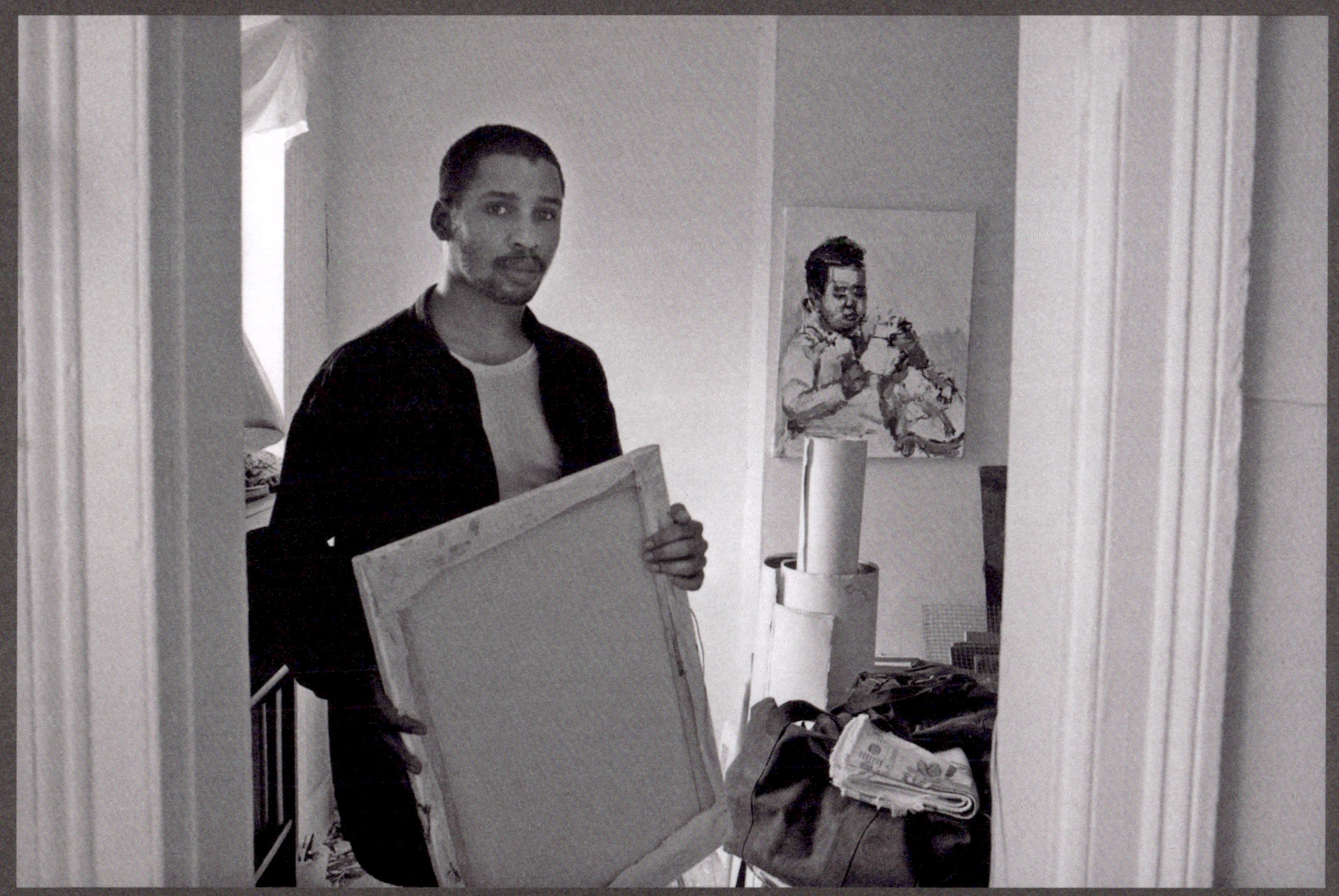

Ellis in his Greenpoint apartment, 1988. Photo by Allen Frame

At its core, the art of Darrel Ellis possesses an exquisite
tension. His painting and photography exude a
sensitivity, a delicateness that conveys pathos, nostalgia,
and longing. His art is quiet and contemplative,
retreating just enough to beckon us in. Yet this work
also powerfully emanates a yearning to resist ideological
reduction. An exceedingly talented artist, Ellis's career
was tragically cut short by his death from AIDS-related
complications at the age of thirty-three in 1992. When
reflecting on the complexities of Ellis's life and work, it
feels almost like a betrayal to distill or pin down the
work's essence, to render its ephemeral qualities legible.
There is a certain violence (if not a presumptuousness)
in the act of bringing something intentionally slippery,
elusive, and personal into knowledge—which is to
suggest that unknowability is perhaps a quality one
should covet and protect. Such a notion contradicts the
commodity logics of the art world: an industry defined
by its economic rapacity and voracious appetite for visual
objects steeped in the intimacies and psychologies of
their makers. Needless to say, this consumptive impulse
grates against the deeply personal nature of artistic
production. The role of the critic is to reveal, but when
looking closely at Ellis's art, this act is corrupted and
rendered almost obscenely voyeuristic, as if the work
both admonishes and dares us to enter the fraught nature
of its intimacies.

    The generative friction within Ellis's work issues
from a fateful event that would shape him, and motivate
his continued return to photographs of a happier past.
Born in the Bronx in 1958, Ellis developed a keen interest
in the photographic medium at a young age, and resolved
to become an artist at the age of seventeen. Inspired by
family photographs taken by his late father, the young
Ellis developed a fascination with reinterpreting images
of memories that were not his own. His father, Thomas
Ellis, was a postal clerk and photographer who, for a time,
ran a small portrait studio. A veteran of the US Marines,
the elder Ellis was tragically killed in 1958 by two
plainclothes police officers. At the time of Thomas Ellis's
senseless killing, his wife was pregnant with Darrel. The
injustice of his father's untimely death had an enduring
and traumatic influence on Darrel, leading him to piece
together the memories and experiences of a father he
had never known. In the early 1980s, the budding artist
began working with the framed photos his father had
taken—leading his mother to eventually give him Thomas's
extensive collection of negatives. The archive consisted
of photos depicting immediate and extended family in
Harlem and the South Bronx. Acquiring the archive in
1981 was a transformative moment in Ellis's development
as an artist, and a major catalyst for his future conceptual
and aesthetic choices.

    In his formative years as a student, museum visits
became a major source of inspiration, deepening his
knowledge and appreciation for Western art. In 1981,
Ellis met artist and writer Allen Frame, who became
a close and enduring friend. During that period, he
was photographed by two important artists, Robert
Mapplethorpe and Peter Hujar. From 1981 to 1982,
Darrel participated in the Whitney Independent Study
Program, where he continued to develop his own unique
formal language. He was actively experimenting with
different photographic techniques, as well as figurative
paintings, primarily from framed and matted prints of
his father's photographs. In 1982, while working as an
instructor for the Whitney Museum's Artreach Program
(1982–85), Ellis visited schools and gave lectures to
students about the museum's collection. By the mid-
1980s, Ellis's career as an artist began to pick up steam.
What followed were more exhibition opportunities,

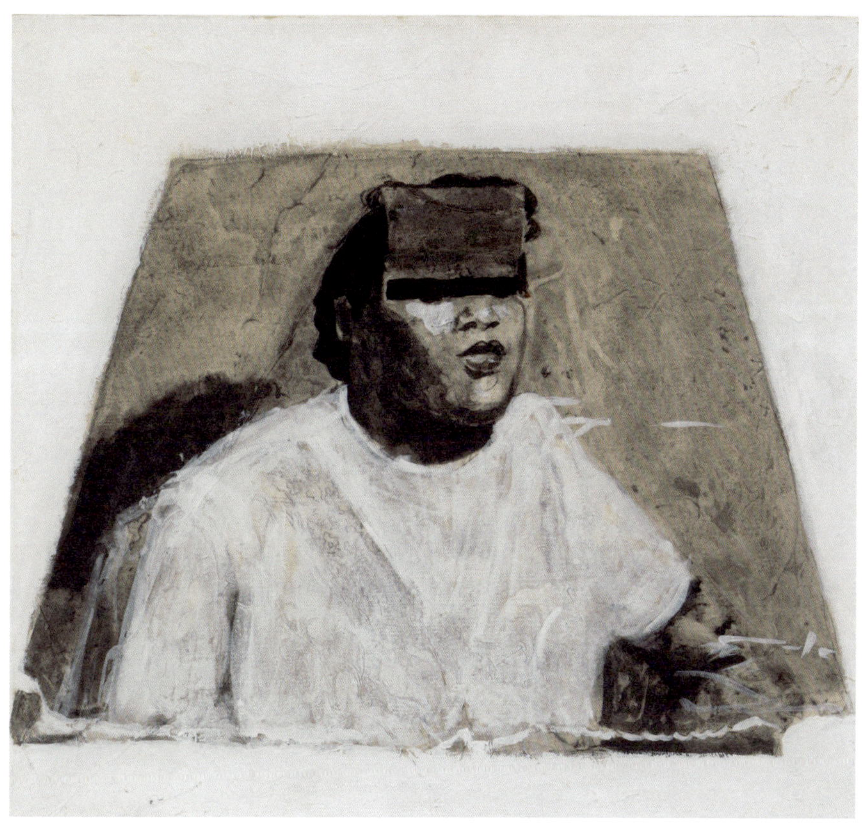

1. *Untitled* (Mother)
ca. 1989–90
Oil, ink, gouache, and graphite on paper
mounted on canvas
25 × 24 inches

including *Drawings from My Father's Photographs*, shown at Fashion Moda and Anichini Gallery in 1983. And in 1984, his work was in a group exhibition entitled *New York Work* in Switzerland, organized by Not Vital, which included artist luminaries Robert Gober and Nan Goldin.

Ellis's artworks have an opacity, and a fragmentary quality reflective of his rather ambivalent attitudes toward his identity, or perhaps more accurately, a desire to resist the limitations often imposed by being Black and gay in an intolerant society. Ellis was outspoken regarding this, stating that he had to deal with race and racism despite his own sense of openness and the vast multiracial spectrum of friends with whom he socialized. Race was a limitation and an imposition on his creativity and social existence in New York, but it also impacted the perception of his artwork. For Ellis, it was a contradiction (if not perceived as inappropriate) to be a Black artist with a European sensibility—especially considering the expectations placed on African American artists. "People often tell me," he said, "sometimes my work doesn't really look like it's done by a Black person."[2] Still, he made a point of resisting any form of reduction or stifling legibility, especially as it pertained to his race and sexuality.

Implicit in Ellis's work is an extraordinary protectiveness. His various acts of obscuring and removal say something quite profound about the violent nature of gazing upon the intimacies of others. Not all is revealed, despite the fact that Ellis works specifically with family photographs. These images, like memories themselves, are warped, distorted, and obscured by the artist, as if to say, "You can look, but you cannot know." We see this quality in Ellis's painting *Untitled* (Mother), ca. 1989–90 (fig. 1), a work based upon a family photograph of the artist's mother. In many respects, it is a classic portrait—a frontal image, reminiscent of the conventional idealizing studio portraits found in family homes everywhere. The painting has a rustic rawness in its complex layers of gouache on canvas. Its grayish and black tonalities have a distinct quality of ominousness, but what stands out are the work's affective resonances. One cannot avoid the conflicted profundity of the photograph source, which images a Black woman of great familial significance to the artist. But Ellis holds back from fully revealing his mother's visage, by obscuring her eyes with a painted rectangular form. This act of removing, or perhaps denying the gaze, creates a psychologically conflicted relation between remembrance and devotion, between intimacy and unknowability. The obscuring of the eyes not only alludes to a denial of voyeuristic consumption, but also to a potentially conflicted relationship to one's own family history. Yet Ellis protects the original negatives or source photographs, never altering or allowing direct access. We see only specters of them. It is precisely the fractured and unreliable nature of our memories, the conflicted and often fraught relations with family, combined with the joys, traumas, and disappointments of our past, that render this work so incredibly poignant.

These protective modulations of the image are equally present in the works which do not seem, on their surface, to distort or obscure. For example, in *Untitled (Self-Portrait)*, ca. 1990–91 (fig. 2), we are faced with an ink on paper, based on a photograph of the artist. In this later work, Ellis stands, wearing a dark hat and loose sweater. This time, the eyes are a focal point: he gazes directly out of the frame with an imploring look, his head cocked to one side. His hands are held up, palms upturned, as if begging. While it contains no specific erasures, the painting, with its thin, ghostlike application of pigment, clearly addresses itself to that which is projected onto him—namely, in this case, the sense of his social standing and worth relative to his AIDS-related changes in appearance and weight loss. It speaks eloquently of appearances.

Ellis was emphatic that his work does not attempt to make a meta-critique of racial inequality, or (in the case of his family-photo-inspired art) to suggest that his family somehow symbolically stands in for all Black

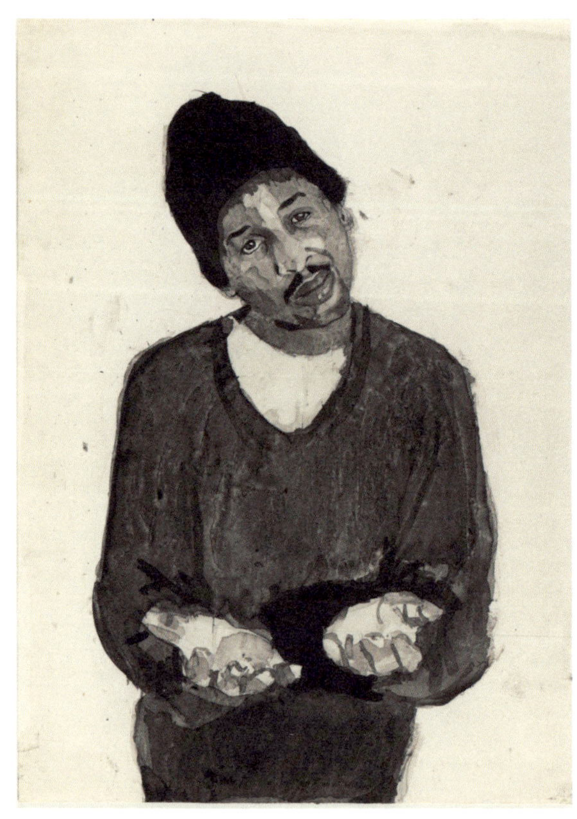

2. *Untitled* (Self Portrait)
ca. 1990–91
Ink and wash on paper prepared with textured ground
24 ½ × 17 inches

families. That need to resist definition is a prominent feature of his formal approach—which emerged from a concern that his images of the African American family would be read by art viewers differently than those depicting a white family. While he admitted that his entire life had been dictated by various forces related to his race, gender, sexuality, and community, he remained invested in the belief that we are all ultimately spiritual beings—though limited by the meanings ascribed to our physical bodies.

The notion of an art that seems to resist its own revealing is admittedly strange—almost as if it challenges the interpreter, highlighting the responsibility they bear as a witness. It would appear that Ellis is abundantly aware of the gaze, and its unique violence: its ability to disclose and expose, but inability, or unwillingness, to humanize. In the early 1990s, French/Martiniquan writer Édouard Glissant theorized this dynamic in terms of a right to *opacity*, championing the right to unknowability while acknowledging the implicit failures of representation to actually *see* certain subjects; that is, to actually understand, which is more about reciprocity and empathy than simply observing.[3] What Glissant located was a core tension, implicit in the representation of difference in social contexts, in which alterity is the nexus for forms of social discrimination. To that point, the fraught relation between visibility and invisibility, between being perpetually viewed and having social value, is a contradiction subtending the perilous terrain of visual representation. Moreover, in the United States, there has always been a cultural thirst for images of difference, but this desire to consume belies the very stark realities of structural inequality, criminalization, and often death. But we need to carefully ponder how we look upon certain bodies, and be cognizant of the unique liabilities of these instances of revealing. The right to opacity is perhaps a means to resist the violence of this incessant unveiling: to defy the ideological reduction of which Glissant speaks. For the other, the right to go unseen may function as a powerful means to resist the limiting scripts and clichéd tropes that overdetermine the representation of difference: that tendency to fetishize images of ennobled suffering.

This struggle between transparency and opacity is at the heart of Darrel Ellis's work. To grasp Ellis's creative production is to appreciate the implicit tensions and contradictions of making visible Black bodies and Black lives in a society that has yet to reconcile its relationship to racial difference. In looking at his artworks, there is a reticence, a desire and longing to connect to his past, to better understand himself—while simultaneously negotiating an art world that demands the right to look (to gaze upon), but not to fully acknowledge or appreciate. The fallacious belief in a conjunction between *visibility* and *value* drives so much of the thinking around racial representation today, but, as Glissant argues, the representation of difference "itself can still contrive to reduce things to the transparent."[4] Ellis directly resisted that transparency through a series of striking formal refusals.

In 1983 the young artist was invited to reproduce his drawings in *BOMB* magazine, where his friend Allen Frame was a contributing editor at the time. The magazine expressed interest in publishing the original source photographs, alongside his reworkings of the images. In support of the growing interest in his work, Ellis's mother gave her son multiple boxes of hundreds of negatives in medium format. It was, as he described it, his "inheritance," his "legacy."[5] Ellis became aware of his father's deep knowledge of photographic history, as well as the technical aspects of the medium. As a multimedia artist, Ellis was not particularly interested in the mechanics of photography, but he drew great inspiration from his father's vast archive and extensive equipment. Exhibition opportunities continued to present themselves, including two group exhibitions in Germany and one in Switzerland. For a time, Ellis lived in Berlin, with the prospect of greater support and success, but this did not materialize as he had hoped, and he returned to New York once his funds were exhausted.

Upon his return, he secured a job at the Museum of Modern Art in 1987 as a security guard. It was initially inspiring and motivational to be among the museum's vast collection, but over time, his mood soured. To be an aspiring artist working at such a major museum as a guard felt demeaning.[6] The experience had a profound impact, leading him to strike out on his own again, moving into an apartment in bohemian Greenpoint, Brooklyn. Living independently was a major boost, giving him the confidence to direct greater energy into his work. However, it was also during this period that Ellis learned of his HIV-positive status, which he did not disclose for some time, but shared privately with Allen Frame in 1991.

In 1989, he was invited by photographer Nan Goldin to participate in *Witnesses: Against Our Vanishing*, for which he made self-portraits based upon the photographs taken of him by Peter Hujar and Robert Mapplethorpe. His work *Self-Portrait after Photograph by Robert Mapplethorpe*, 1989 (p. 118), was often reproduced in the critical press for the show, and received an unusual amount of attention due to various controversies connected with the exhibition. Specifically, the turmoil was caused by the NEA's attempt to revoke its support of the show, as part of its notorious attack on the federal funding of art deemed to be obscene or indecent. Ellis's self-portrait work was well received and he began producing similar works, based upon photographs taken of him by others. In Frame's recollections, Ellis found motivation in the success of his self-portraits, but he was also "self-conscious about seeming narcissistic as the self-portraits proliferated; on the other hand, he was aware of the political impact of asserting his Black male presence and of attempting to redress the paucity of such images seen in anything other than a negative context."[7]

According to Frame, Ellis's self-portraits "questioned the idealized images of his youthful self, as well as confronted his own mortality."[8] These interlocking concerns coalesce in *Self-Portrait after Photograph by Robert Mapplethorpe*, 1990 (fig. 3), a second version of the self-portrait, which is among the most powerful works in his oeuvre. In its formal qualities, it recalls similar works by painters Luc Tuymans, William Kentridge, Gerhard Richter, and Marlene Dumas, as well as Andy Warhol's more whimsical photo-based works. There is a tradition in which artists engage in a painterly reworking and manipulation of photographs, or draw direct creative inspiration from them. In the late twentieth century, an interest in the hybridization of photography and painting emerged: a kind of interdependency between seemingly disparate mediums. Ellis tended to engage with photographs in a manner that worked against the medium's spatial logics. For example, with the 1990 *Self-Portrait*, his painterly approach flattened the mechanically produced three-dimensionality of the photographic image. It is precisely that spatial/formal depth that gives the subject (particularly with portraiture) its affective resonance. As Frame recalls, Ellis found the original Mapplethorpe image to be cold, yet despite the flattening of his reworked image, the result contains a greater pathos and interiority—as well as a stillness,

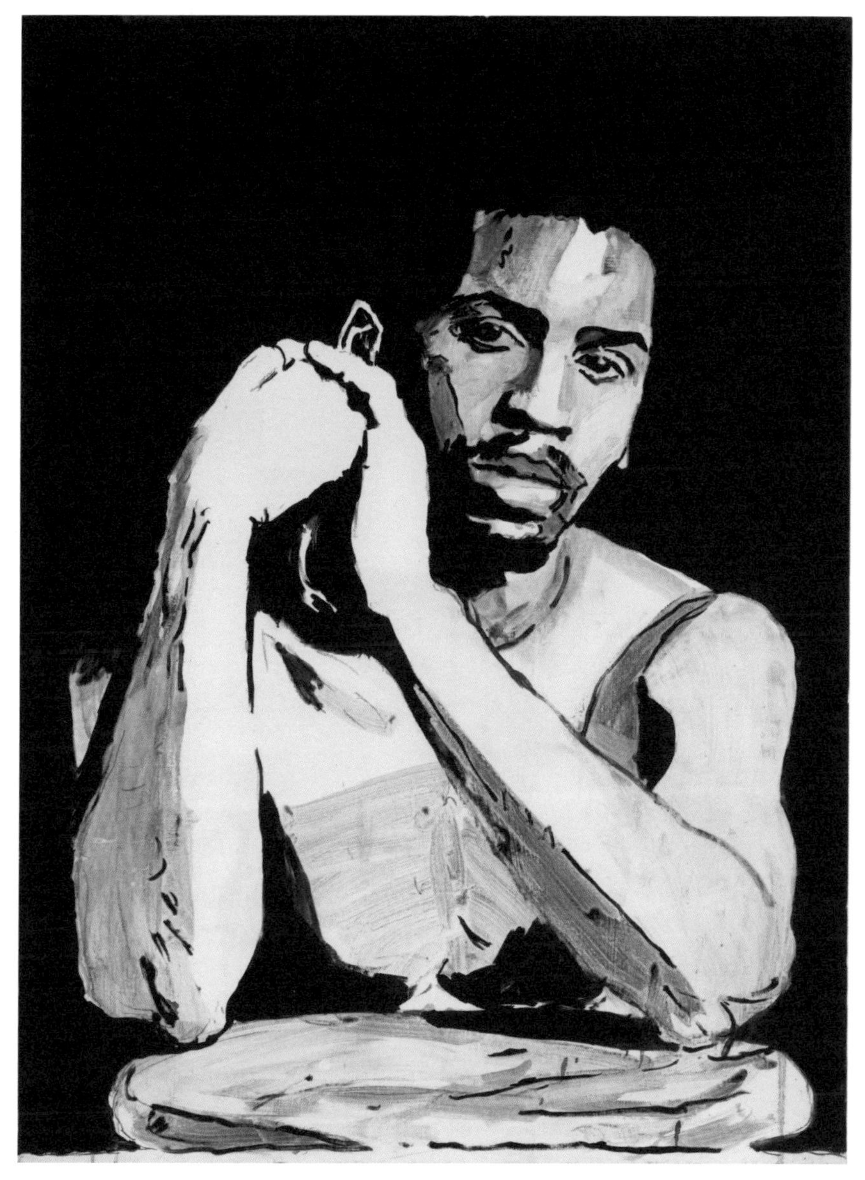

3. *Self-Portrait after Photograph by Robert Mapplethorpe*
1990
Acrylic and charcoal on canvas
60 × 42 inches

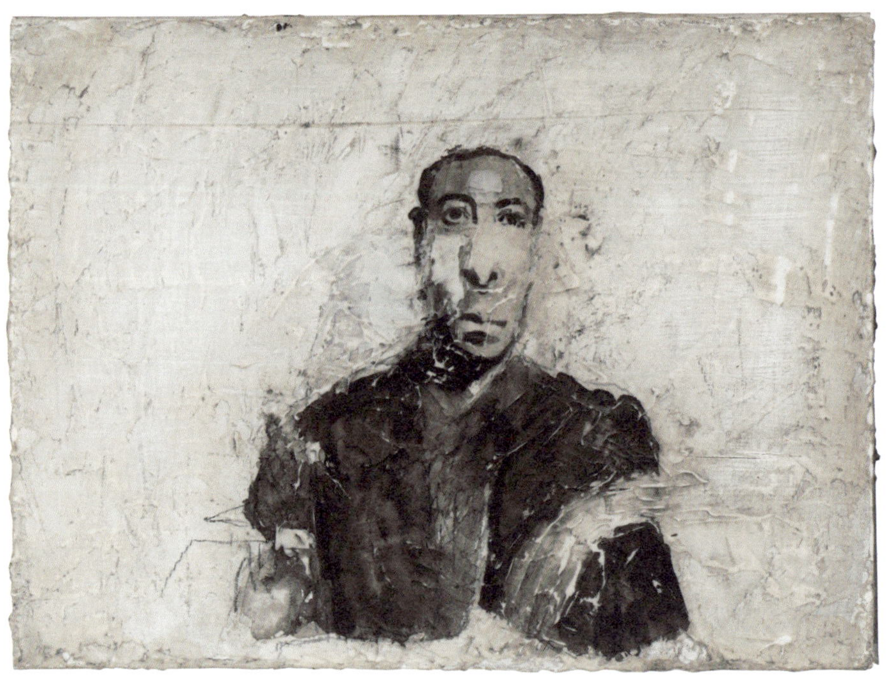



or perhaps a muted quality that is more emotionally revealing than his intentionally detached family-oriented works. In the Mapplethorpe-inspired self-portrait, the tonal washes of gray, black, and white have a certain formal directness, rendering the image almost iconic. But it also has a starkness and flatness that renders Ellis's gaze particularly piercing. The rendering of the eyes, which has a painterly simplicity, is almost disturbingly connected to the viewer. As a result, the quality of its interiority and self-reflection is heightened through the forcefulness of the returned gaze.

But there is also a quality to Ellis's painting that is in direct dialogue with photographic theory. In curator Helen Molesworth's writing on the photography-inspired paintings of Luc Tuymans, she reflects upon Roland Barthes's indispensable volume on photography, *Camera Lucida*. In her critical framing of the Belgian painter, Molesworth argues that the photograph implicitly meditates on the inevitability of loss:

*Camera Lucida* transformed the spatial indexicality of "I was *there*" into a temporal condition: I *was* there. Barthes described the relay between the historical reality of the photographer in a particular place and time and the inevitability of the photograph's freezing of human life into a slice of time as the dialectical tension between the *studium*—photography's evidential domain—and the *punctum*—the realm of details that prick our affective states into a meditation on the inevitability of loss. In both registers the psychic realm of the photograph is death, an affinity of time, signified by an endless path and a yawning futurity, in which the present is turned into the past by the click of the shutter.[9]

Like Tuymans, Ellis mobilized this psychic realm of the photograph to great effect, gathering up the intensities already present in images of his family and himself, and building upon them. This is conveyed in the 1990 *Self-Portrait*, which could be described as a meditation on the inevitability of dying; yet, as the curator suggests, this quality isn't necessarily imbued by the artist, but is implicit in the photographic medium itself: within the temporal condition "I *was* there" is an acknowledgment of death's imminence. The painting contains a strong sense of reflection, a pondering of one's youthful self, at a time in the artist's life when he was faced with the realities of his mortality.

The quality of loss permeates all of Ellis's photography-inspired works. In *Untitled* (Great Uncle Joseph Tansle), ca. 1988–92 (fig. 4), rendered in ink and charcoal on wood, Ellis recreates a photographic portrait of his great uncle, Joseph Tansle, originally taken by his father. The painting is incredibly rich in its materiality and the gestural brushwork has a sculptural quality, a thickness that feels extremely labored, as if the surface was built up over time. Layers were added, scraped away, and then reapplied laboriously, creating a dense history of mark-making that gives the work an aged quality. In the center of the painting is the distorted portrait of Tansle, as he looks forward impassively. Like so many of Ellis's works, the subject's face is formally obscured. In this instance, the face is elongated and morphed almost to the point of unintelligibility, while still retaining the original photograph's representational conventions. The washed-out and muddy tonalities in sepia-toned white give the painting a sullied quality, as if it had been exposed to the elements. But when encountering these works, what stands out are Ellis's formal refusals that take shape in the figures' distortion. Despite the artist's claims that he engaged with his father's archive without sentimentality—as if the lives depicted were not entirely knowable—there is still the sense that he conceals and protects while simultaneously revealing. As viewers, we are given only a limited view, but the intimacies of his family's history are altered just enough to deny full access to his familial legacy. Tansle's visage, which is rendered in stark blacks and washes of gray and white, is altered just enough to obstruct full visual recognition and access. The revealing and inviting intent of the family photo as a vernacular expression—as posed, stilted, and composed as it tends to be—is denied and kept private by the artist. Yet Ellis still effectively invokes a sense of the impenetrability and unknowability of family.

Themes of refusal and obfuscation run through Ellis's reworkings of his father's photographs. For example, *Untitled* (Laure on Easter Sunday), ca. 1990 (fig. 5), depicts Ellis's sister Laure as a child. She stands somewhat awkwardly outdoors, all dressed up for an occasion. In her hand she carries a stuffed bunny toy. The black-and-white photograph is typical in many ways; it's a cliché of similar photographs in family homes around the world. It is strikingly specific, yet entirely generic. Once again, the artist has chosen to both distort and obscure. In this instance, the young Laure's head is elongated and two rectangular forms, rendered in white paint, partially obscure the child's face. It is an odd image, yet it exudes the artist's explicit commitment to portraiture. His work functions as an accounting of a family struggling to remain intact, despite the realities of racism, economic challenges, and tragedy.

This was a period of greater maturity and creative sophistication for Ellis. His work evolved, but he was also living alone, supporting himself and contending with the realities of his health status. Ellis projected photographs onto a surface, where he utilized pencil, ink, watercolor, and gouache to render the images on canvas. The results were striking. He was utilizing his father's archive of family photos to stunning effect. As Frame describes it, Ellis "let them speak universally, as haunting icons, as poignant emblems of an era, as intense cameos of familial bonding, and as riveting markers of individual struggle."[10]

Ellis would eventually divulge that he chose to work with his father's images because of his familial connections—suggesting that, as an artist, he must feel something for his subject. However, he was frank about the fact that, while there was love and compassion that compelled his engagement with his family's photographs, there was still a sense of detachment. Ellis was clear that, despite the conveyed intimacy, he didn't have sentimental feelings about the images themselves, because they depicted a life he never experienced.[11] Ultimately, his father's pictures enabled him to keep a certain distance from the realities of the elder Ellis's death. This impassiveness expressed by Ellis tends to counter our sense of the intimacy implicit in his creative engagement with family memories that, considering the loss of his father, reads as an attempt to visually reconstruct his family. On the contrary, Ellis was emphatic that he utilized the images generically, because he could never fully understand the photographs his father took in the 1950s. In the end, that life was simply foreign to him, and emblematized a kind of representational gulf that

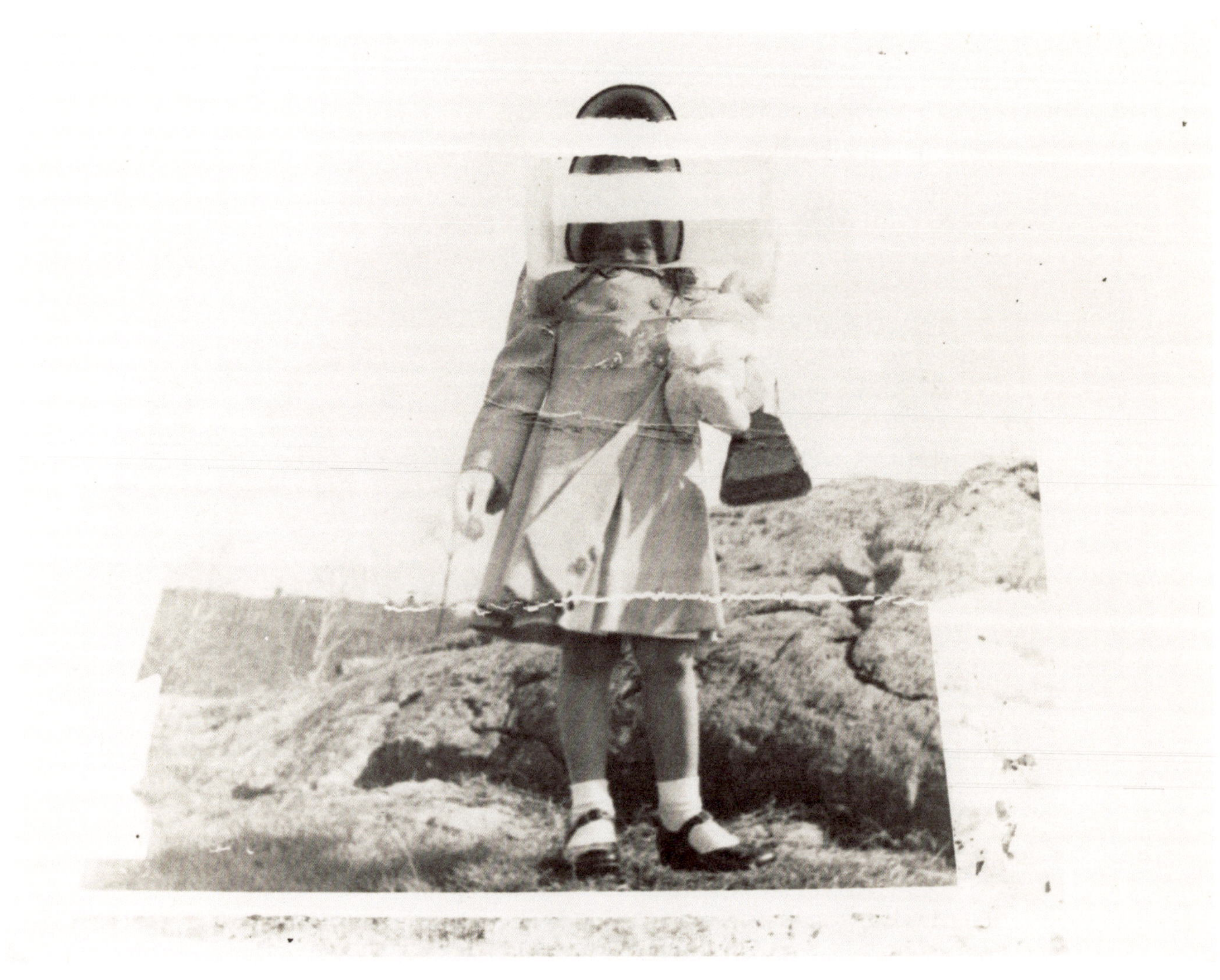

5. *Untitled* (Laure on Easter Sunday)
ca. 1990
Gelatin silver print
11 × 14 inches

could never successfully be bridged.

Despite the evocativeness and potency of his family-based works, there is something eerily prescient about the self-portraits produced toward the last years of his life. *Untitled* (Self-Portrait after Allen Frame Photograph), ca. 1990 (p. 9), is a large painting of the artist, produced with ink on paper. Like so many of Ellis's illustrative works, it is painted in shades of black, gray, and white, and in a reductive painterly style. The image is somber in tone, as it depicts Ellis from his head to his knees, posed at a three-quarter angle. He is slightly slouched, shoulders hunched forward, as his arms drape down. The young artist's head is slightly tilted downward, giving him a kind of sheepish disposition—and his expression appears melancholic, or perhaps retreating. There is a distinct air of sadness and despondence. But like all spontaneous portraits, the image is merely a snapshot taken of the artist by someone else, a fleeting instance and therefore potentially misleading in its resonances and significations. Nevertheless, what is so powerful about the self-portrait is Ellis's interest in recreating it: his fascination with contemplating how others see him—and what the act of recreating the image will reveal about himself.

Toward the end of his life, he continued to exhibit his work, but declining health posed many challenges and uncertainties. His 1991 solo exhibition at Baron/Boisanté Editions in New York was a high point, but that same year he was hospitalized for the first time. While in the hospital, he revealed his HIV status to his family. Still, he felt well enough to continue living and working in Brooklyn, supported in part by a generous grant awarded to him in 1991 by the New York Foundation for the Arts. Months after Ellis's death in 1992, Peter Galassi, chief curator of photography at the Museum of Modern Art, included his work in *New Photography 8*. This was a turning point for Ellis's legacy, which led to many other exhibitions in the United States, Europe, and Canada.

There is something incredibly powerful in Darrel Ellis's ability to explore the beautiful and often tragic pageantry of everyday life. Despite the volatility of his time, reflected in structural racism, an anti-gay legal culture, and the terrifying realities of AIDS, Ellis managed to turn inward, to tap into the inner workings, longings, joys, and forms of loss experienced by families. In many respects, these are the most universal and distinctly human themes one could explore: a kind of visual sympathy with the human banalities that bind us. Darrel Ellis's artistic journey was marked by absence and loss, beginning with the unjust murder of his father—a man he never knew. But his practice of veiling those familial images from viewers gently insisted on a refusal to be reduced, the denial of transparency, and the right to representational opacity.


Notes

1   Édouard Glissant, "For Opacity," in *Poetics of Relation*, trans. Betsy Wing (Ann Arbor: University of Michigan Press, 1997), 189–90.

2   Darrel Ellis, interview by David Hirsh, January 21, 1991, Visual AIDS Archive Project, New York.

3   Glissant, "For Opacity," 189–94.

4   Ibid., 189.

5   Darrel Ellis, interviewed by Miriam Hernández, October 16, 1990. The Museum of Modern Art Exhibition Records, 1637.12. The Museum of Modern Art Archives, New York.

6   Allen Frame, "Our Family Legacy: Variations in Black and White," in *Darrel Ellis* (New York: Art in General, 1996), 17.

7   Ibid., 18.

8   Ibid.

9   Helen Molesworth, "Luc Tuymans: Painting the Banality of Evil," in *Luc Tuymans* (New York: Distributed Art Publishers, 2009), 23.

10  Frame, "Our Family Legacy," 18.

11  Ellis, interview by Hirsh, 1991.

# The Faces & Forms of Darrel Ellis

# Tiana Reid

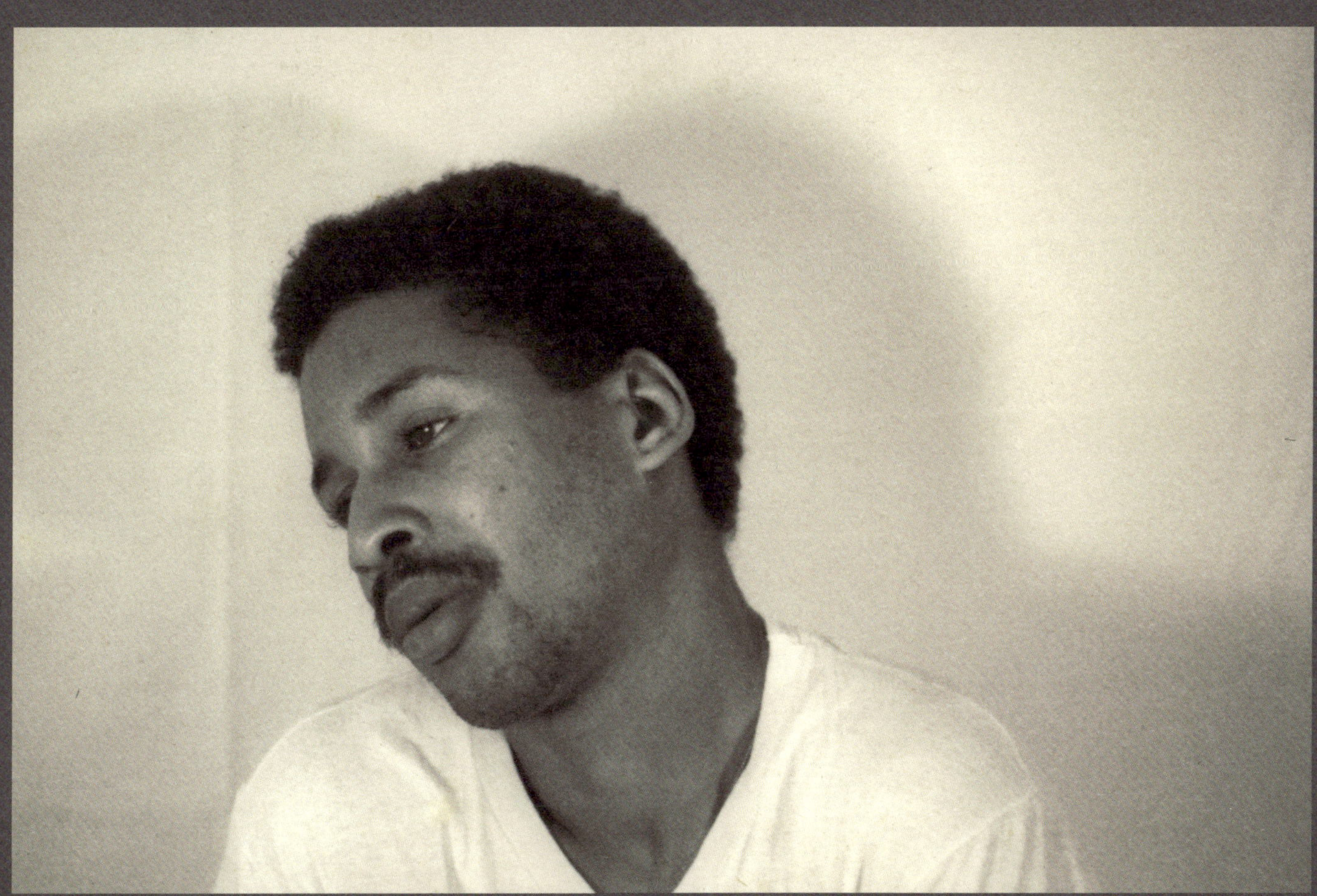

Self-portrait from the artist's archive,
ca. 1990–91

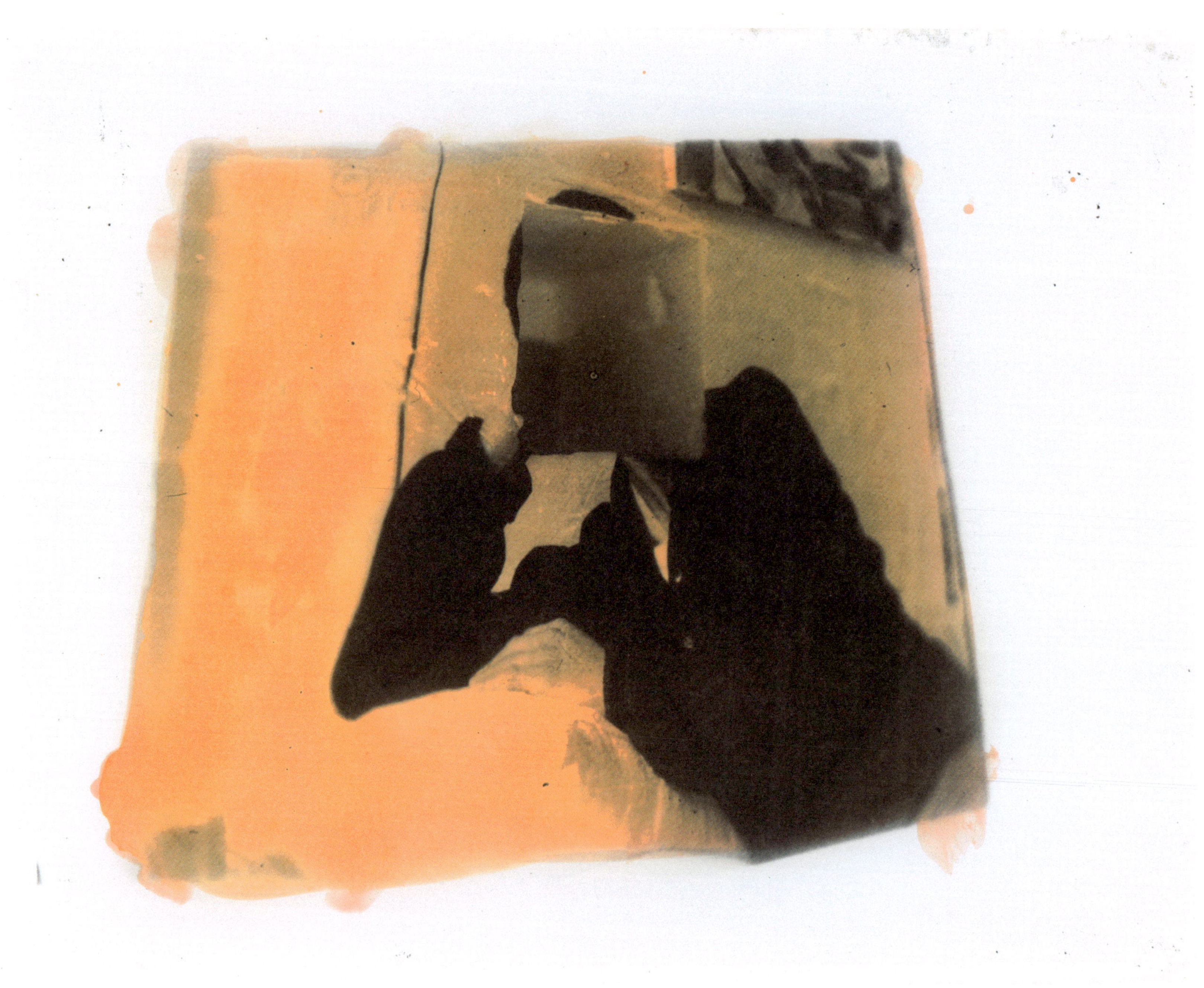

Studying the work of Darrel Ellis is like witnessing the eruption of an inner life, multiple lives captured through one work of art. All that tension and little release. Here, he sits on a couch. In a print with colored ink, *Untitled* (Self-Portrait after Allen Frame Photograph), ca. 1990 (fig. 6), he wears a dark cardigan, buttoned three-quarters of the way up. His right elbow slopes on top of the couch; his hand is propping up the right side of his head. Draped over the cushions, his left hand is curled up, fingers like a shell. Ellis leans into the sofa. He is comfortable, but he is also deliberately and intentionally posing. On the wall behind him, a piece of art edges out from the corner of the photograph. The scene is washed in a pastel orange-peach ink, an atmospheric light rubbing up against the darkness of the sweater and the stiff edges of the hung painting. Most notably: flush over Ellis's head is a blurry square that blocks out his facial features. The shape of his skull is only slightly visible, making it so that a human face is referenced but the details, the shadings, the peculiarities of individuality are missing. This practice of face-blocking, engendering a flash of apprehension and longing, is typical Darrel Ellis.

A major pleasure of encountering Ellis is noticing him encounter himself—often, through a mass of repetitions. *Untitled* (Self-Portrait after Allen Frame Photograph) is preoccupied with an absent presence that both gestures to and erases the self in self-portrait. Ellis's absent presence outlines what is not there. Indeed, to call the artist faceless here would deny the quietude and harmony of expression that vacancy holds. "The way to go: Lightness. Spirit as opposed to matter. Get the viewer to experience lightness and immateriality," he writes in his journals. "This is a very hard task[.] It upsets our notions about existence, and negates the reliance upon pyschical [*sic*] perceptions."[1] Other iterations from this same series reveal his face to various degrees—each work utterly unique and yet clearly serial, a sequence that relies on movement, on continuation, on incompleteness, on practice in a kind of Surrealist automatism. Even with this range of precision, this vacillation in sameness and difference seems to give off a telltale mood: weathered, textured, exposed, soft. Intellectual acuity a visceral impulse: "Material must be used[.] We are matter, but we must use it to convey reality[,] that which is beyond our present physical consciousness[,] our limitations."[2]

Ellis's series of self-portraits on the couch offers not a photographic representation of Ellis, but rather the very mechanics of representation. Troubling the self-portrait, Ellis focuses on those formal characteristics that draw our attention to the aesthetic decisions that come "before" the finished portrait: the seated subject, the placement of the hands, the expression of the face, the direct gaze of the eyes. The "before"—the process of staging, revision, and revisitation—becomes a difficult aftermath.

Ellis's inclination toward this mode of absent presence has been noted by his friend Allen Frame, who has stewarded Ellis's estate since he passed in 1992. In his essay "One Family Legacy: Variations in Black and White," Frame notes that Ellis returned to an experimental photography technique he had developed earlier in his career, in 1987, after a disappointing trip to Germany. "He used geometric forms—circles, squares, and horizontal bars—to obliterate central parts of the image, creating mysterious symbols that suggest both discord and harmony," Frame writes. "The overlaying geometric forms act as an aggressive intervention, yet help resolve and complete compositions that, unlike his father's, are vaguely defined."[3]

When this technique is applied to the face, Ellis works out a poetics of the self-portrait. Framing is part of the image itself, framing its own location of the self-portrait, disrupting what's there and what's not there. His self-portraits are slant in that they are interpretations of another image. And yet the multiplication of experiments sidesteps any claim on an "original" image. What unifies these self-portraits is the present-absence of the face, the self—fractured and fragmented—as a site of improvisation. Ellis identified the self through the fact of seeing, as abstracted and fictional, as bits and pieces.

In 1987, after Ellis landed a full-time job at the Museum of Modern Art as a security guard, he moved from his mother's apartment in the Bronx to Greenpoint in Brooklyn, to live on his own. As a guard, he worked long hours, during which he studied the canonical works of the museum's collection. His interventions, now, weren't only against the self but also exhibition culture. Using his MoMA ID photograph as a source image, he positioned himself not *as* art but *with* or *attending to* the canonical art he was tasked to guard. In *Untitled (Self-Portrait after Museum Guard Photograph)*, ca. 1990 (p. 108) he's wearing a black suit jacket and polka-dotted tie, and has a thick mustache; the face is at once scrunched up and long. A white ladderlike T breaks up the space where the eyebrows should be. His bottom lip swells. He has no neck at all, just a deformed dome bulging out from his shirt collar. This image makes evident that Ellis saw his photography as a sculptural act, building on a shifting set of forms.[4]

Ellis here is mediating an image of himself that does not belong to him, tearing up the hyper-individuality of the ID. Photographs capture, and photographic identification captures to the nth degree. A historical technology—of domination, exclusion, sovereignty, citizenship, authentication, and governance—ID photos track, document, surveil, and individualize. Of course, the ID can also be an artifact of pride and pleasure: proof of employment or education, the stamp of a name-brand institution next to one's face, the freedom of movement. (In 1989, Ellis used his MoMA ID to open a bank account.)[5] The ID lives in the realm of proper nouns, of what's finished, what's printed, what's passive, what's formed, what's stable, but Ellis's practice is a verb: moving not toward finality but toward unforming and unbecoming.

This undoing is something of a burden. In her essay "In Our Glory: Photography and Black Life," bell hooks writes, "Such is the power of the photograph, of the image, that it can give back and take away, that it can bind."[6] Ellis recognized the binding nature of a photograph—the power and threat in representation—and pulled back the curtain. While the face is supposed to set people apart from one another, it's often as if Ellis worked from an already subverted self, remaking the self, initiating the multiple faces we carry around with us.

By fragmenting, manipulating, and layering, Ellis defamiliarized the familiar world through a serial poetics, reiterating, repeating, over and over again. In an early photograph (fig. 7), we see one of Ellis's siblings, Katrina, in a small bedroom. Drawing the dark drapes with one hand, she looks out the window. Her back is turned to us, while the images framed within the window and the television are obliterated by a seismic whiteness. We cannot discern the outlines of any buildings in the distance, the weather, or the TV show on the screen. The figure opens herself up to plenitude, to the heights of nothingness, an optical expanse with no limits, exquisite loss. The domestic space is marked by estrangement—its channels to the outside (the window, the TV) are formed into an unmapped world, an overexposed terrain of possibility and projection. In this mise en abyme, the blankness suggested by this sequence of overexposed surfaces threatens to eviscerate the entire image. Like the woman at the window, or the artist pondering the world before him, we too are poised at the lip of the abyss, waiting for the final image to reveal itself. Here and elsewhere, Ellis worked by covering up in order to reveal, seeking maximum intensification and achieving a disquieted mood only equaled by the sense that an even stranger image lies just over some beyond.

Notes

1    Darrel Ellis, sketchbook (1987), n.p. My thanks to the Visual AIDS Archive Project for providing me with scans of Ellis's sketchbooks and journals, courtesy of the Estate of Darrel Ellis.

2    Ibid., n.p.

3    Allen Frame, "One Family Legacy: Variations in Black and White," in *Darrel Ellis* (New York: Art in General, 1996), 17.

4    In another sketchbook, Ellis writes about the relationship between sculpture and photography: "The geometric shape introduces the element of touch, feel—the basic element of photography[.] By rephotographing the photograph with an sculpture form [*sic*] I emphasize the materiality of physical reality." Darrel Ellis, sketchbook (ca. 1988), n.p.

5    Darrel Ellis, sketchbook (ca. 1989), n.p.

6    bell hooks, "In Our Glory: Photography and Black Life," in *Art on My Mind: Visual Politics* (New York: New Press, 1995), 56.

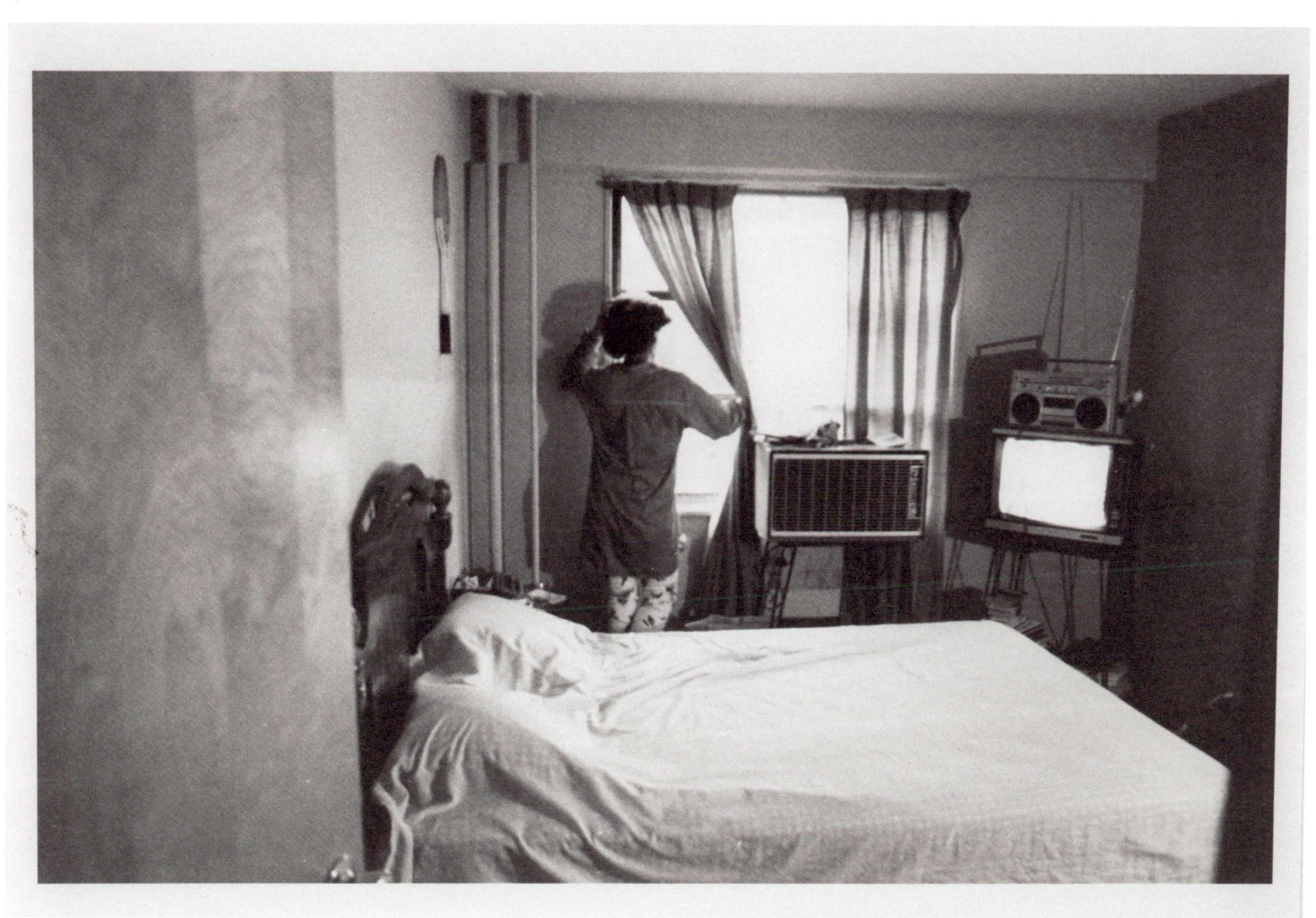

7. Katrina Stewart, Ellis's sister, at the window of her mother's bedroom, ca. 1985–88. Photograph by Darrel Ellis

# A New Sensibility

# Interview with Darrel Ellis by David Hirsh

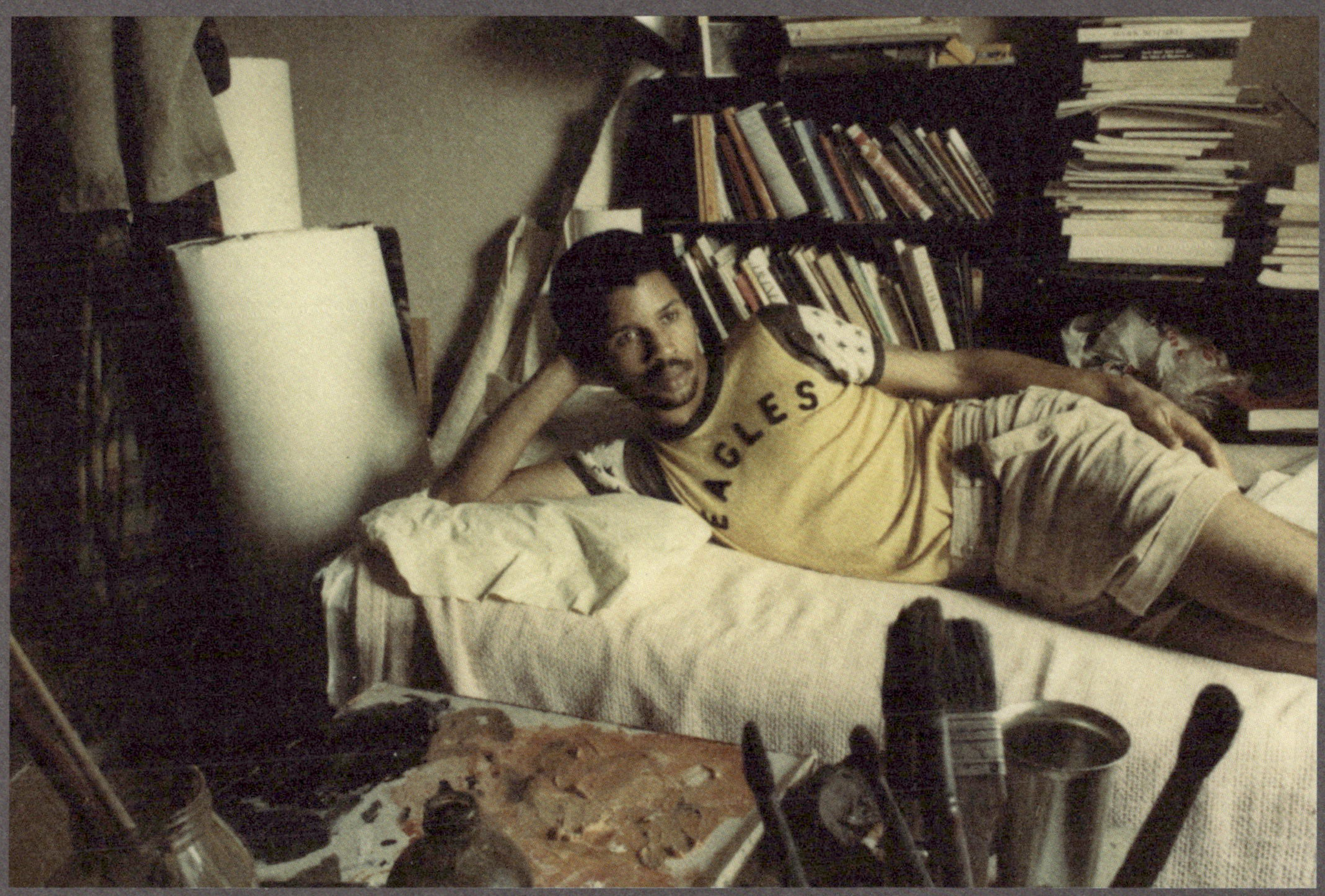

"I use images of my family because they affect me so strongly;
they're just something I know extremely well, very deeply."
— Darrel Ellis

On January 21, 1991, David Hirsh interviewed a thirty-two-year-old Darrel Ellis in his apartment in Greenpoint, Brooklyn, on the occasion of Ellis's solo exhibition at Baron/Boisanté Editions. In the months following this conversation, Ellis would go on to receive a major grant from the New York Foundation for the Arts, participate in a touring exhibition, and earn the attention of Peter Galassi, chief curator of photography at the Museum of Modern Art, who acquired two of Ellis's photographs for the museum shortly after Ellis's death.

When Hirsh was introduced to Ellis, he was working as an arts writer at the *New York Native*, a gay biweekly newspaper, for whom he recorded dozens of interviews with gay and lesbian artists in the late 1980s and early 1990s. In 1994, Hirsh, alongside the painter Frank Moore, helped document and archive the work of artists with HIV and AIDS, developing what eventually became the Visual AIDS Archive Project. At the time of the interview, Hirsh had not yet begun working with Visual AIDS, and, while Ellis knew his HIV status, even his closest friends didn't know he was living with AIDS until he was hospitalized several months later.

In the interview, Ellis discusses his childhood growing up in the Bronx and his relationships with his family and his father's photography. He also shares insights about his artistic process as well as his fascination with the European painting tradition, and the expectations placed upon him as a Black artist. The transcript published here has been edited for clarity and length. The full recording is available to researchers through the Visual AIDS Archive Project. It is the only known audio recording of Ellis.

**David Hirsh:** Where were you born?

**Darrel Ellis:** I was born in the Bronx, New York, on December 5, 1958, which makes me a Sagittarius.

**Hirsh:** What are some of your earliest memories?

**Ellis:** Well, I grew up in the South Bronx. It was a nice place in the sixties; it was clean, we lived in a new building. I was a very isolated kid. My mother had two children after I was born, after she remarried, so then she had five children, and I was in the middle, the third one. I always grew up with the feeling of not really being connected to anybody else in the family. I developed as an artist from spending a lot of time alone and being very introspective. I always loved to draw, especially cars. I've always been a very dreamy person. My grandparents thought I was being too affected by "white culture."

**Hirsh:** Oh really?

**Ellis:** Yeah, my grandmother anyhow thought that, because, during junior high school, I had a number of friends who were white, and she grew up in the Deep South. I can think of some of the things she said to me, and her attitudes: "Darrel, you live in a very, very racist society, you're in big trouble. Everything that's happened to you in this world so far, a lot of it is because you're Black." As a teenager, you don't want to hear that, you're very idealistic and you love everybody. My mother was also that way and she didn't talk race in the house, but her mother did. So, at the time, I didn't get along with my grandmother, but now that she's gone and I'm grown, she knew what she was talking about. Even though I feel a little bit of protection from above, it's very dangerous in this world being Black, because we're the enemy in this country.

**Hirsh:** As I understand it, your father was killed one month before you were born. If you feel free to talk about it . . .

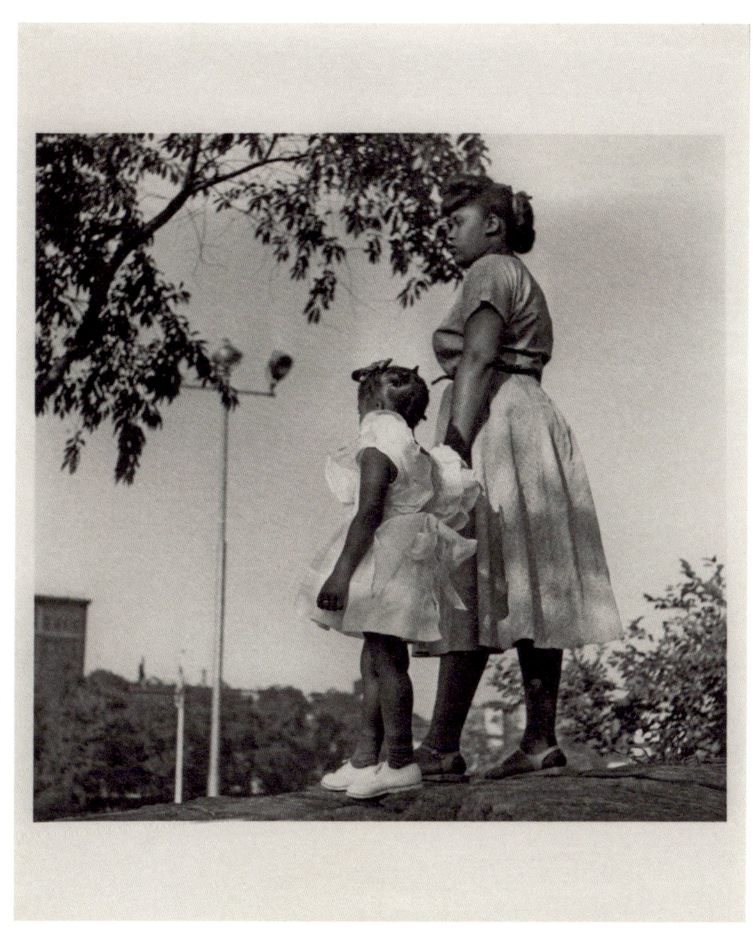



Ellis: Yes. Yes, he was. My father was beaten up by cops in 1958. Yeah, police brutality, way back then. My father, from what I've heard about him through my family, my grandparents, my mother, my sister, and what I feel in my heart and what I see in his large body of work that he left, was a good, honest, hardworking, responsible, idealistic, optimistic war veteran. He was what we consider a good man, and for him to be beaten up by cops . . . the situation was that the cops were doing something they shouldn't have been doing, and he was there and the cops were drinking and they just beat him to death because he was in the wrong place at the wrong time. They were in a car, blocking my father from trying to get in front of them. He was having difficulty driving to get ahead of them, they got into a brawl, so that's how he died. An ironic thing about the whole story is that my father was working in the post office, but he had applied to become a policeman, and he was due to report to work as a policeman the following day, after his death. So that's the irony of that. I never knew the man. I get kind of sad now as I talk about it, and it's kind of a painful thing.

Hirsh: He obviously devoted a lot of attention to photographs.

Ellis: Yes, he did. He was very involved with photography. He knew the history and he had an enormous amount of equipment. He left literally hundreds and hundreds of negatives and pictures behind.

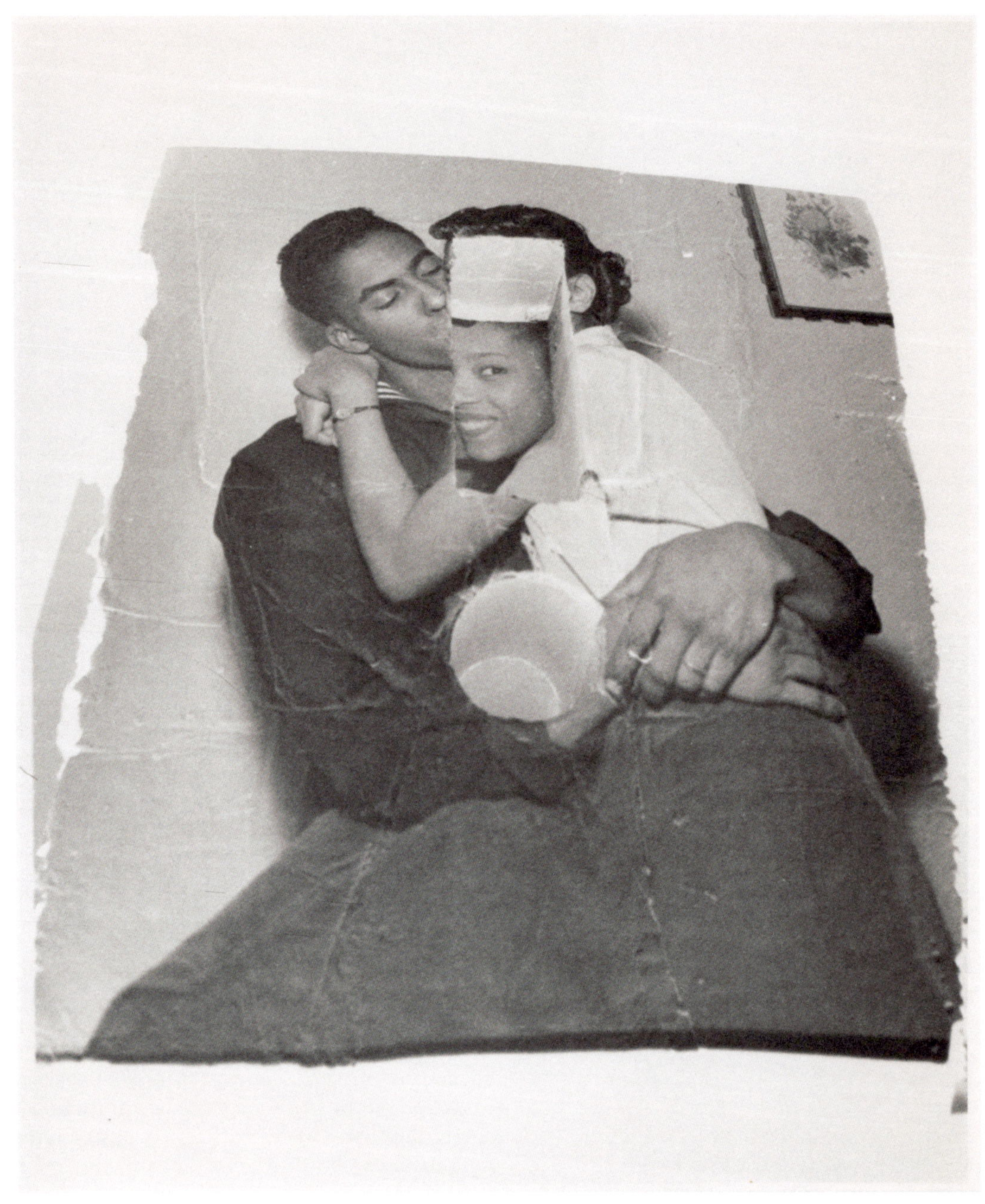

9. *The Kiss*
1990
Gelatin silver print
20 × 16 inches
Collection of Joshua P. Smith

Hirsh: Were they almost all of family groupings?

Ellis: Yes, he took a lot of pictures, devoted a whole lot of his time to photographing. He had a huge encyclopedia of photography, the most up-to-date volumes on the history of photography, all the best cameras. What he would think about my work in photography?—forget it, it would be a laugh. He was serious—an expert, you know—and he was just like the Museum of Modern Art. When I showed them my work, it was like a joke to them—not as much now as it used to be.

Hirsh: But at the same time, you're continuing where he left off.

Ellis: Definitely. It's a mystery to me because my work is very melancholy. His work is very optimistic. It's close-to-war America and my work is something else; my work looks like it's collaged or cut up, but it's only an illusion—nothing is destroyed. The photos, the negatives, are perfectly intact. I only project the image, I don't touch the negative, and the surfaces I use, they're all intact. Everything is intact. It's just that they come together and they marry for a while, then they split up, but they're still intact. The whole process is very ephemeral; the images are very ephemeral. They're in line with my beliefs, inasmuch as I feel that, even though we live in a physical world—we live in a real world and we're made of flesh and blood and everything—deeper down, the reality of human beings is that we are in fact spiritual beings. We're connected to some source, some infinite, intangible source of life and creation.

Hirsh: And yet it's referring to something very specific and very real—that is, a family. How did you decide to start using your father's photographs?

Ellis: Well, first off, in order to make a work meaningful, I feel that an artist has to really feel something about the subject. Something to give the work life. I use images of my family because they affect me so strongly; they're just something I know extremely well, very deeply. As for using my father's pictures specifically, it helps me to keep a certain amount of distance and detachment from the reality I know, growing up after my father's death. The world he photographed was one I didn't know, because I wasn't born yet. I grew up in the South Bronx, in the sixties, seventies, and eighties. I don't know any life from the forties and fifties with their picnics and their beautiful clothes and everything is so nice and perfect and wholesome. The subjects in my father's photos are my mother and sister, and my grandparents,

who I knew very well. When I look at pictures of them, I see that life changed them so much, I can't help but have some reaction.

I wasn't a happy child and I was dissatisfied a lot with my family. But that was the reality. You always want to make something to your liking if you can. So I've always tried, through my art—because I could never do it in real life—to make the family to my liking somehow. In order to do that, you have to really look into it, deeply. I feel strongly that deconstructing is all right. But what's more important is reconstruction. It's very cerebral work, very mental work, and, in a way, very soulful work.

Hirsh: Aren't you also doing other things to distort the images?

Ellis: The forms I use to project upon are all different, and the negative, when it interacts with the form that I'm projecting upon, causes certain kinds of distortion. Some of the forms I use are round, some are rectangular, some are biomorphic. That one straight photographic image representing people and a picnic—I project that image on this geometrical shaped form and you get a totally different image than if I project it on something that's more biomorphic. They're all different, the photos; they're like regeneration, regenerated. From one you get many. And that works as a metaphor for the family.

Hirsh: Why don't you choose one image that's currently showing and just talk about it from any perspective you want, in terms of what you felt about it when you were making it, or what you feel about it now. Or, if you don't mind, why don't we talk about *The Kiss*? (fig. 9)

Ellis: When I think about *The Kiss*, I think about my extremely handsome uncle. The photograph shows his first wife, who was extremely beautiful, and they were a beautiful, beautiful couple. I can't help but think about my memory of growing up, and my uncle, what kind of person he was. In the photograph, my uncle's kissing nothing—there's no head there, there's no lips; it's just a white square. And then you see my aunt's face way down under his, looking out at us, the viewer. I can't get into the symbolism of that. People can read into it what they want. I don't have any reading of it. The only thing I see is my uncle. It's a very personal thing. It's hard to explain, but I do feel a real connection to it. You could talk about a lot of things with that image, of course: a kiss, but there's nobody there. The illusion you're kissing; the whole feeling of creating the lover. It's not so much who this person really is, it's that they fill a void for you, they live up to your expectations or they conform to your desire, your ideas.

I want the work I make to affect people, which seems to be getting harder and harder, to really affect people any more, with images, with pictures. Who knows? But I would like to affect people, as an artist.

Hirsh: What sort of change would you like these photographs to effect in people?

Ellis: I just want them to know, this is Darrel Ellis, this is his family. Maybe I'll feel differently at another point in my life. But right now, it's a very raw, kind of primitive feeling. I don't want any separation between what I'm creating and how I feel and the viewer, and how he feels. We're all one human, we're all one being. We're all together in this world. We're all the same, we're all one. That's what I want to effect in people.

It's probably no coincidence that I've chosen my family as the subject. When I look at those photographs sometimes, all I see are holes. It bothers me. I say, "God, there are so many holes in these pictures"—that's what I told the gallery—"God, I can't take this." I guess because it reflects a truth or reality, that search for wholeness and completeness, but it doesn't exist. The photos showing picnic scenes and a beautiful day and the family gathering, Black women having a good time, everything being very upbeat and positive and kind of opulent. You have this strong juxtaposition of this ideal Black family life with all these disjunctions and holes, so, in a way, it's back to why I use my father's work: because that's the raw material I need to talk about, the fact that it's gone, that it doesn't exist anymore.

There's so much racism naturally in the art world. And people don't know how to react to you a lot of times, as a Black artist, they don't know how to react to your work. It's a big issue, and it's one that I guess I don't really think about often—Black, the race thing—even though I know it's there. Maybe I should look at it more because I have to see myself in a context, in another reality, my social context, which I never do. But it's very naive of me to be that way because it's affected my whole life.

Hirsh: Well, that's true. But, on the other hand, white artists don't have to. They can put forward personal work that they expect to have ramifications for a broad audience. So why shouldn't you expect the same?

Ellis: Well, I always have. I grew up loving the European history of art. It's my true love, my education, my background, and that's where so much of my feeling about art and being an artist came from. Bonnard can paint his wife at the kitchen table. This is natural to me to do because I always felt that was the subject matter: the people I was around, my family. I just always assumed that that's what art came from. It's a very gut feeling; it's your life. And I just didn't know any better. What did Giacometti paint all of the time? His brother, his wife, his studio, his mother, the landscape he was born in. Or Balthus? These are all Europeans. I'm a little embarrassed because I'm supposed to be so Black and everything. Not embarrassed, but that's a reality, and it's a very European one.

Hirsh: And it raises questions.

Ellis: Yeah, it raises questions, but I felt Giacometti's work is powerful work, and so is Balthus. Powerful work on so many levels, and I could identify with those guys, along with Lucian Freud and Frank Auerbach. That's always been my inspiration, but as I get older and more experienced, then I begin to question all of that. I also think that's because, hey, maybe finally I'm moving into my time.

It's a contradiction, being a Black artist with very European sensibilities, and given the subjects I'm using, I think my photos of my family—they're very subversive. They're subversive to me because they're challenging my whole belief system and sense of reality that I still hold on to, these very old, unreal ideas about the world that don't exist anymore.

I'm glad that I'm still around and I'm still evolving and growing. Right now, I'm a free spirit. If I'm so lucky as to be commercialized and become a famous artist, I won't refuse it. I'm looking for success as an artist on every level because I feel like I deserve it. This is critical times we're living through; we're approaching ground zero. Everything is moving very quickly, all the systems are running down in order for something else to happen. You look at the art world, and that's certainly clear. All the boom times of the 1980s, that's pretty much gone, but that also allows you to see that it was garbage anyhow. Now is a new time, a new beginning, a new sensibility, a new everything. I'd like to be part of that.

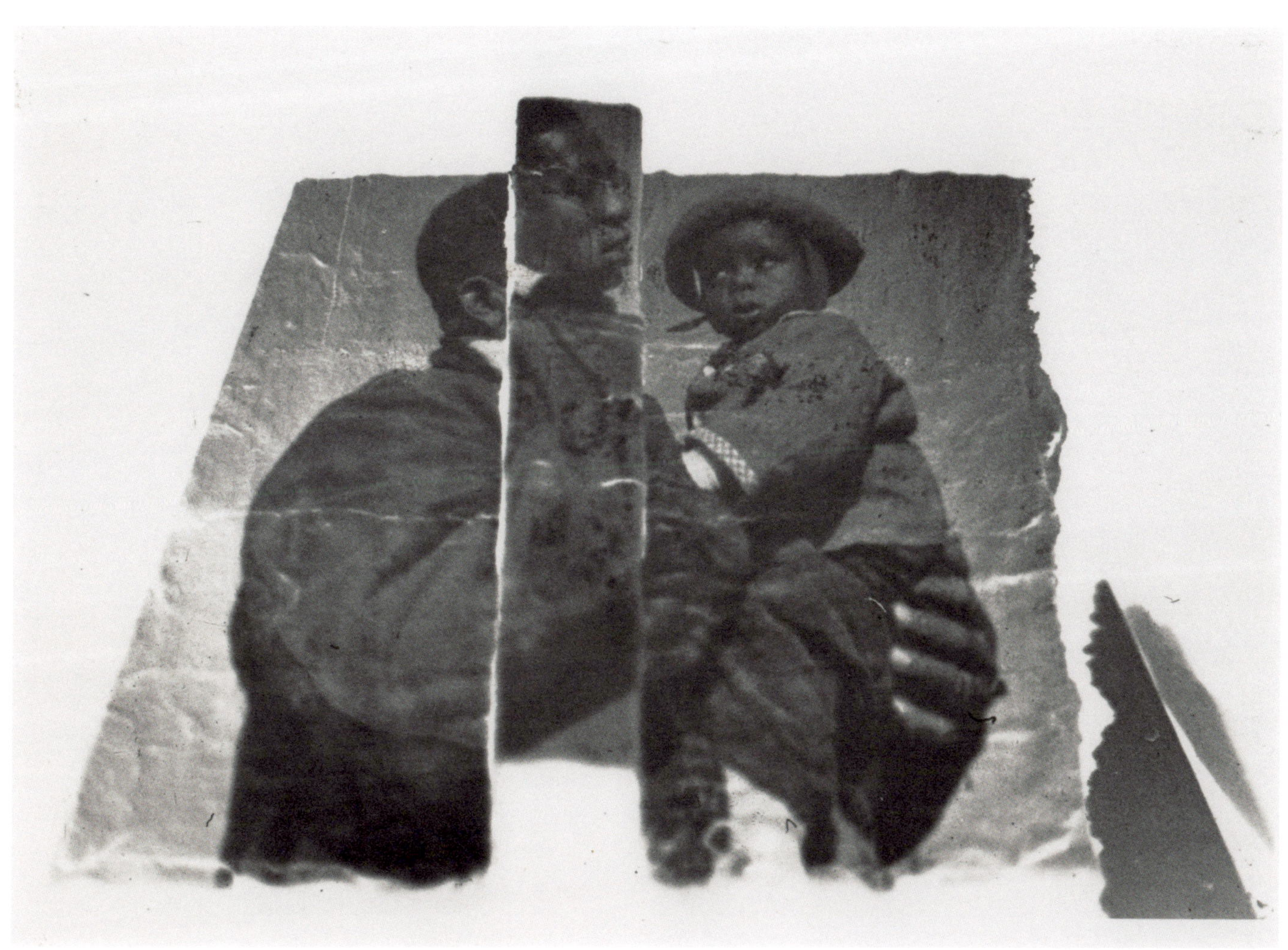

10. *Untitled* (Grandfather Thomas and Cousin Irving)
ca. 1988–92
Gelatin silver print
7 ½ × 9 ½ inches
The Baltimore Museum of Art

# Works

Darrel Ellis did not consistently sign, date, or title
his artworks. Descriptive titles have been added in
parentheses for works that were not titled, based
on information provided by the Ellis family and
Allen Frame. Where there is no direct evidence
for an artwork date an approximate date has been
assigned based on stylistic considerations.

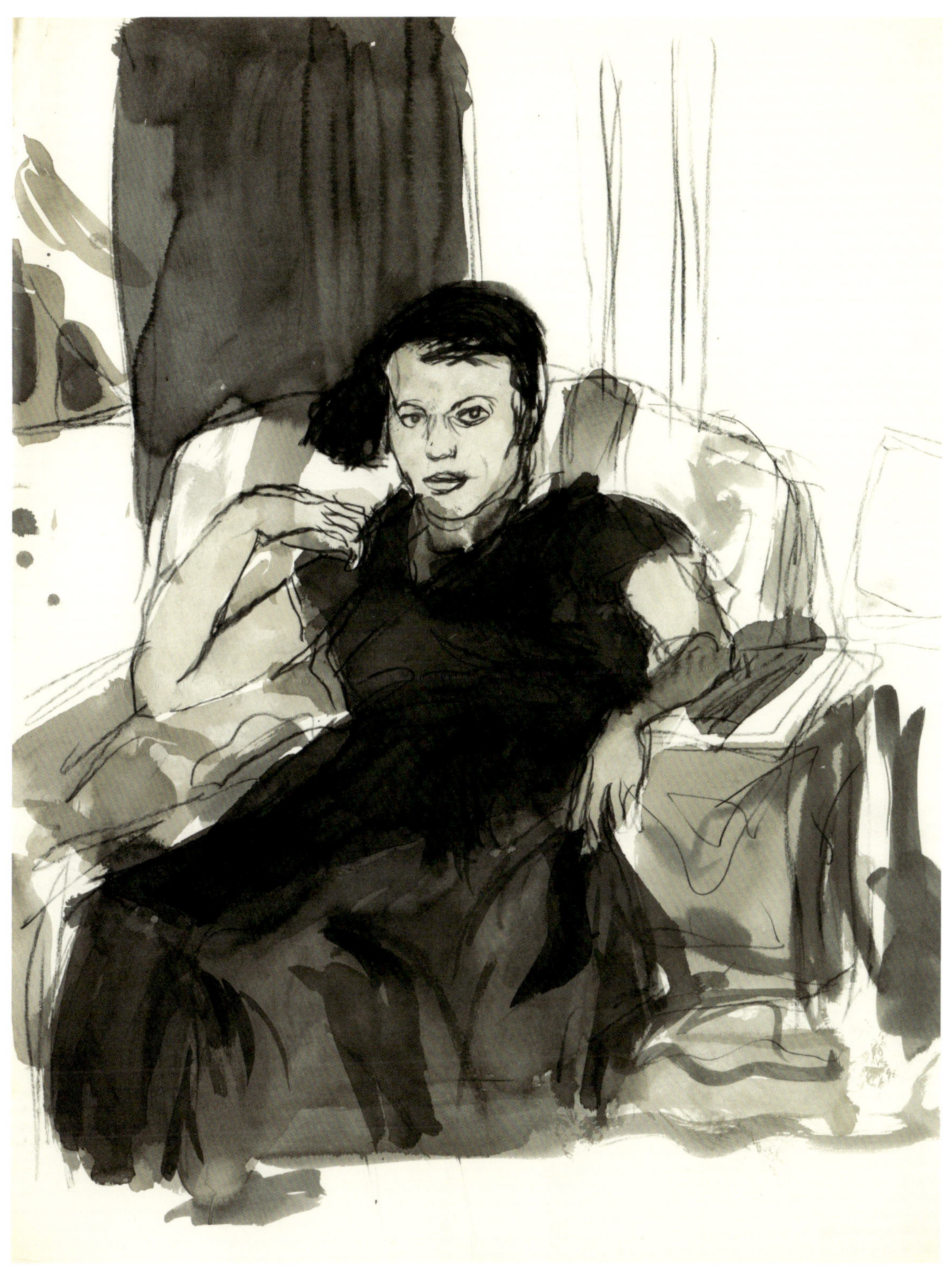

*Untitled* (Woman in Chair)
ca. 1981  85
Ink, wash, and charcoal on paper
29 × 22 inches

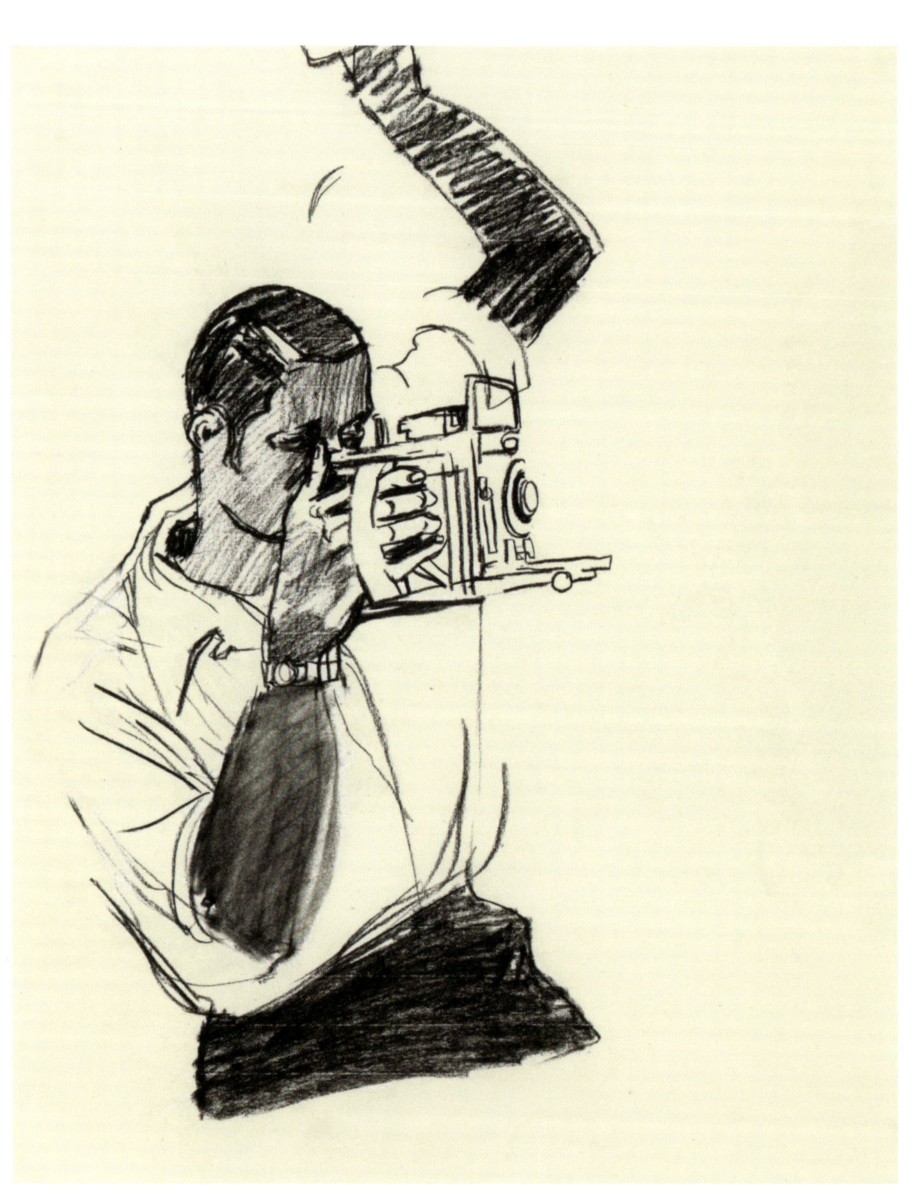

*Untitled* (Father with Camera)
ca. 1981–85
Charcoal on paper
25 × 19 inches

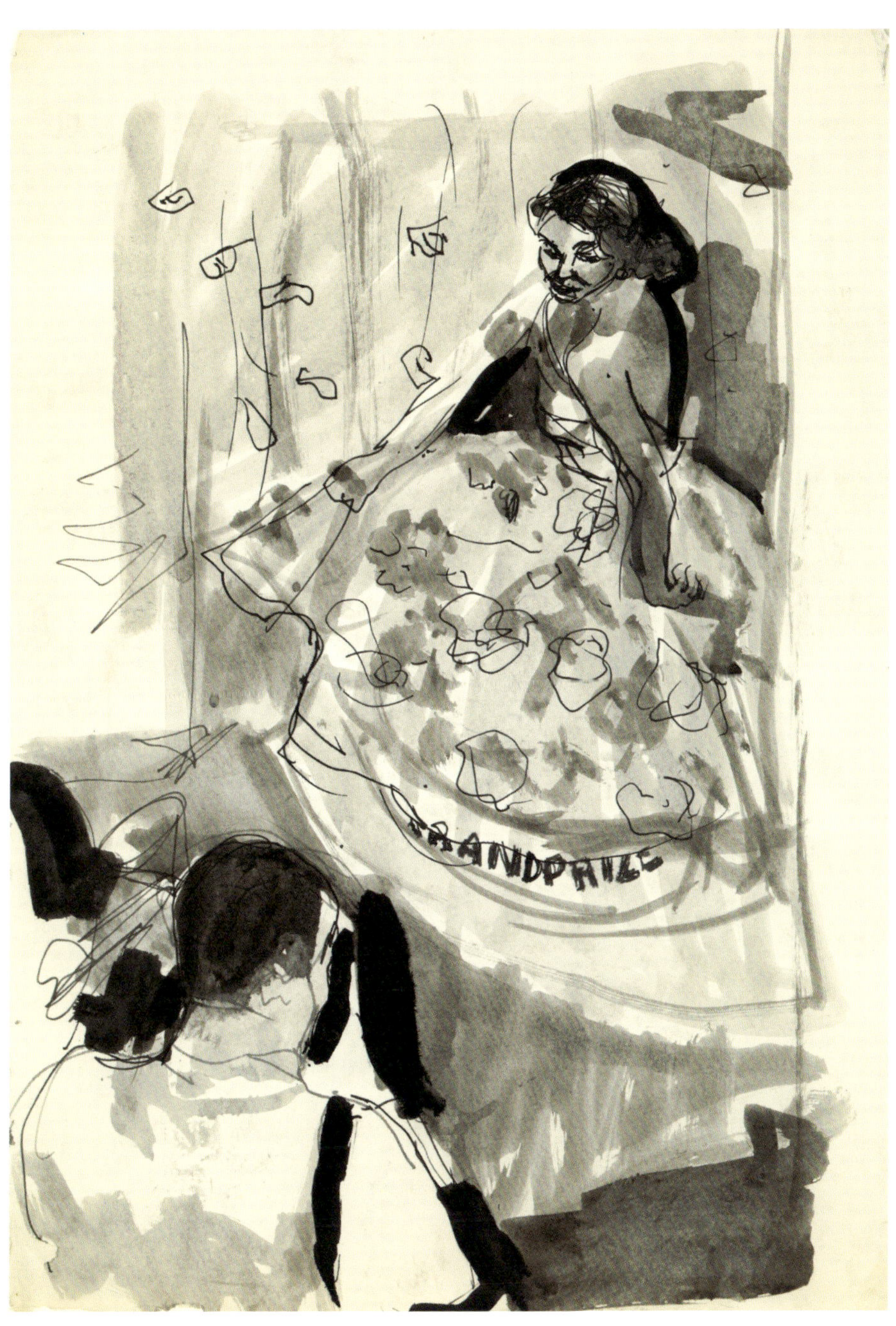

*Untitled* (Grand Prize Beauty Contestant)
ca. 1981
Ink and wash on paper
17 × 11 ¼ inches

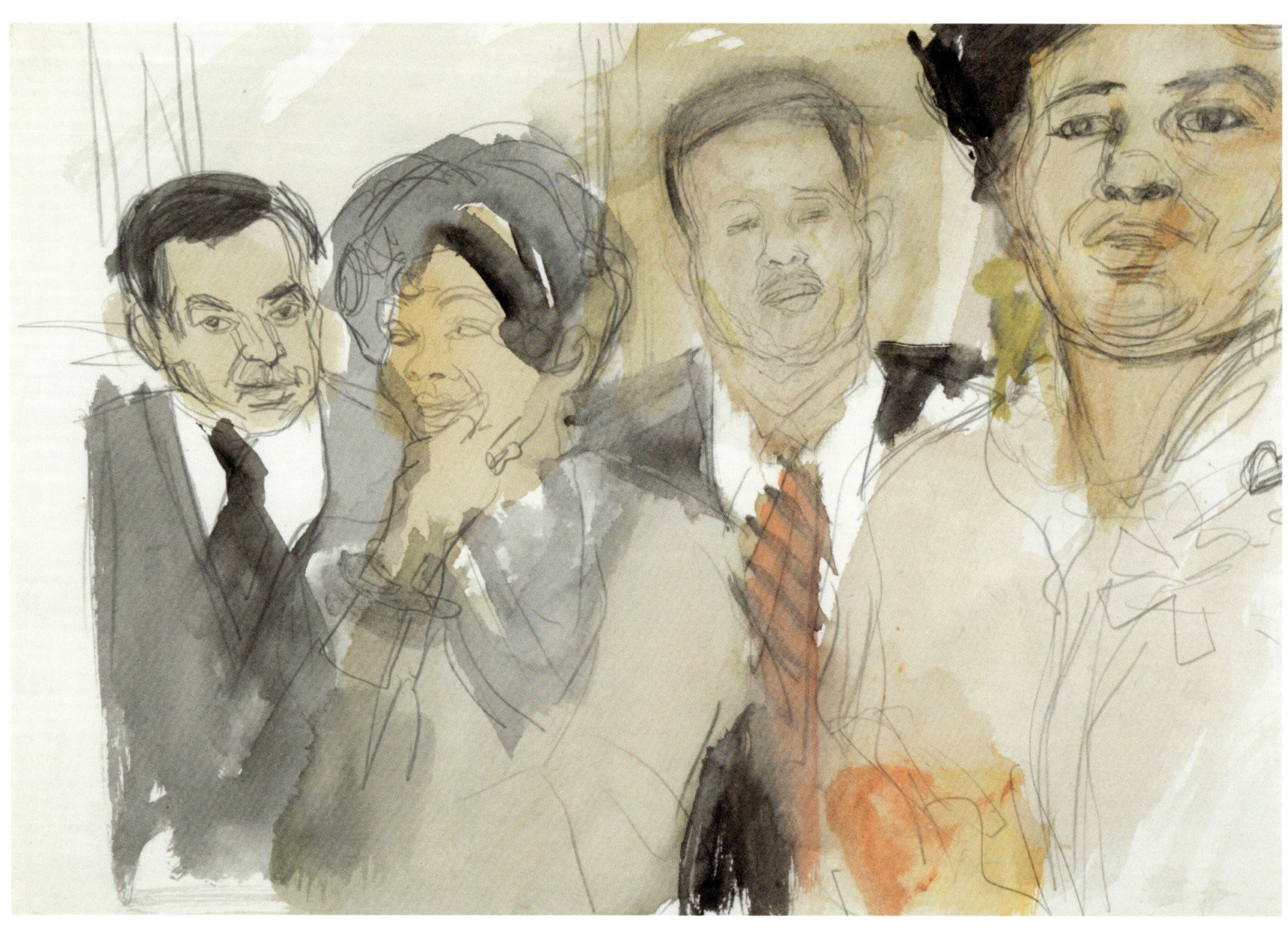

*Untitled* (Four Figures)
ca. 1981–85
Watercolor and graphite on paper
11 × 15 inches

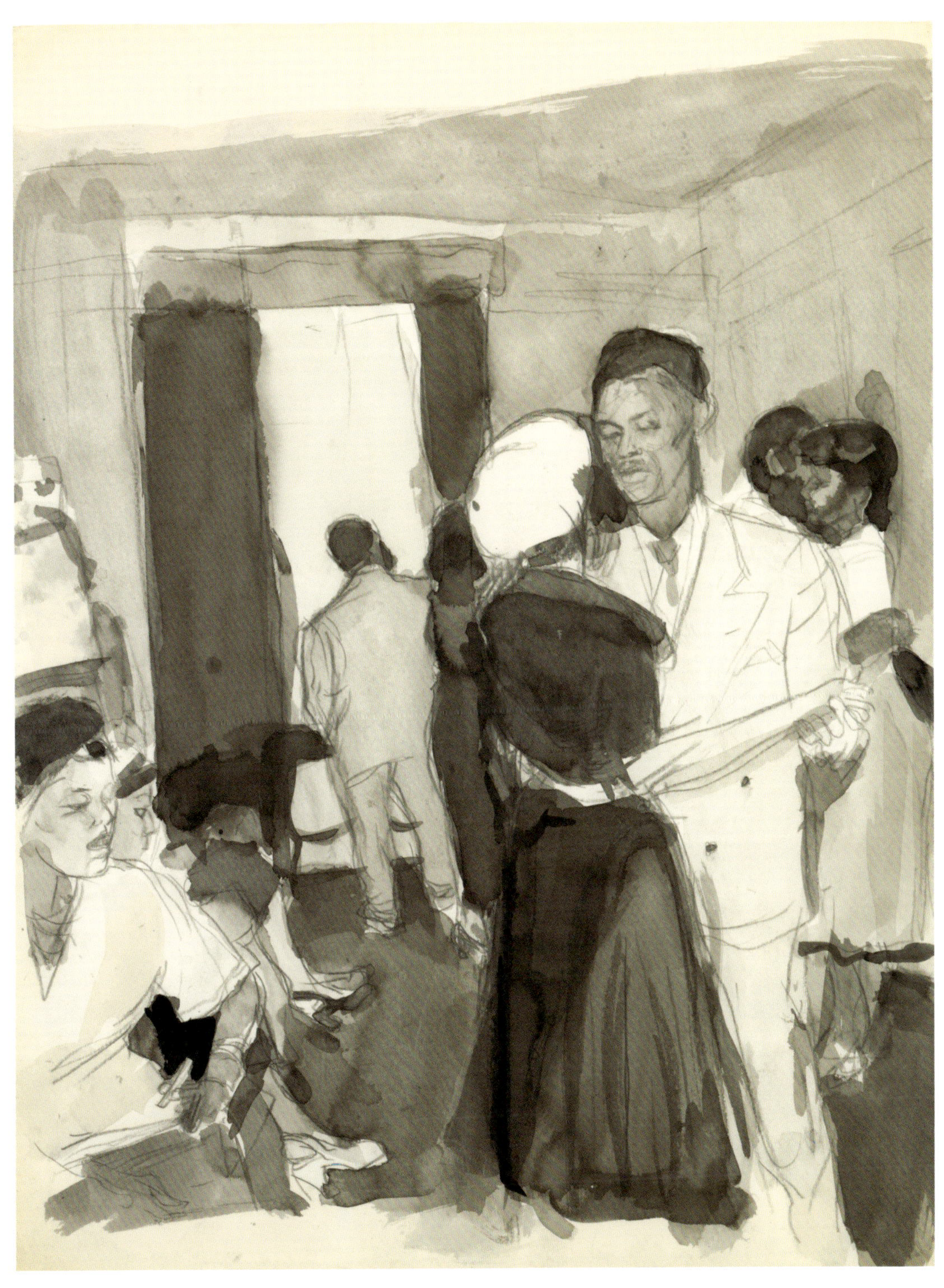

*Untitled* (Dancing Couple)
ca. 1981–85
Ink, wash, and graphite on paper
30 × 21 inches
Collection of Dr. Kenneth Montague /
The Wedge Collection

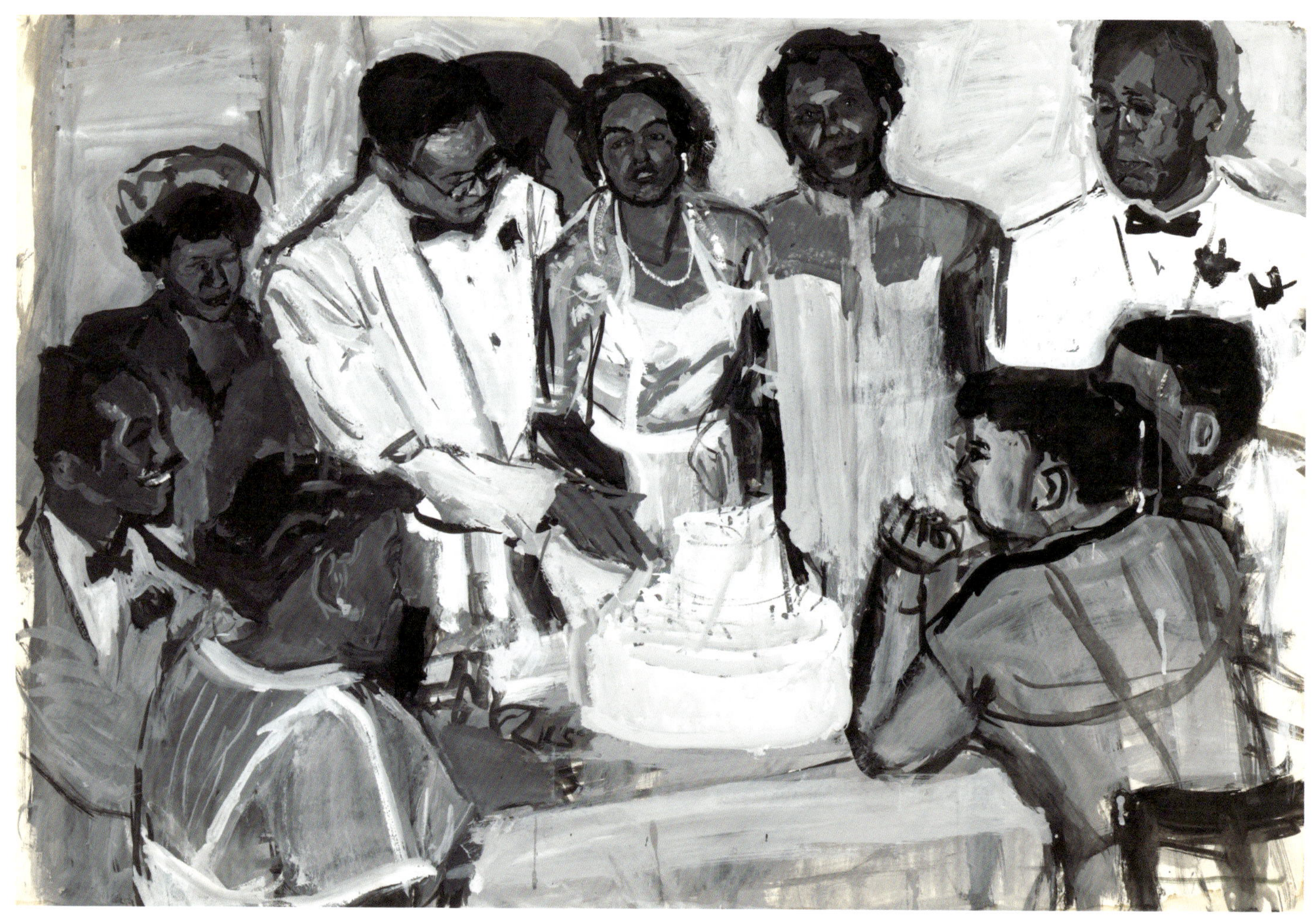

*Untitled* (Group at Aunt Lena's Wedding)
ca. 1981–85
Gouache and ink on paper
30 × 43 inches

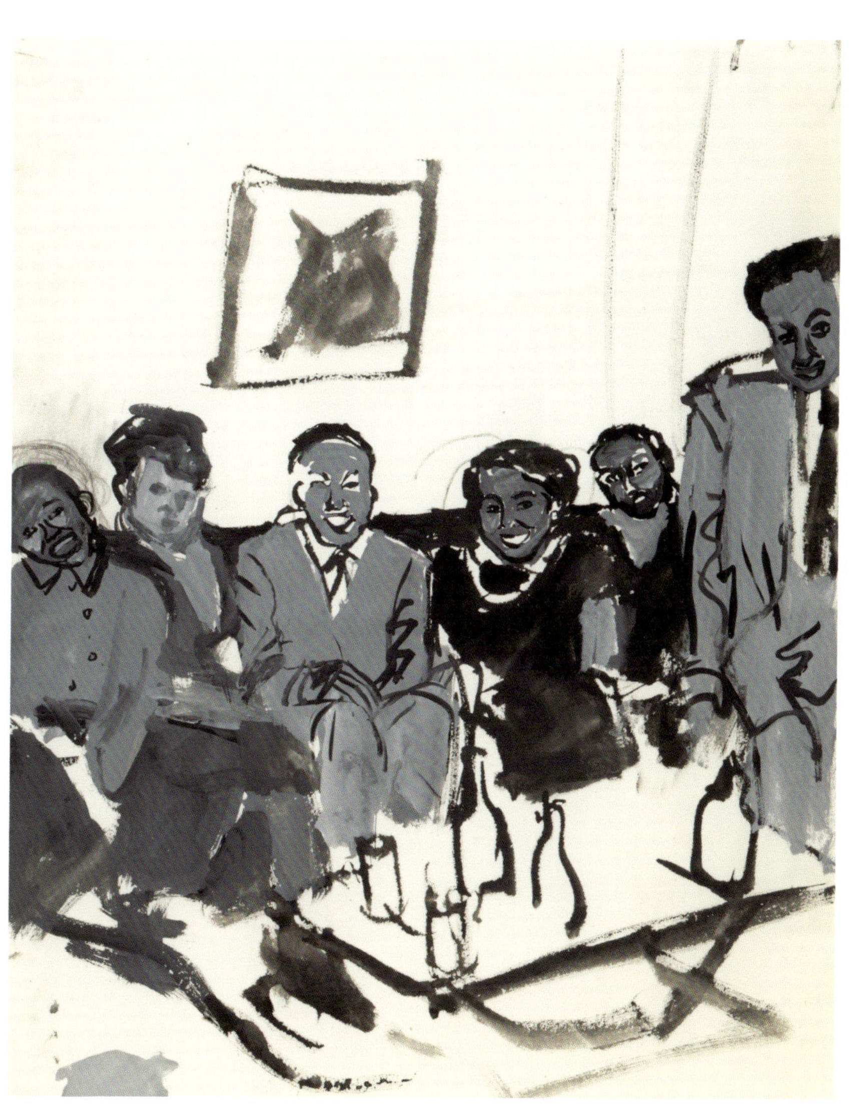

*Untitled* (Group at Party)
ca. 1981–85
Gouache, ink, and graphite on paper
23 ½ × 18 inches

*Untitled* (Grandparents Dancing)
ca. 1981–85
Gouache and ink on paper
22 × 30 inches

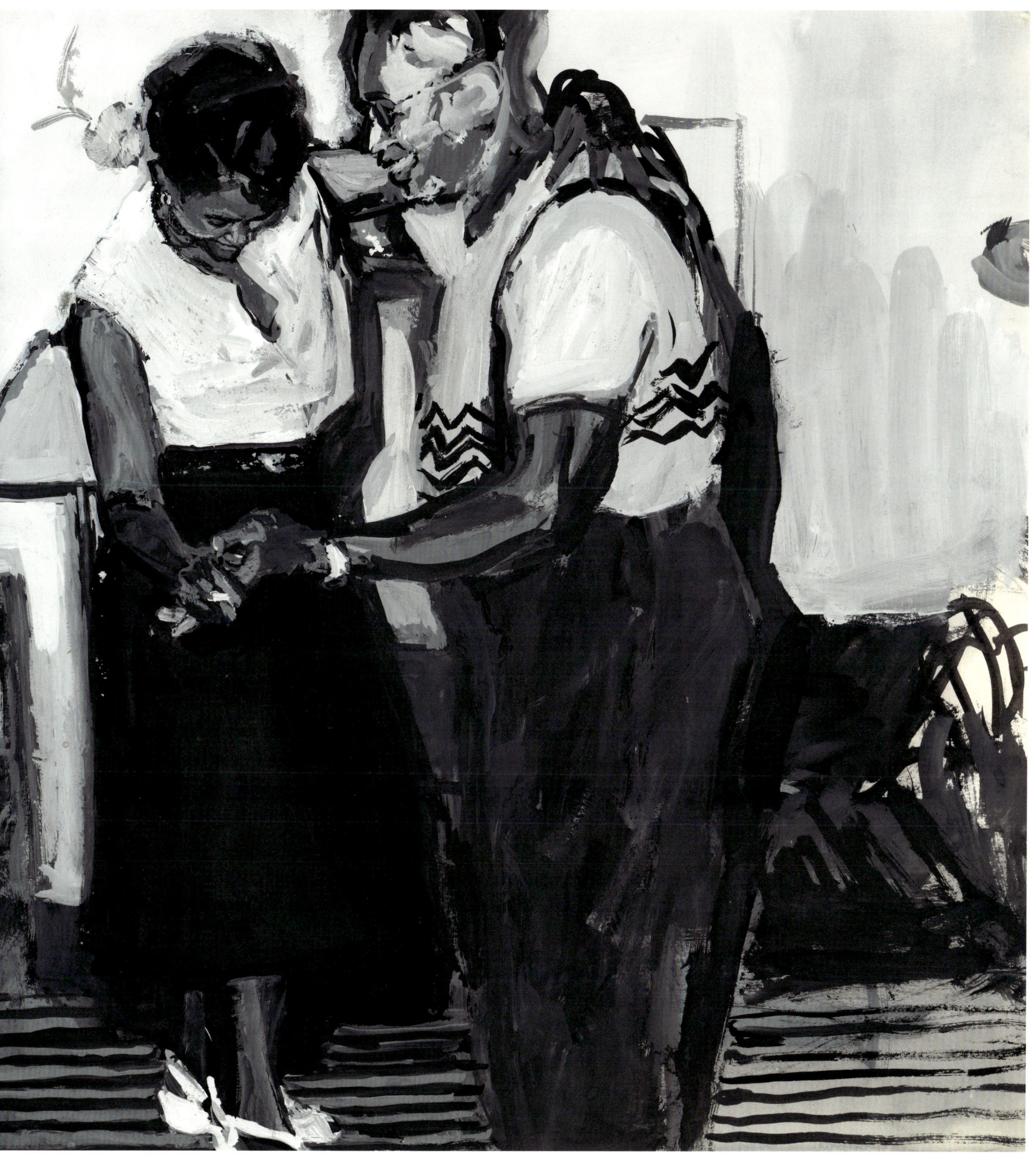

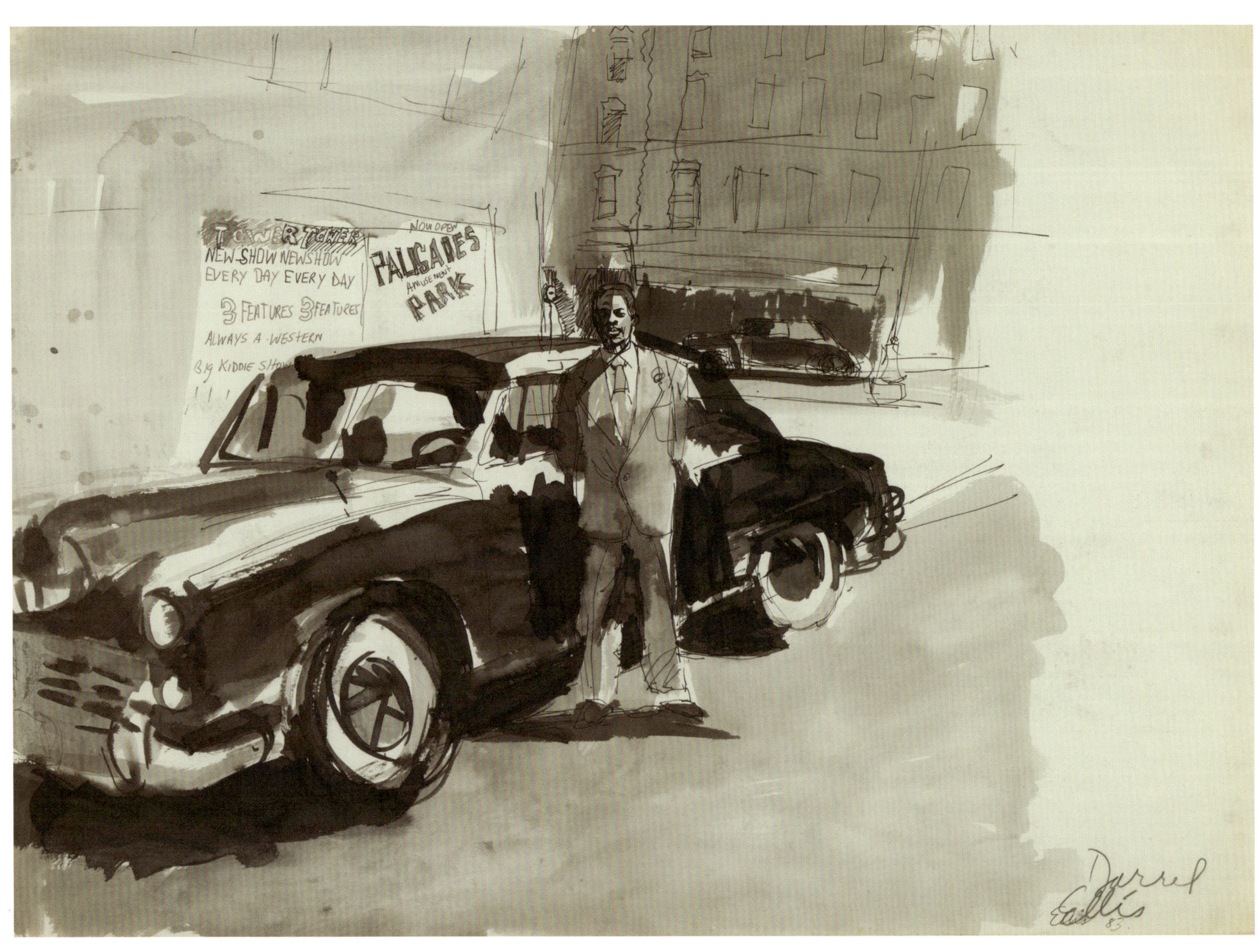


*Untitled* (Man with Car on Street)
1983
Ink and wash on paper
22 ½ × 29 ½ inches

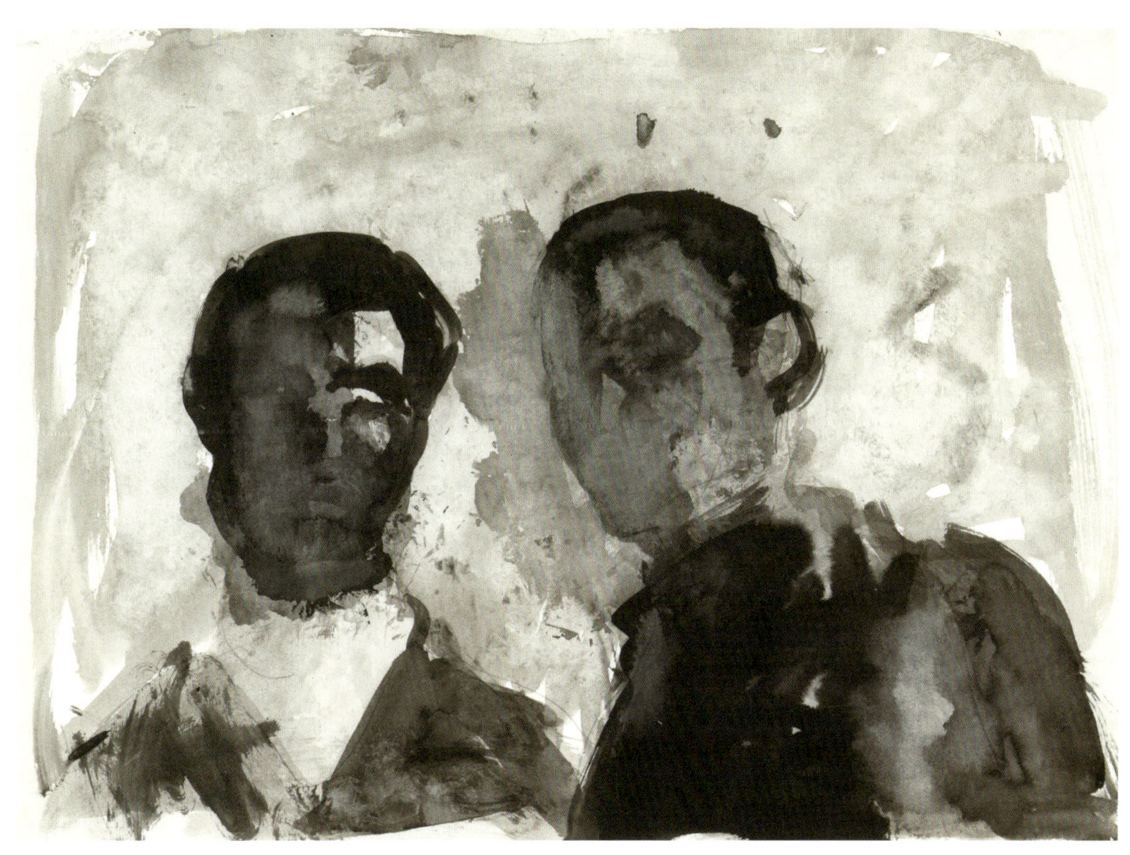

*Self-Portrait with Guard*
1981
Ink, wash, and graphite on paper
18 × 24 inches

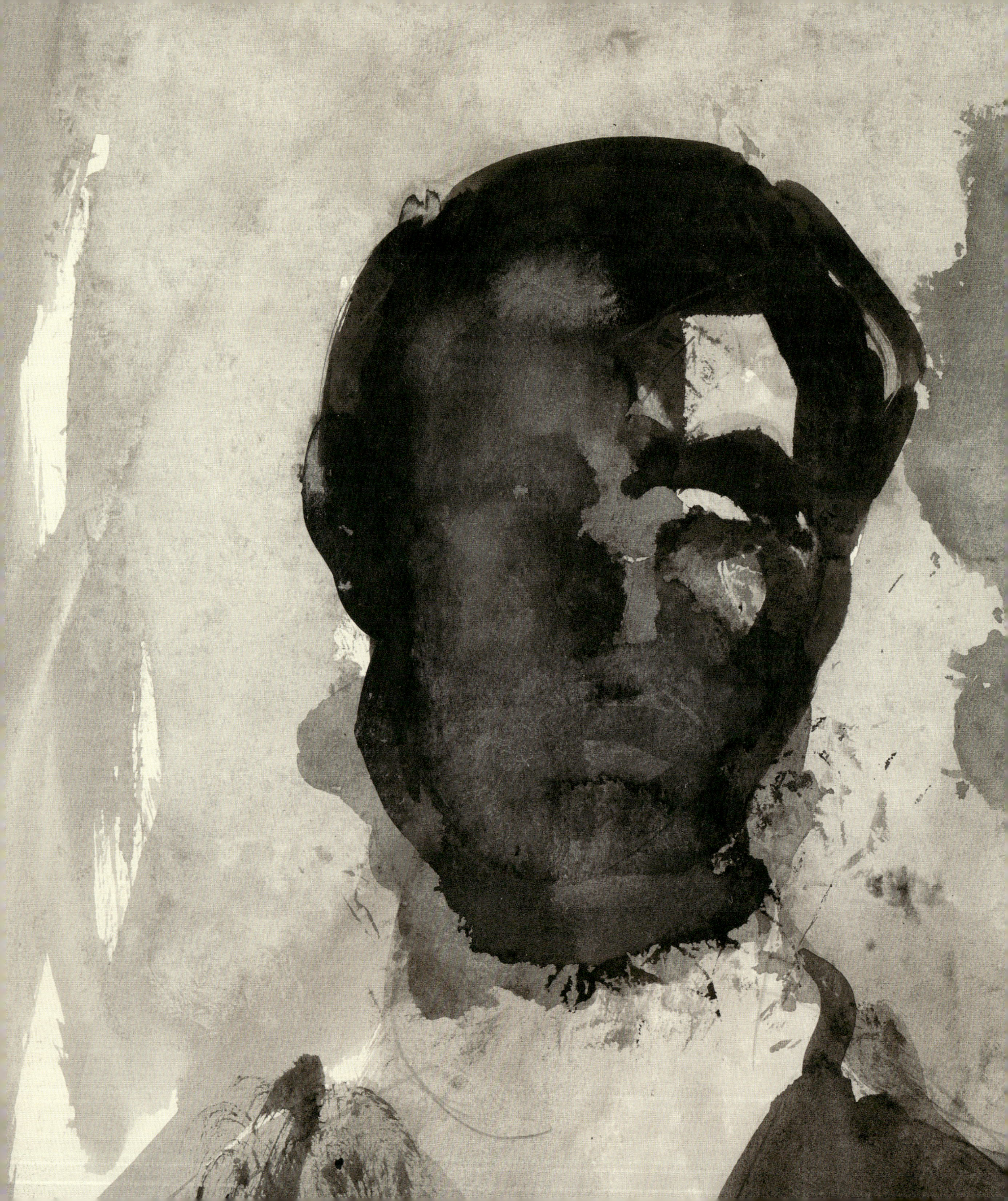

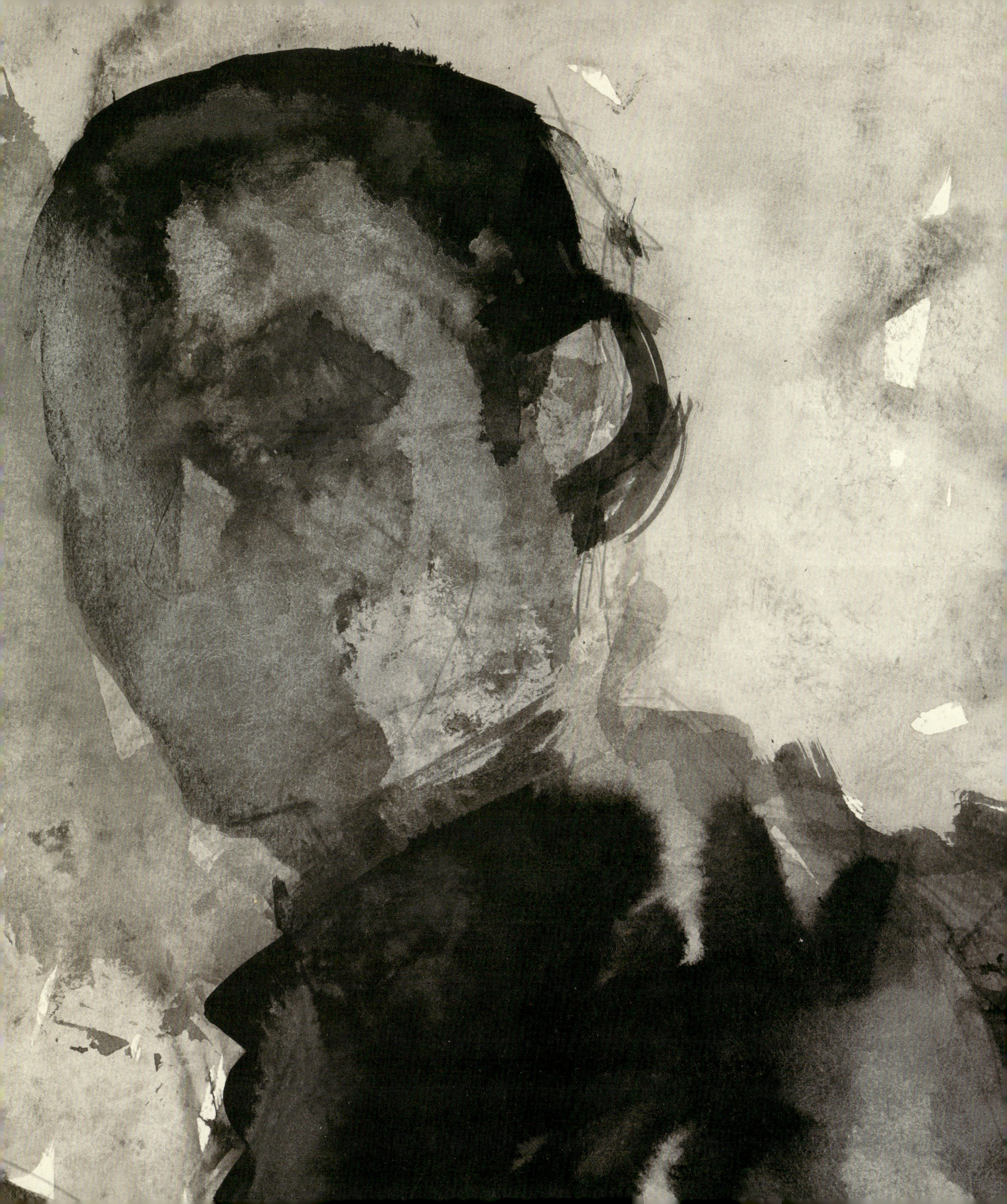

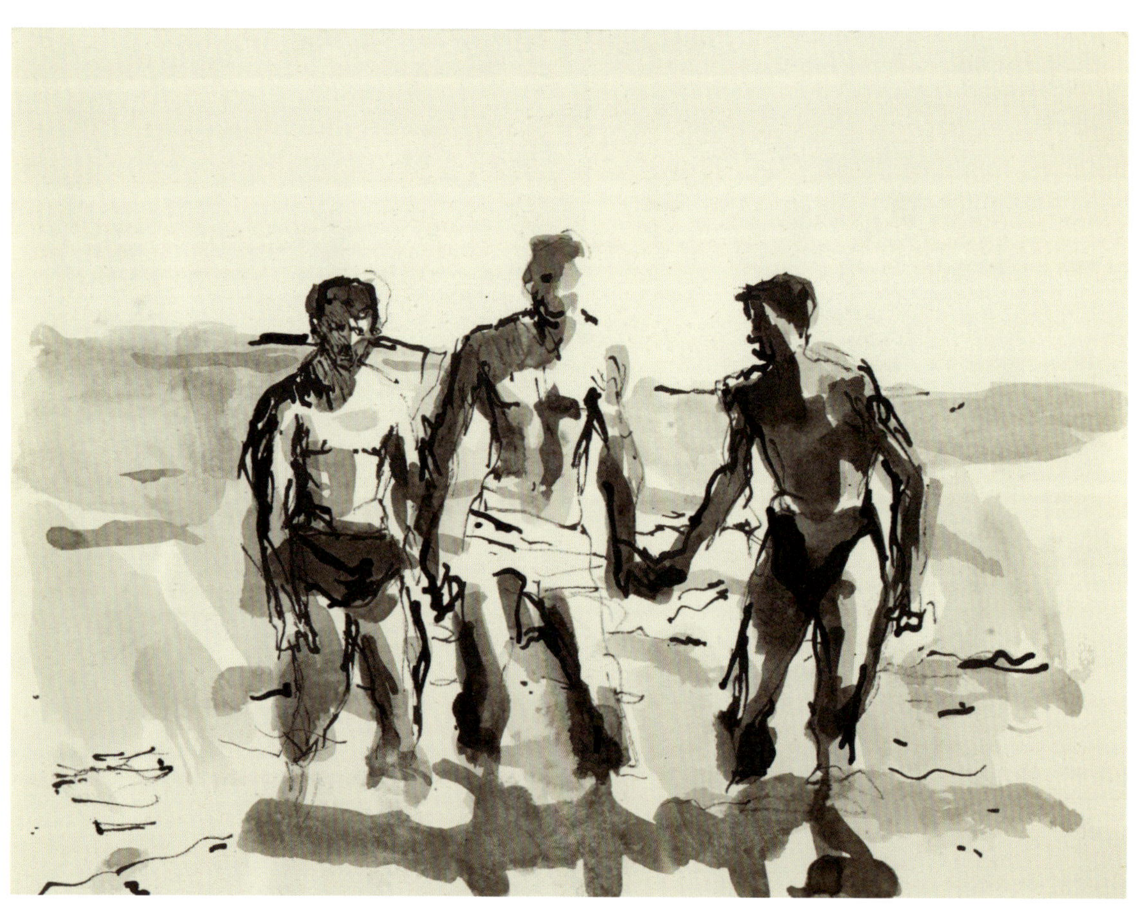

*Untitled* (Bathers)
ca. 1981–85
Ink and wash on paper
11 × 14 inches

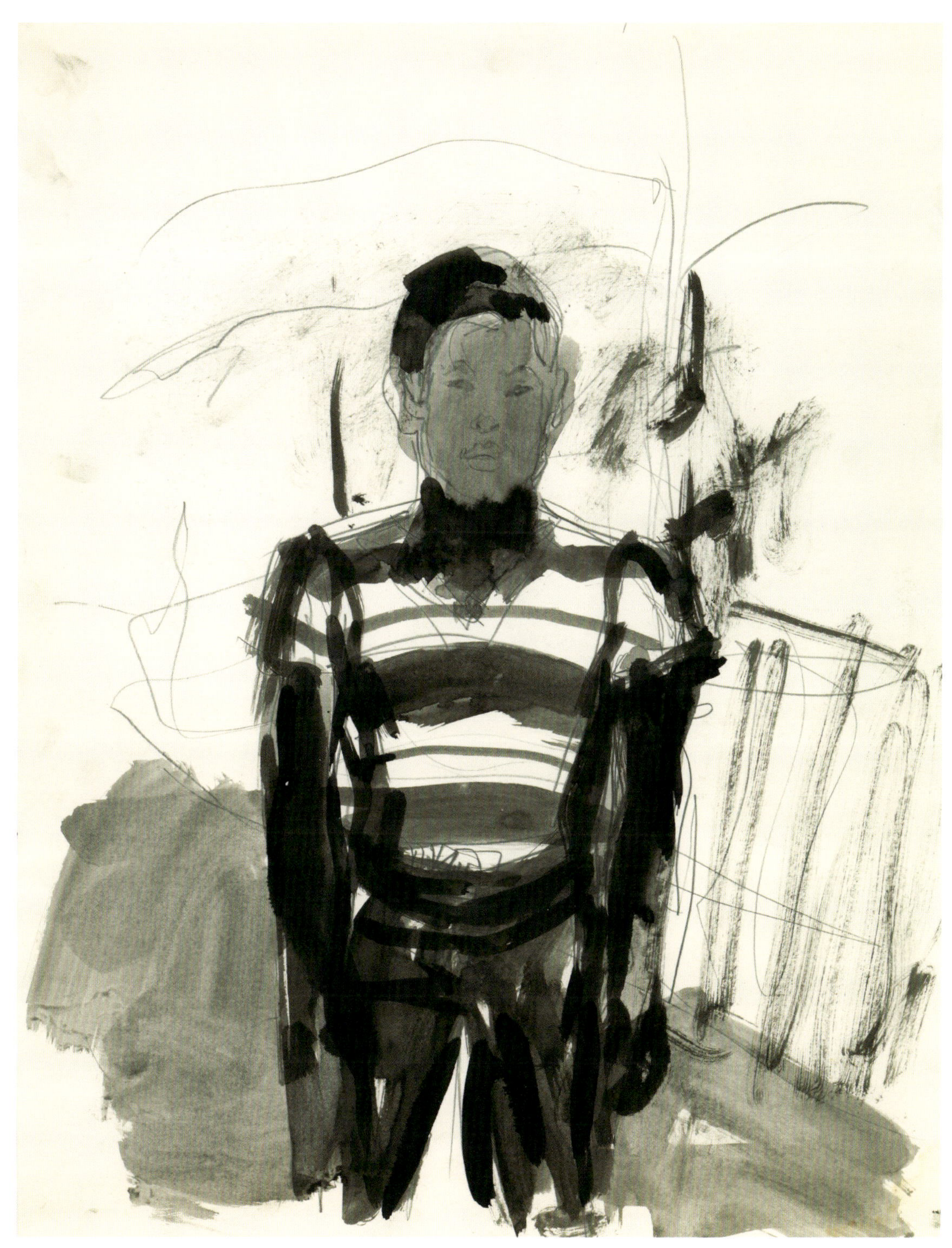

*Untitled* (Child)
ca. 1981–85
Ink, wash, and graphite on paper
24 × 18 inches

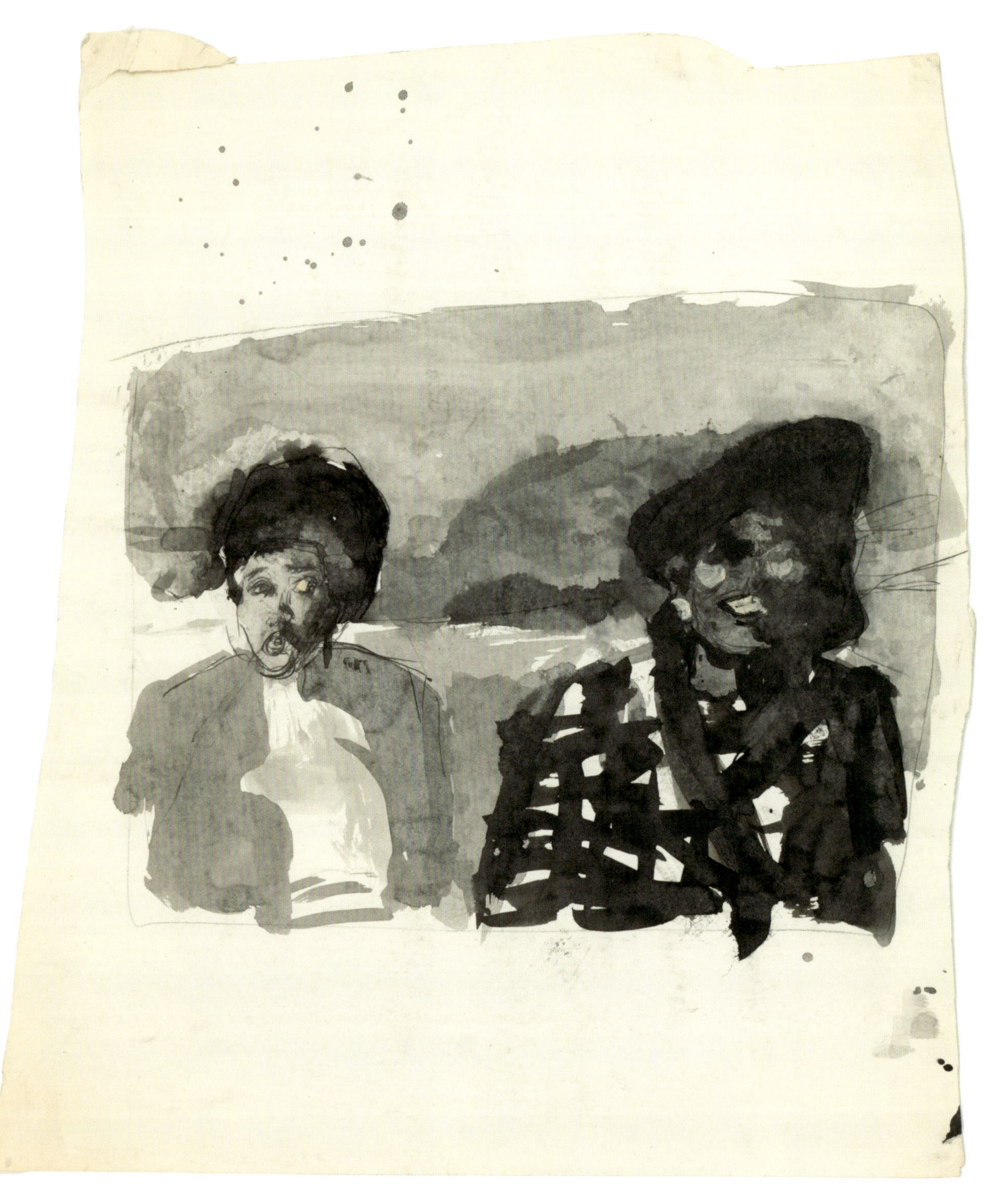

*Untitled* (Two Women)
ca. 1981–85
Ink, wash, and graphite on paper
21 × 16 inches

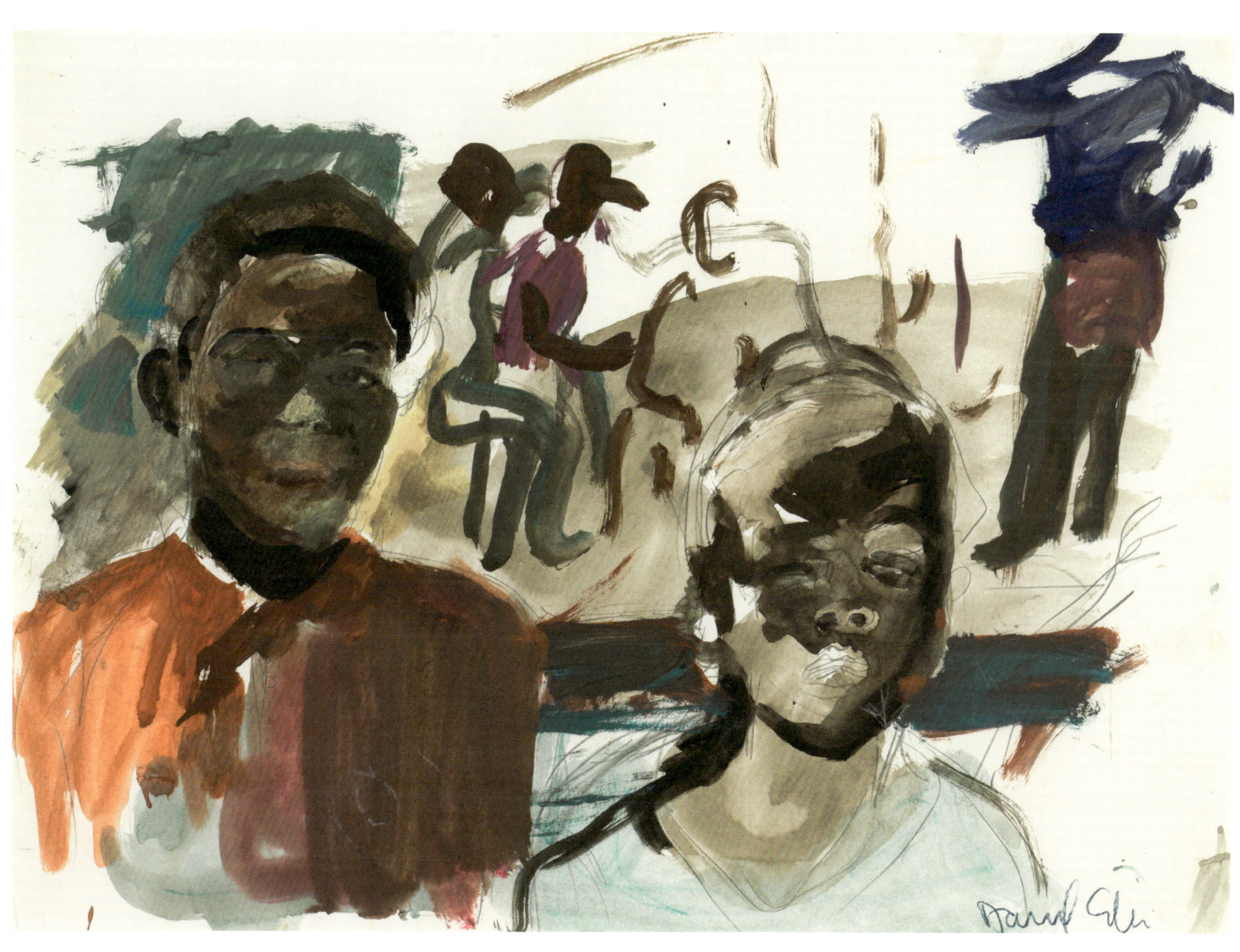

*Untitled* (Children)
ca. 1981–85
Gouache, ink, and graphite on paper
18 × 24 inches

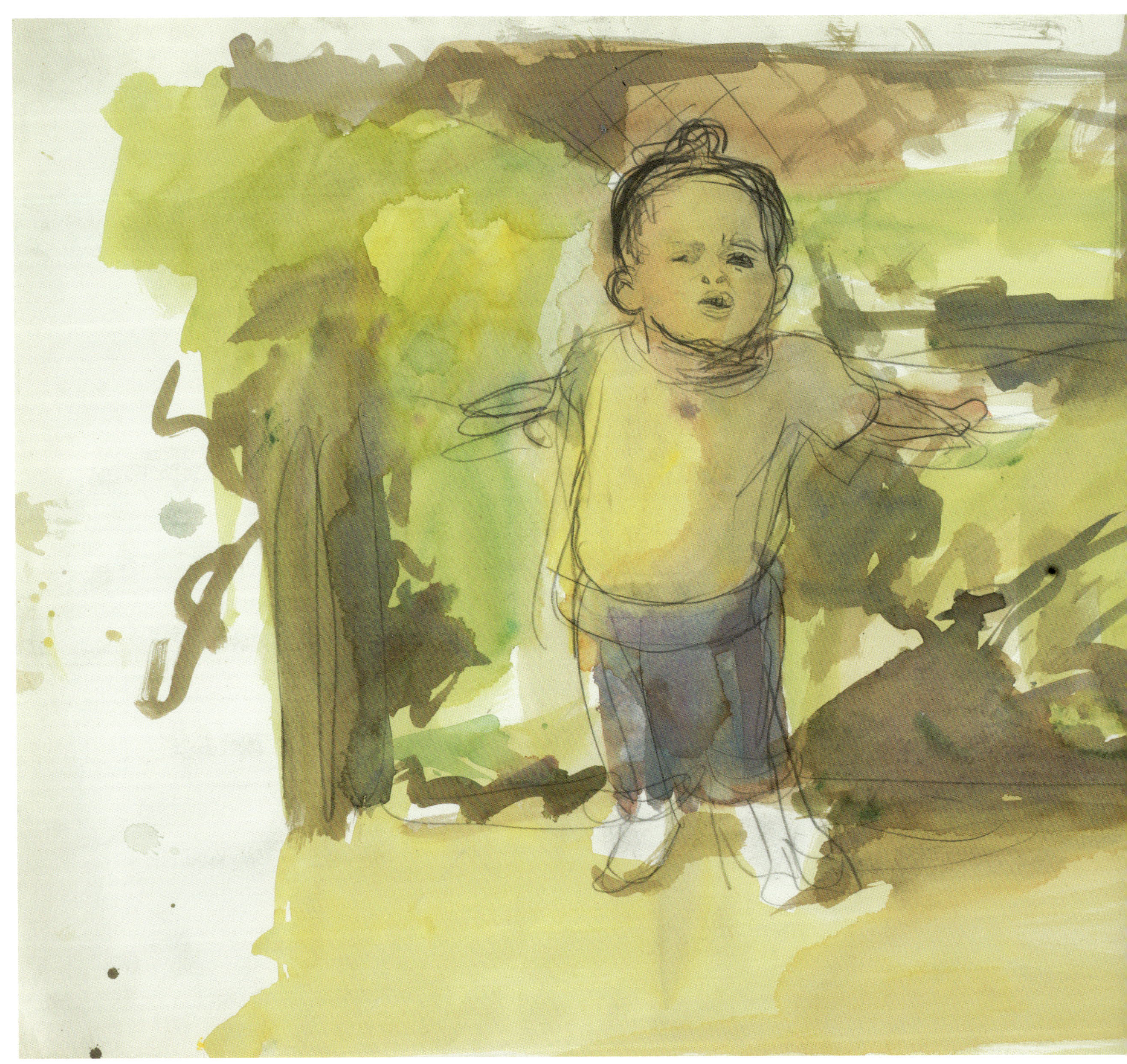

*Untitled* (Baby)
ca 1981–85
Watercolor and graphite on paper
22 × 30 inches

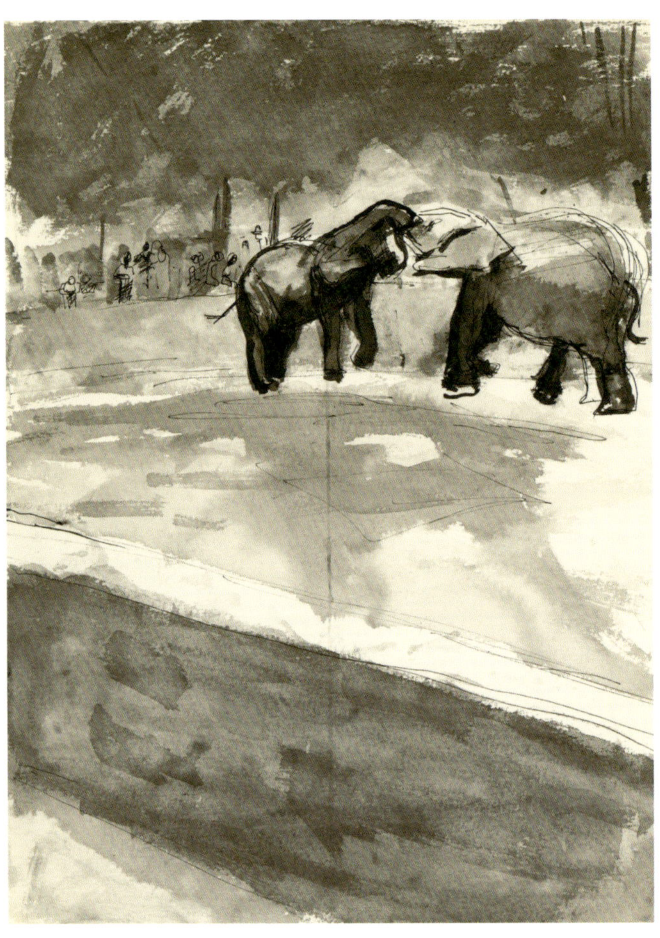

*Untitled* (Elephants)
ca. 1981–85
Ink and wash on paper
20 ½ × 14 ½ inches

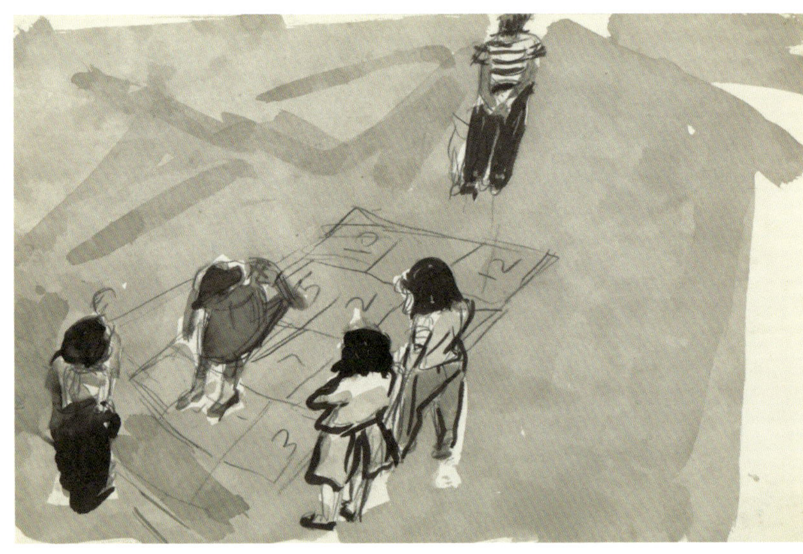

*Untitled* (Hopscotch)
ca. 1981–85
Ink, wash, and graphite on paper
12 × 18 inches
Collection of JoAnn Gonzalez Hickey

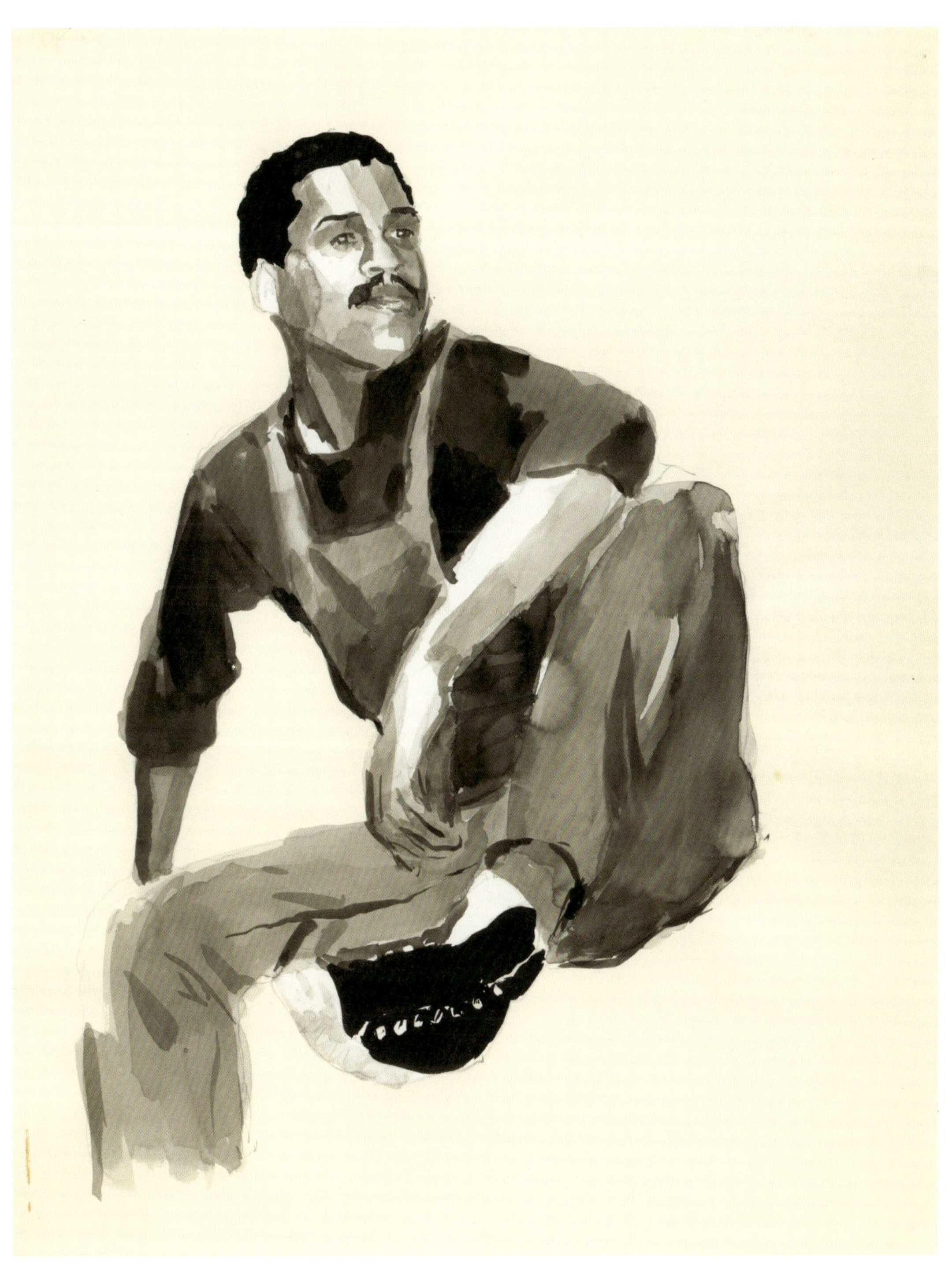

*Untitled* (Self-Portrait)
ca. 1981–85
Ink, wash, and graphite on paper
30 × 23 ⅛ inches

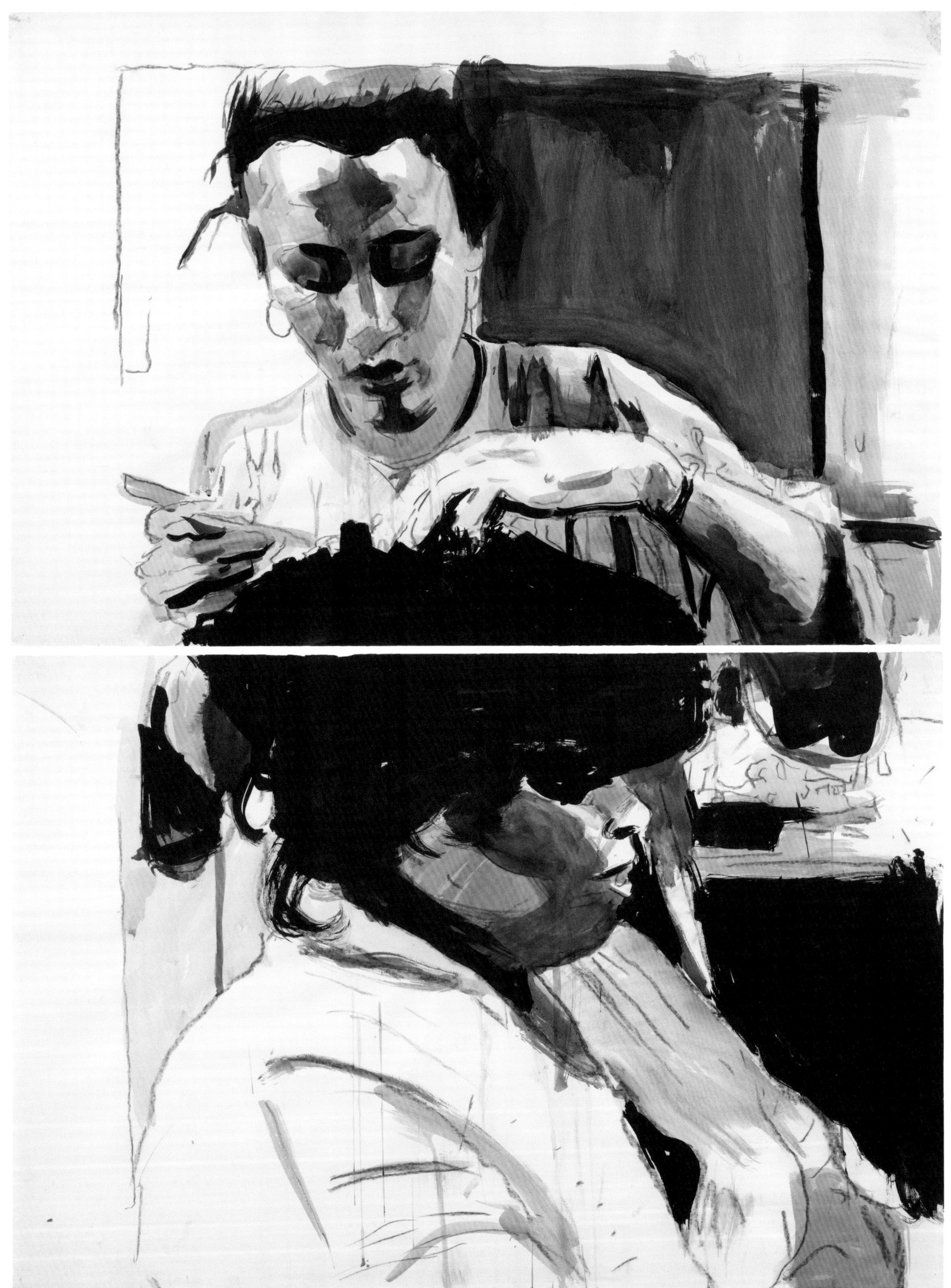

*Untitled* (Katrina Styling Linda's Hair)
ca. 1985–88
Paint, ink, wash, and charcoal on paper
55 × 39 ½ inches

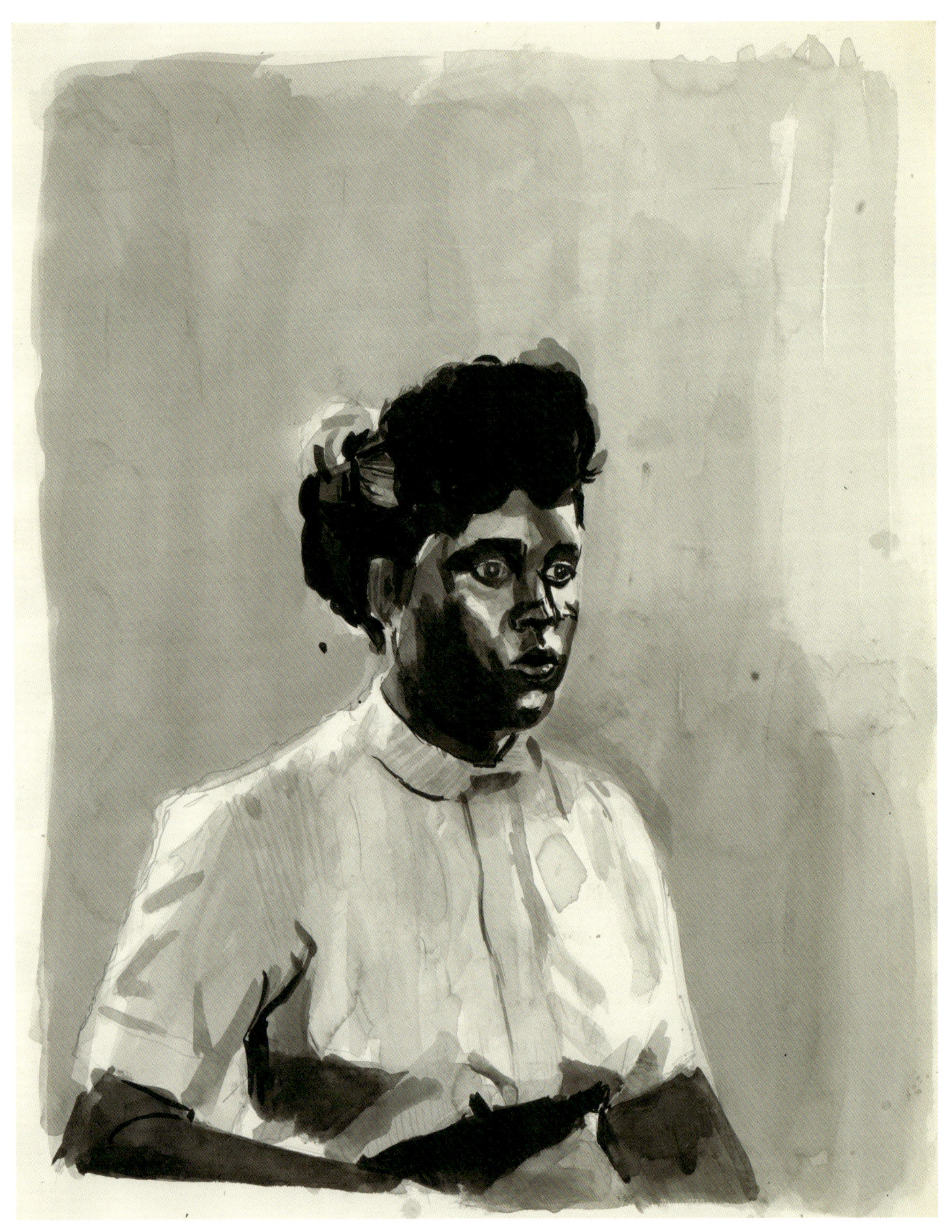

*Untitled* (Mother)
ca. 1989–91
Ink, wash, and graphite on paper
28 × 23 inches

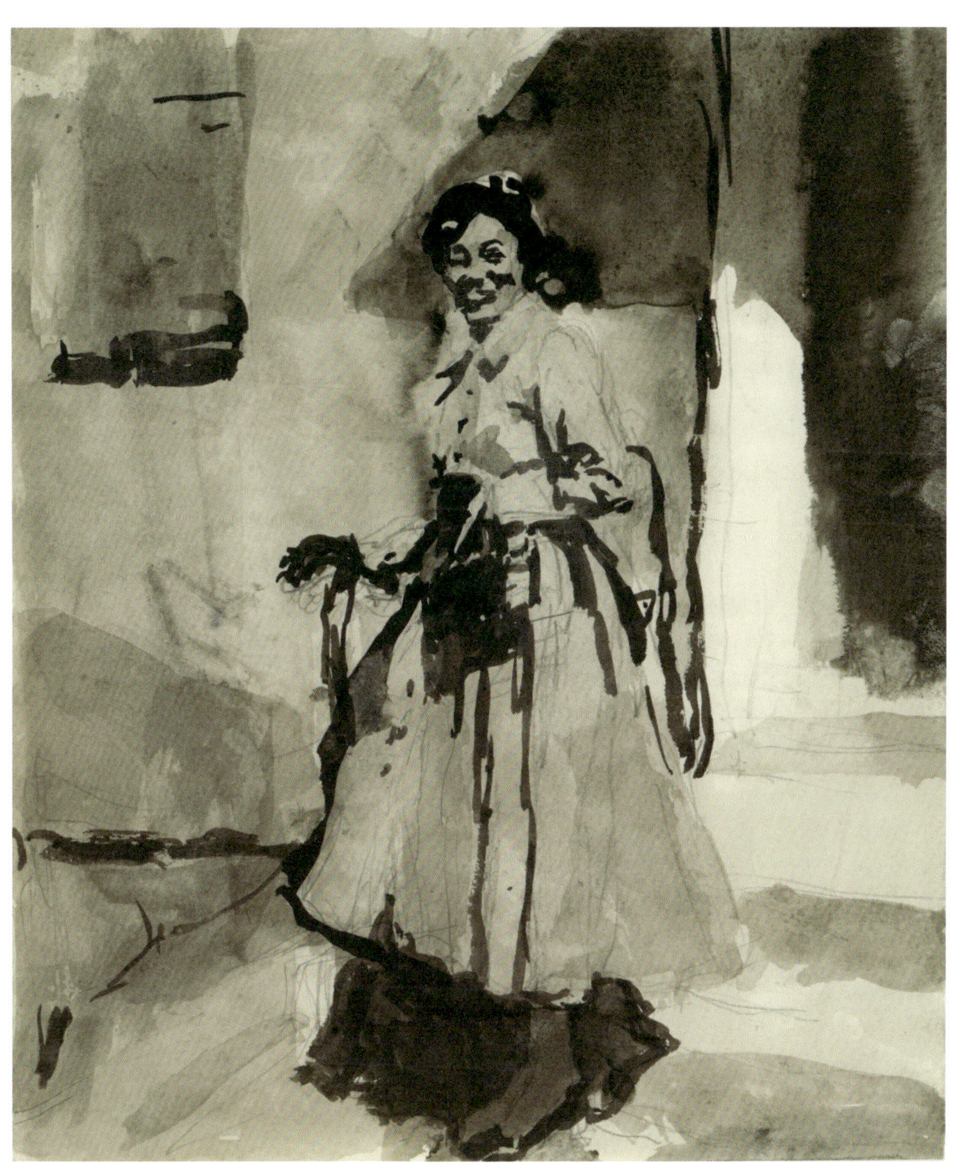

*Untitled* (Grandmother Lillian Ellis)
ca. 1981–85
Ink, wash, and graphite on paper
12 ½ × 10 ½ inches

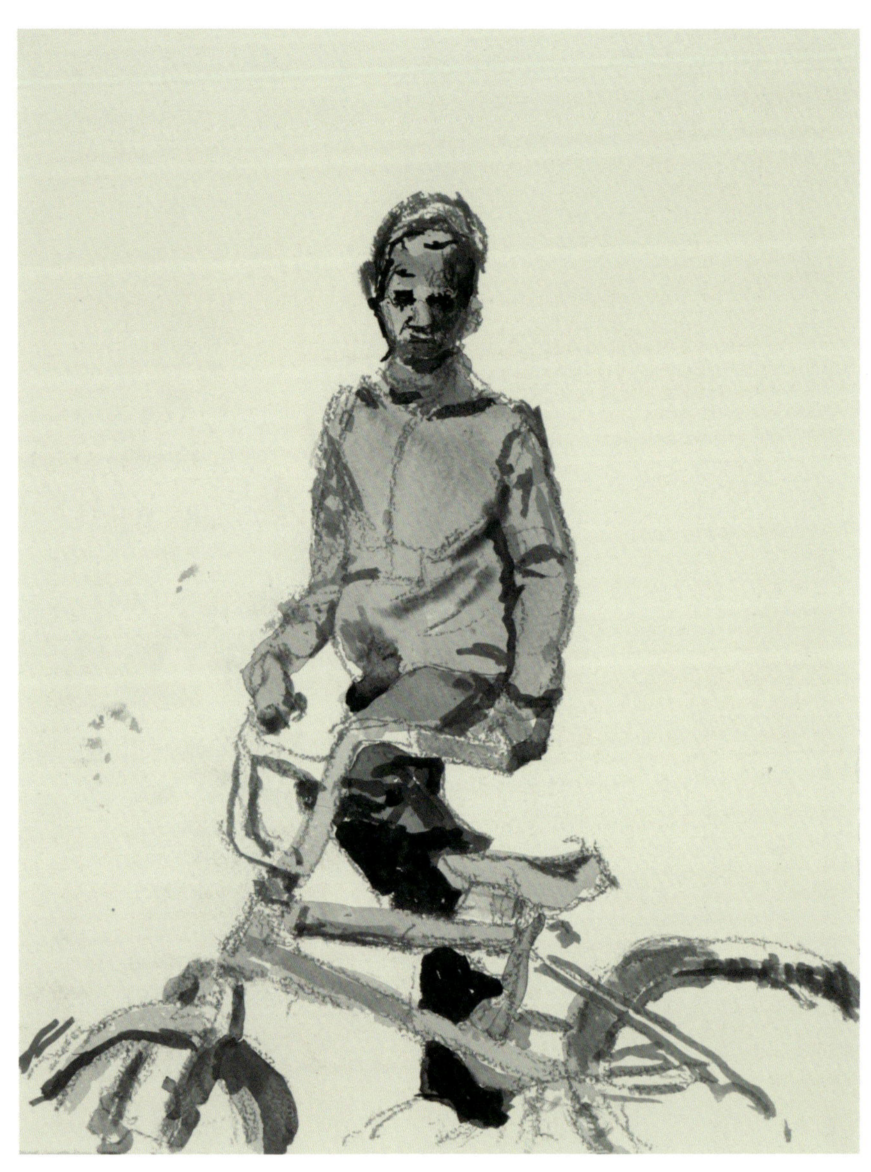

*Untitled* (Boy with Bicycle)
ca. 1981–85
Ink, wash, and graphite on paper
14 × 10 inches

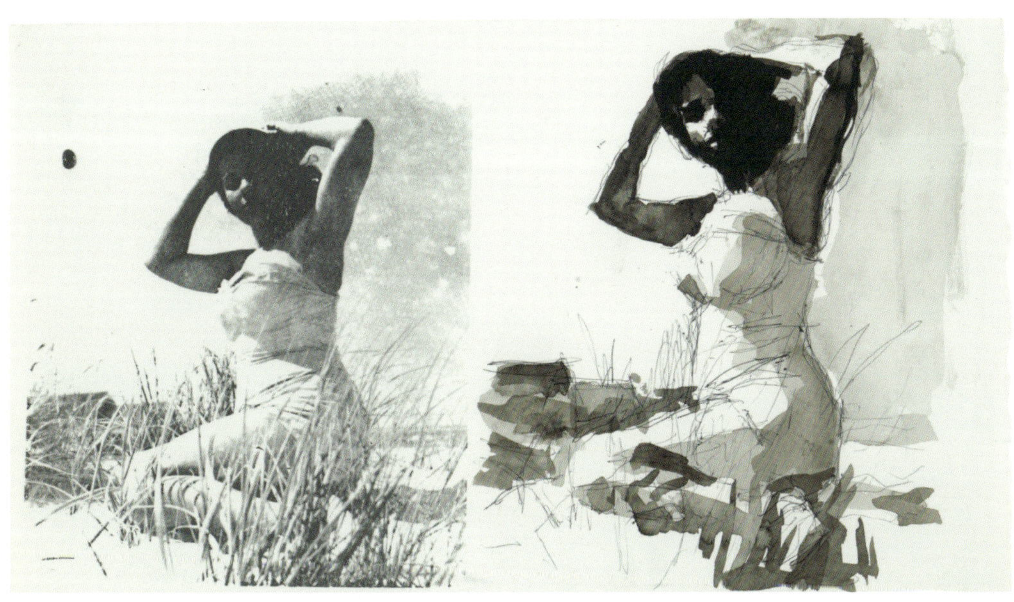

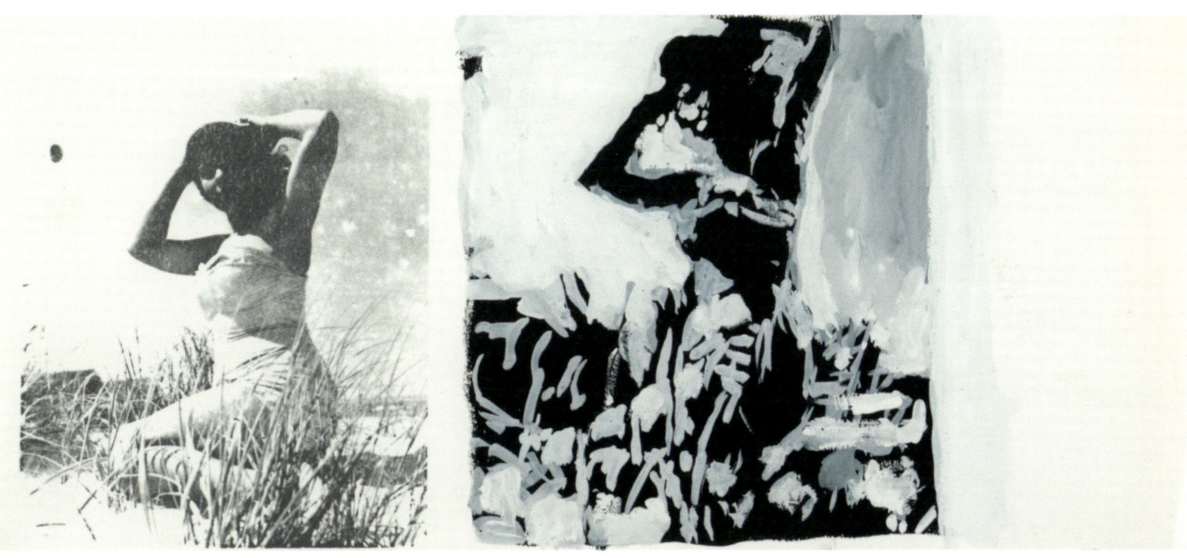

*Untitled* (Bathing Beauty)
ca. 1985–88
Silkscreen with ink and wash on paper
10 × 17 ¼ inches
Collection of Beth Rudin DeWoody

*Untitled* (Bathing Beauty)
ca. 1985–88
Silkscreen with ink and gouache on paper
10 ½ × 22 inches

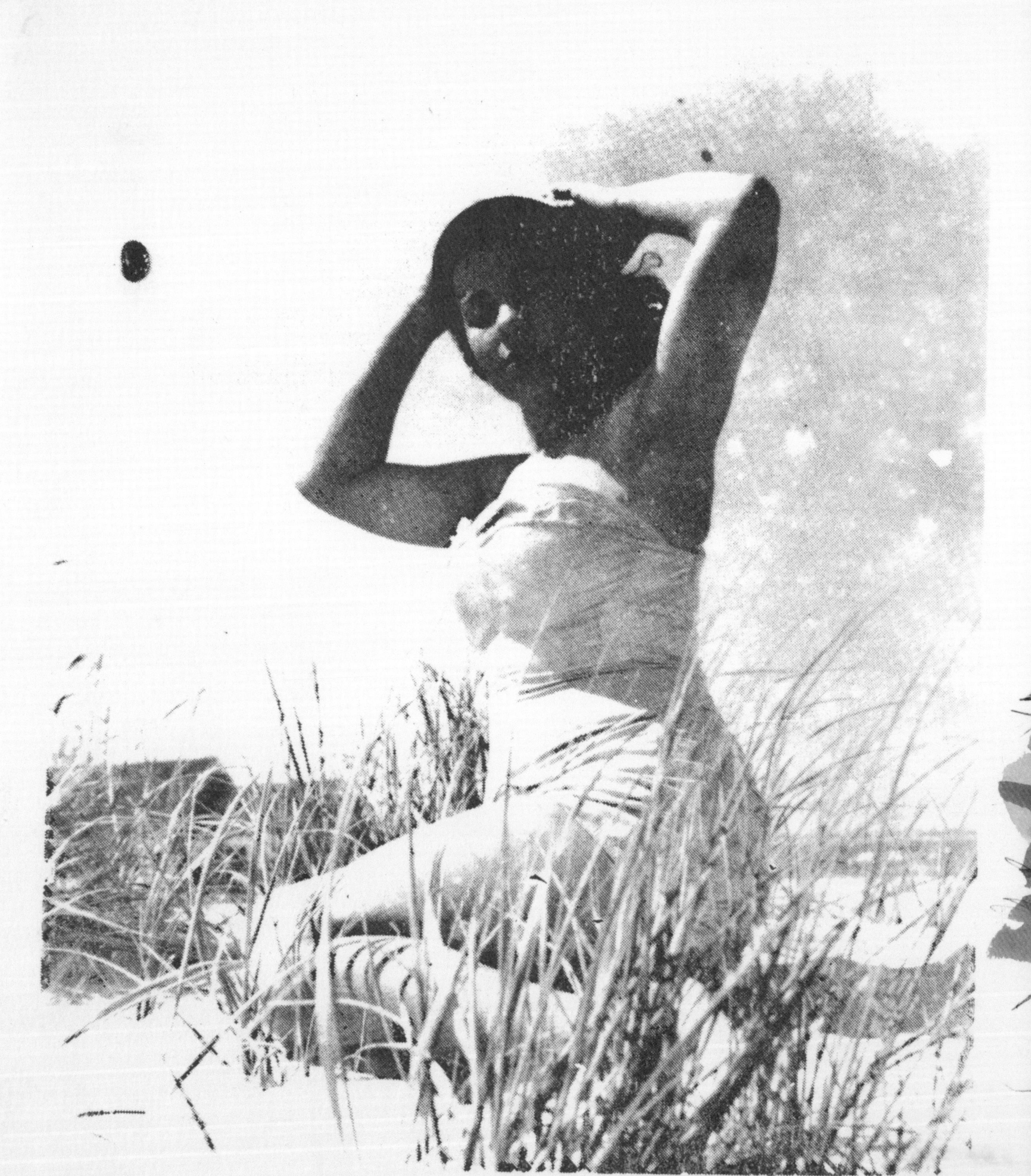

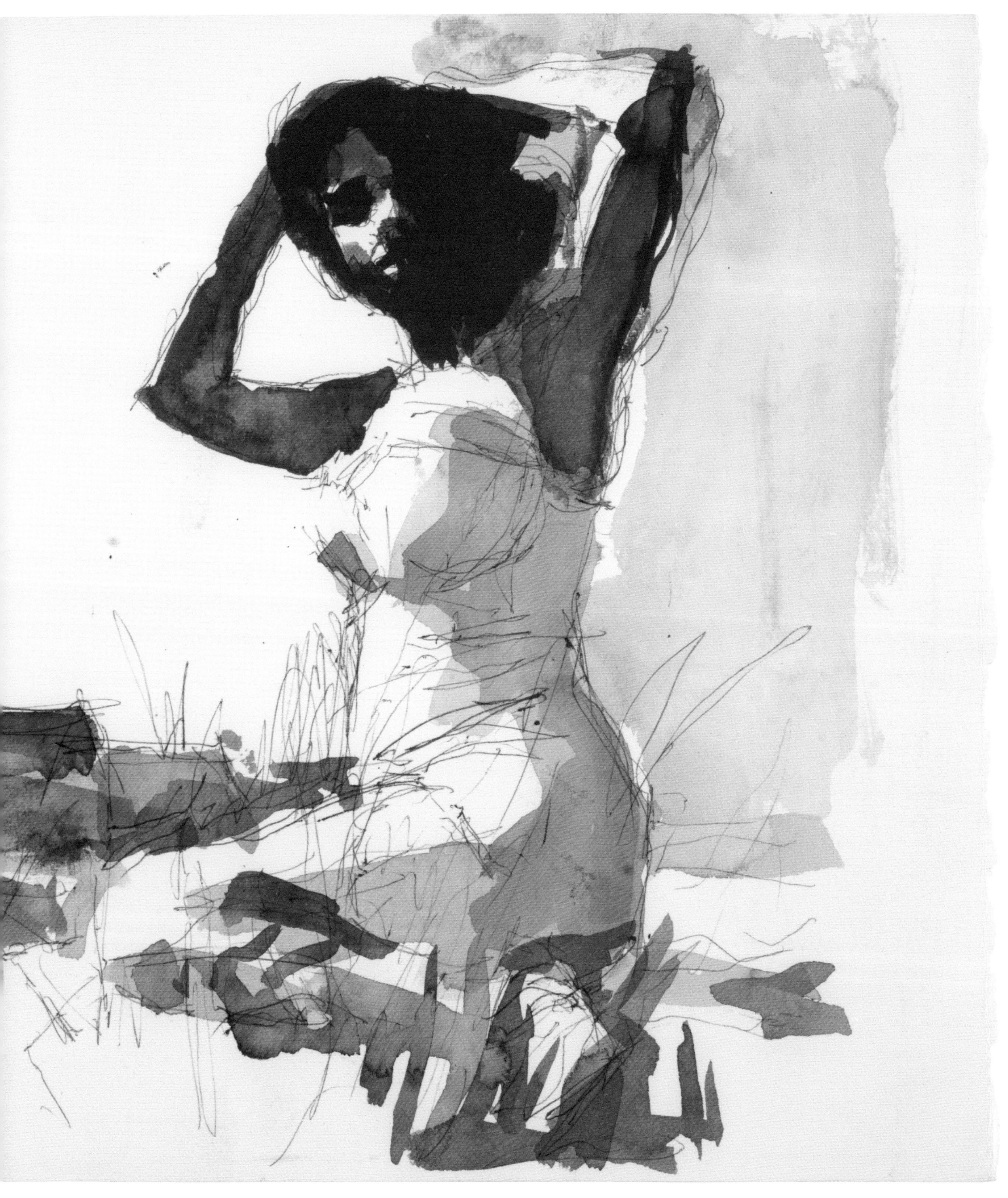

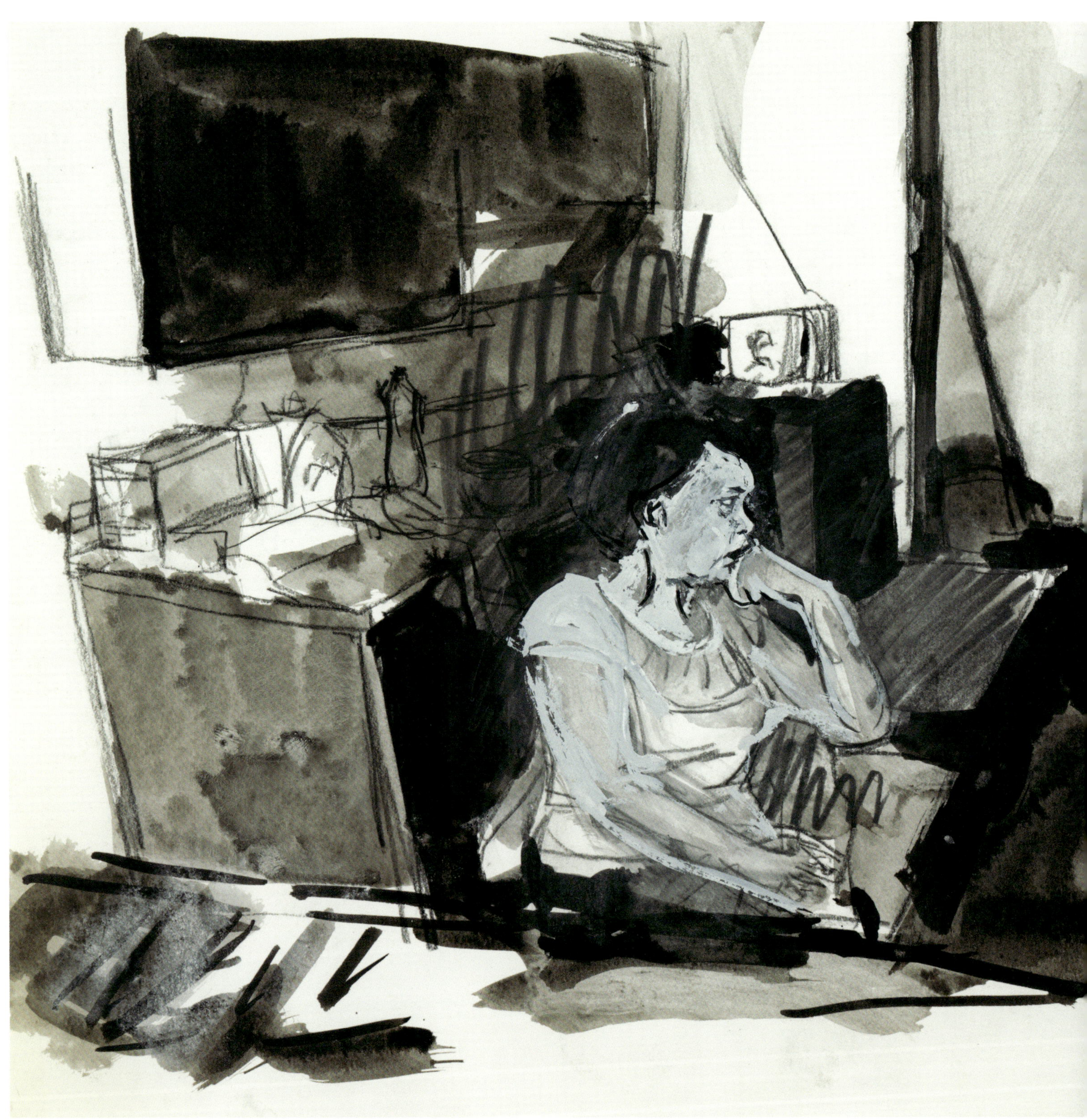

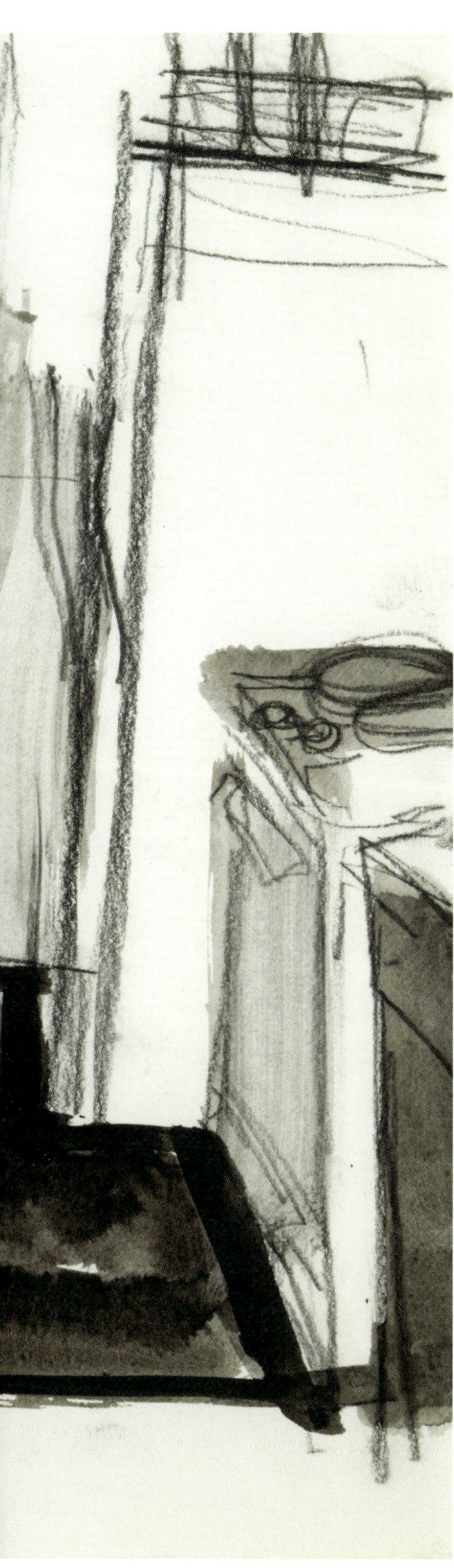

*Untitled* (Mother)
ca. 1985–88
Ink, wash, graphite, charcoal, and acrylic on paper
11 ¾ × 15 ⅝ inches

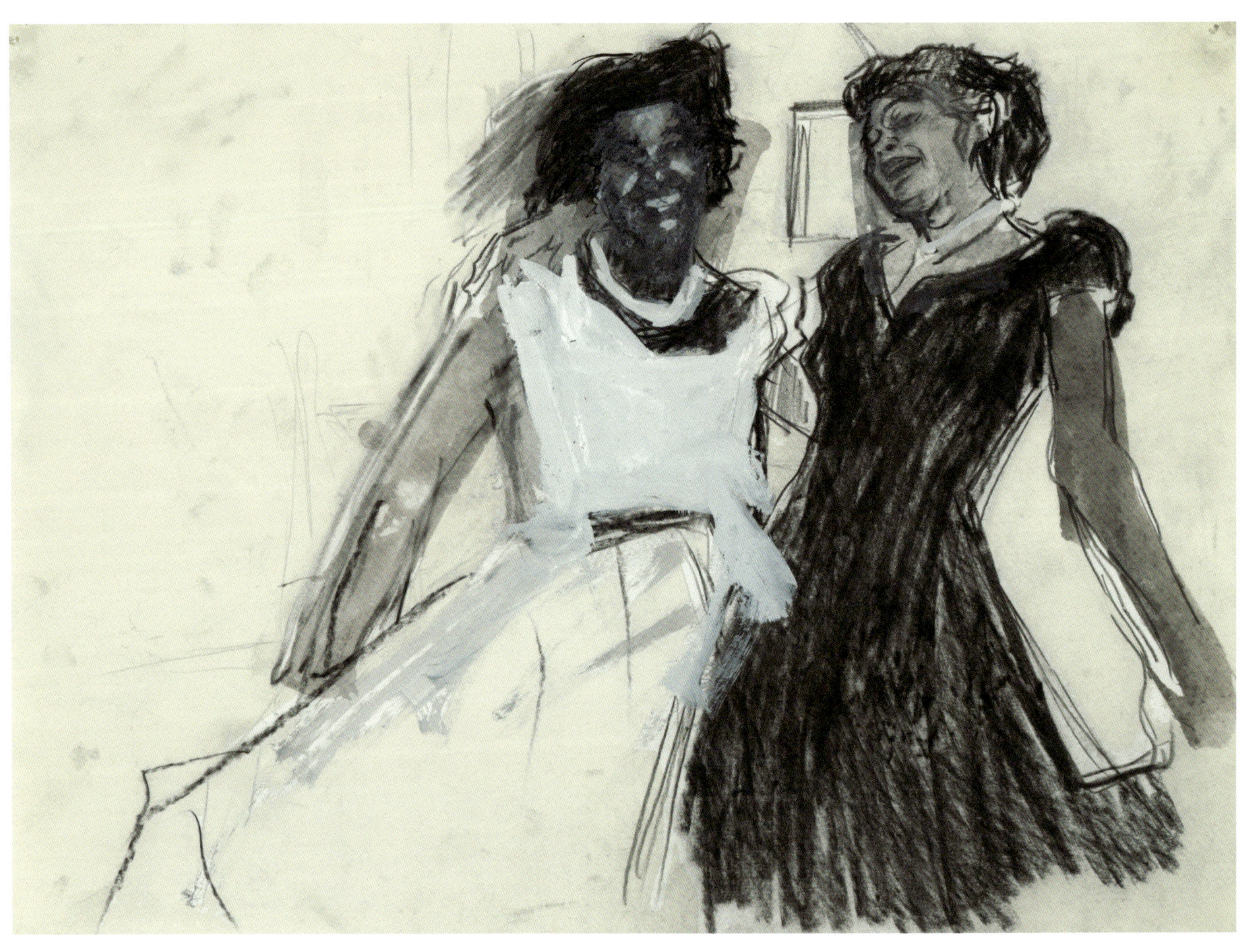


ca. 1983–88
Charcoal, ink, acrylic, and crayon on paper
11 × 15 inches

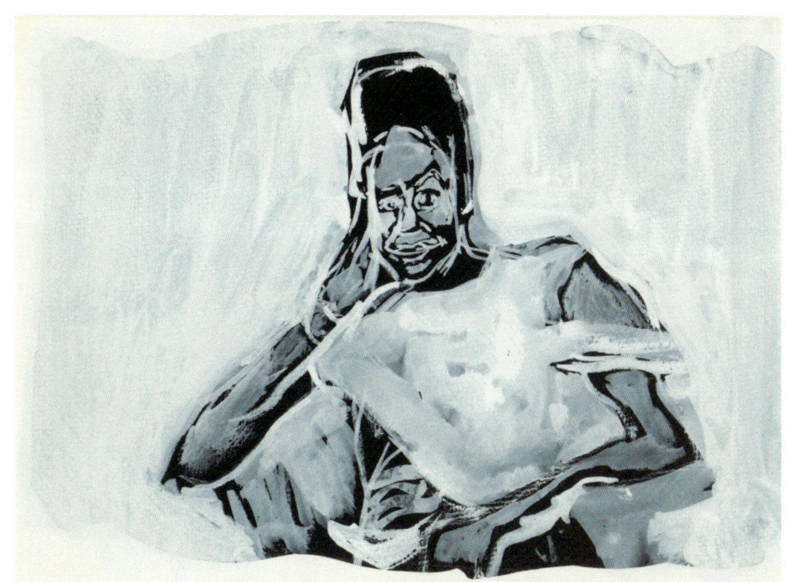

*Untitled* (Birdie Seated)
ca. 1988–92
Gouache and ink on paper
8 ¼ × 11 inches

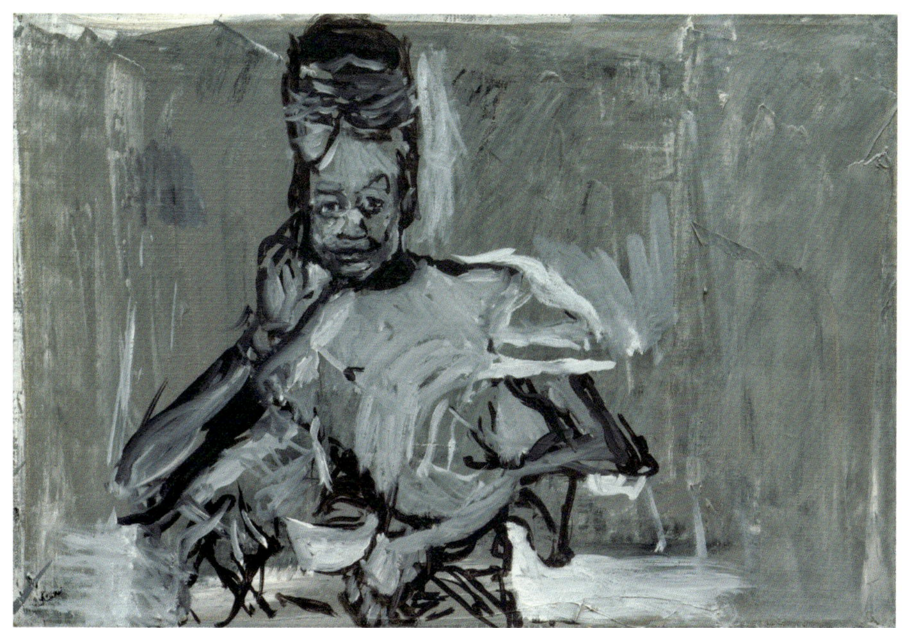

*Untitled* (Birdie Seated)
ca. 1988–92
Paint on canvas
12 ¼ × 17 inches
Collection of Sebastian Daub

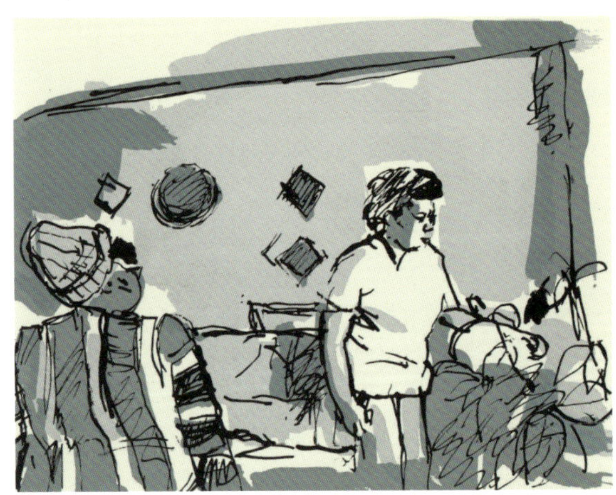 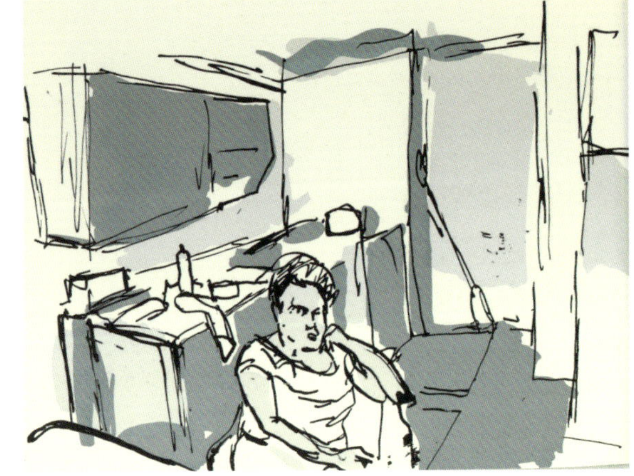

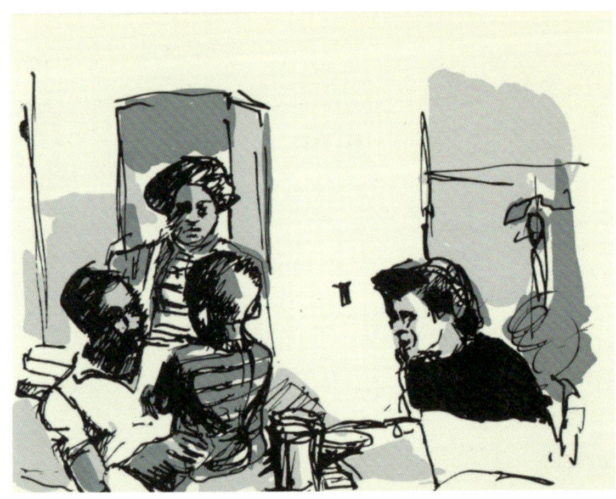 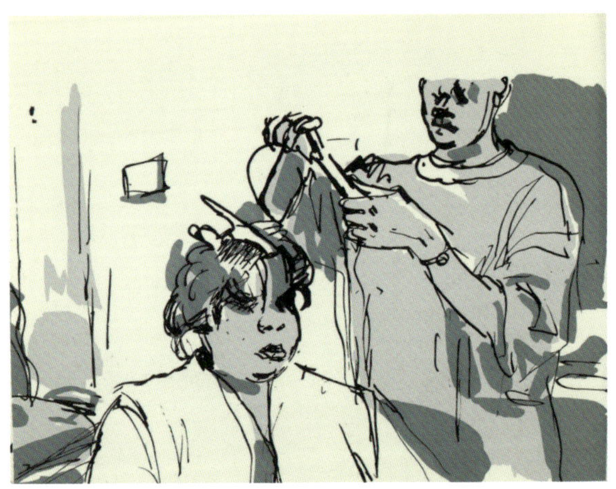

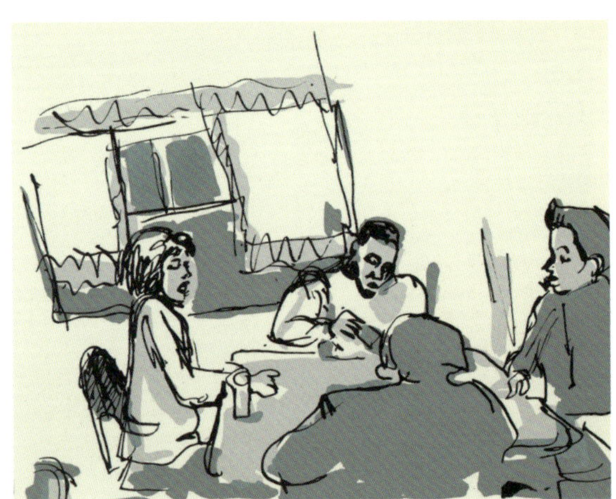 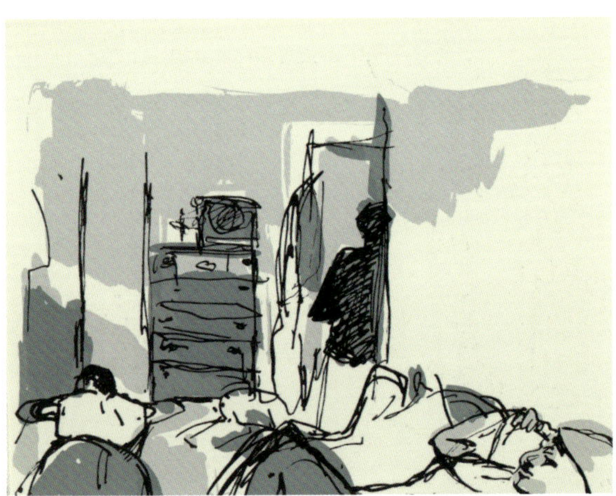

*Darrel Ellis*
1986
Artist's book published by Appearances Press
11 silkscreen prints, each 7 × 9 inches
Edition of 100

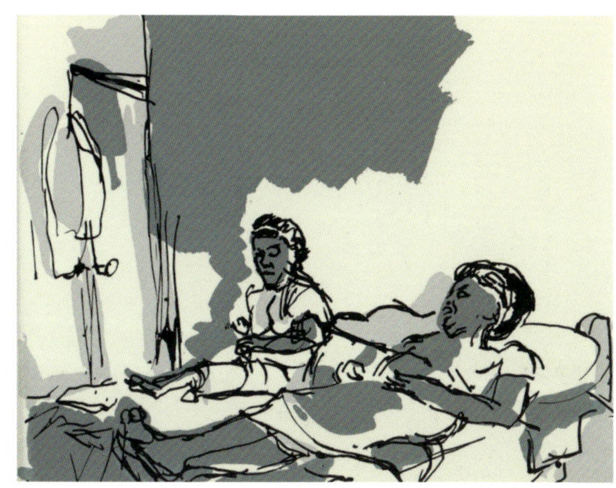

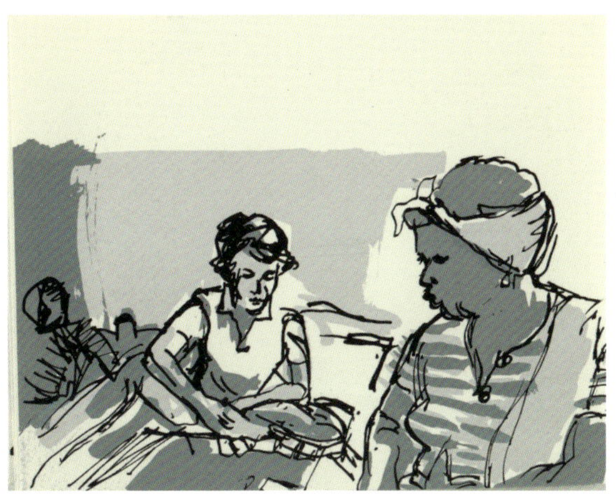

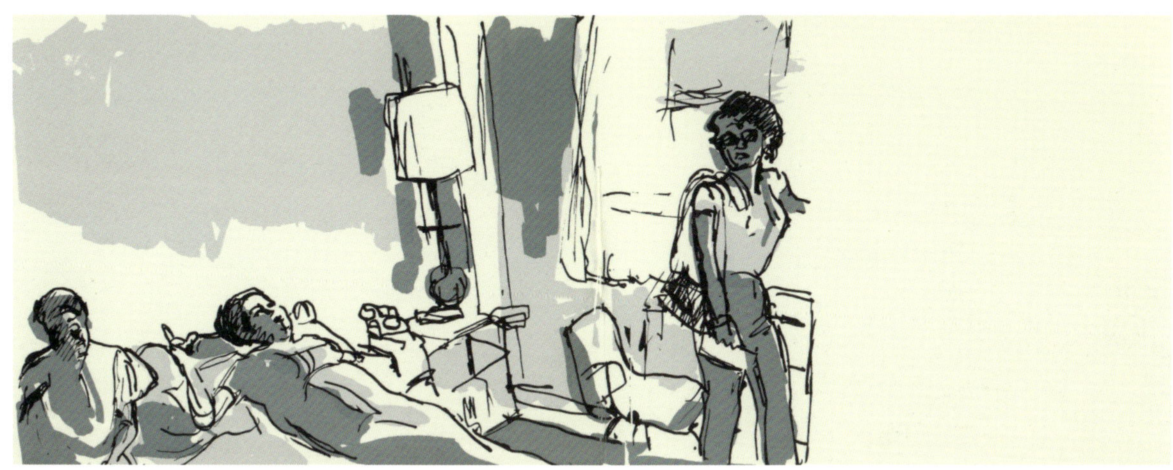

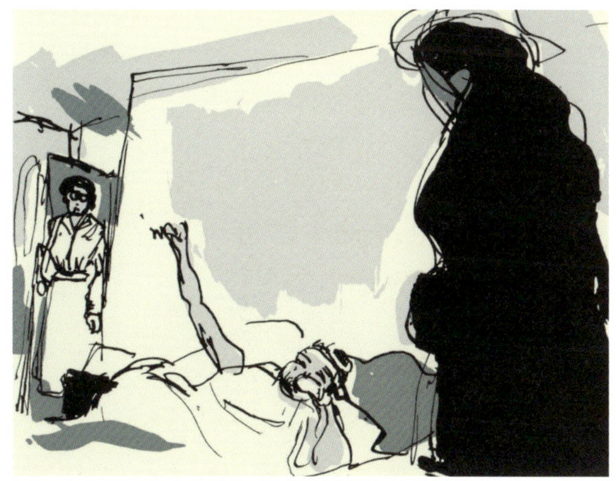

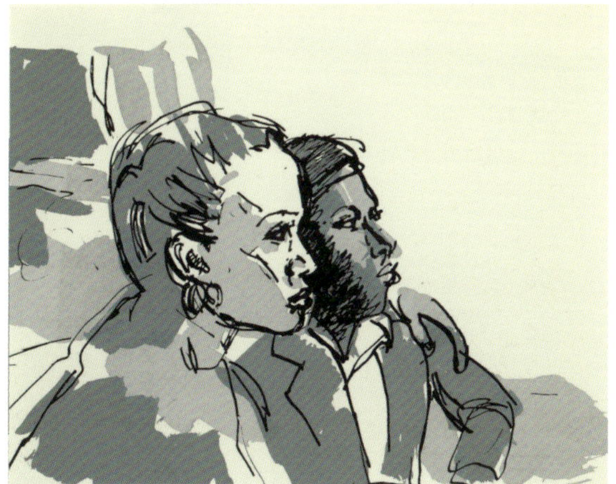

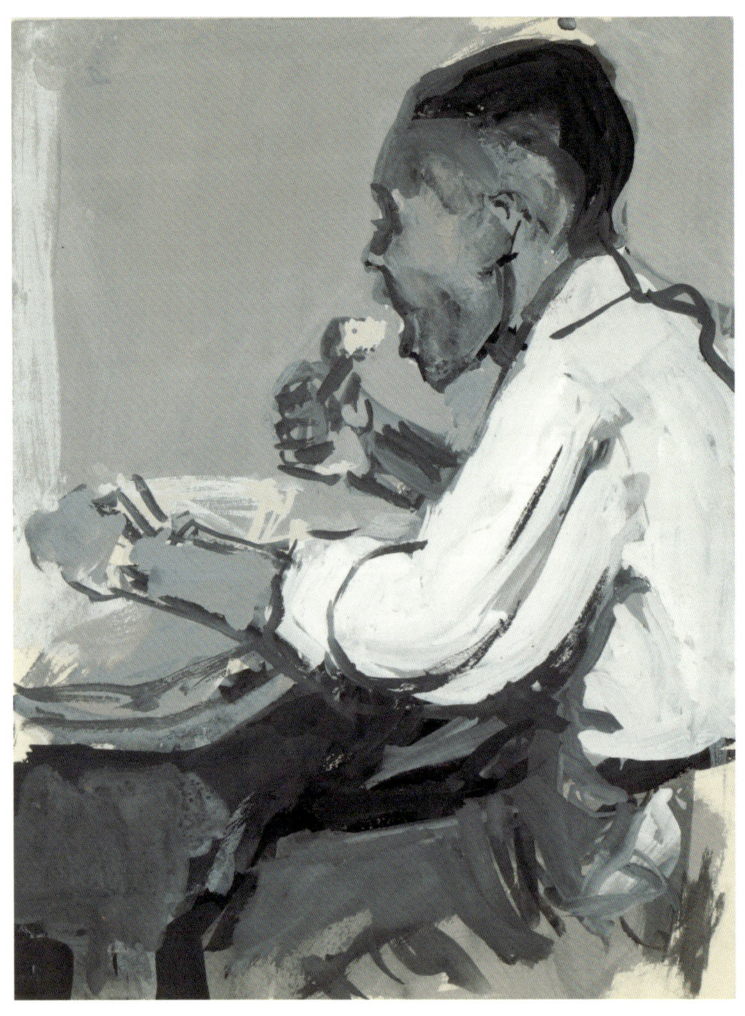

*Untitled* (Uncle Donny)
1983
Acrylic on paper
15 × 11 inches

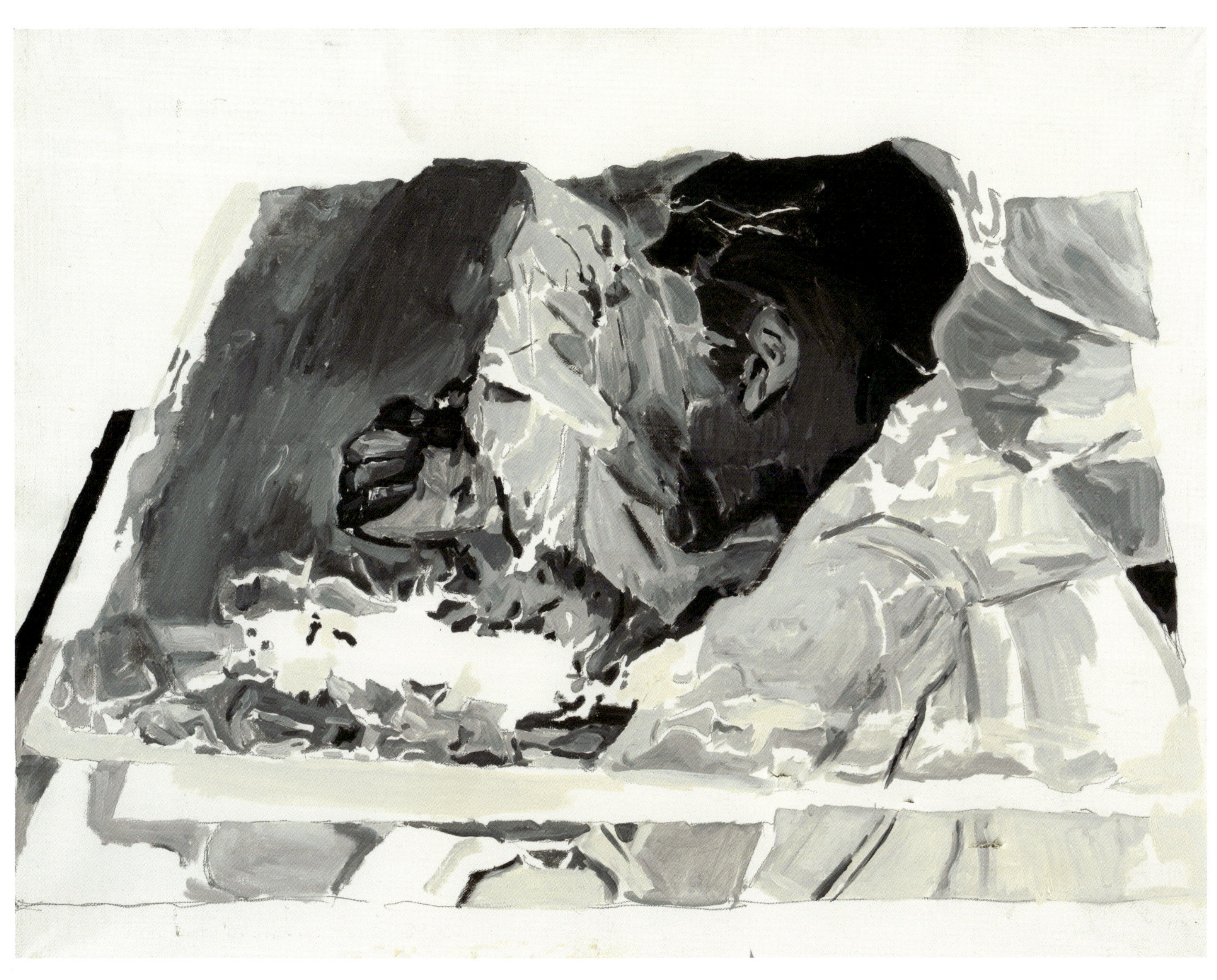

*Untitled* (Uncle Donny)
ca. 1988–92
Acrylic and graphite on canvas
19 × 25 ¼ inches

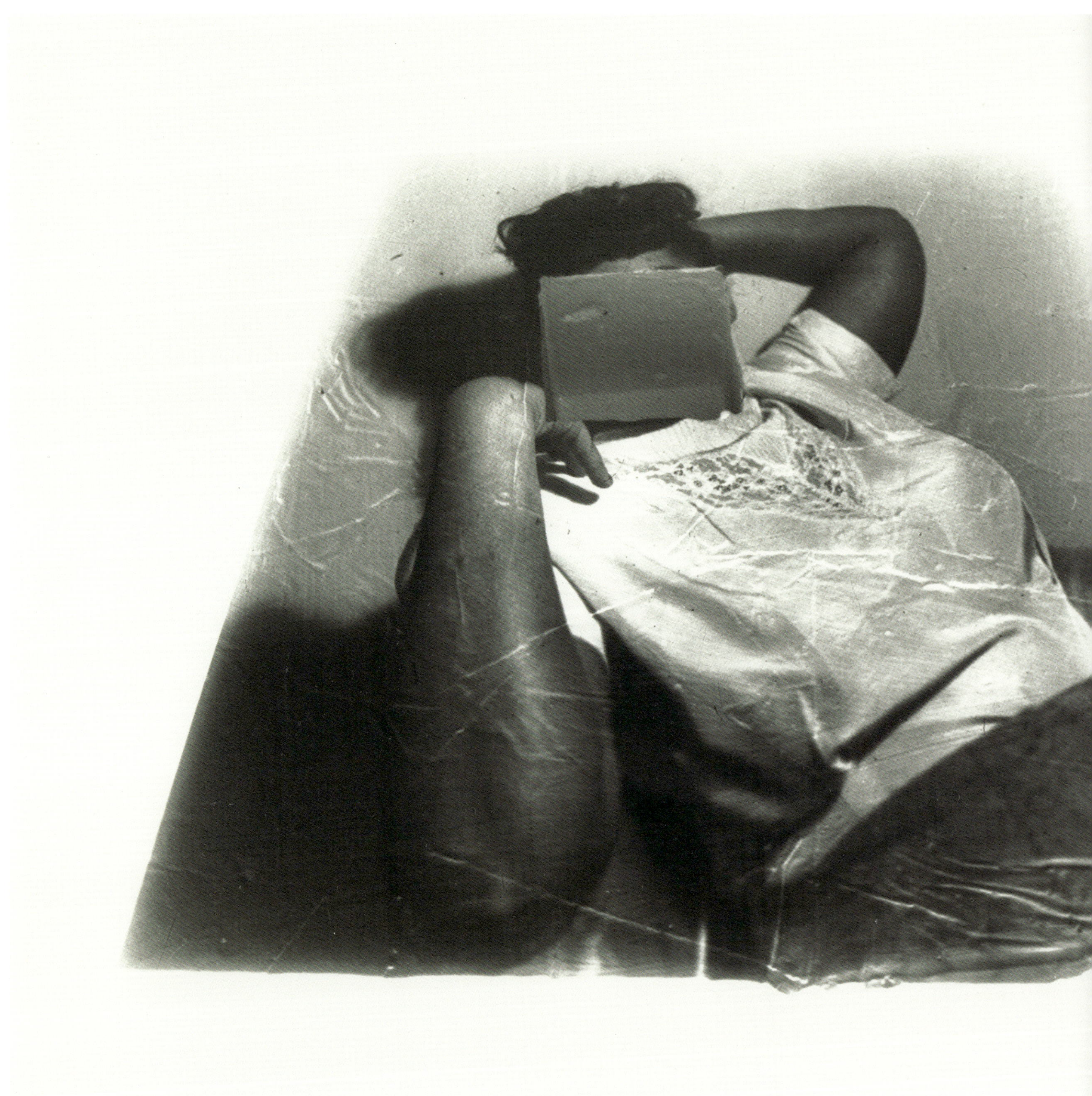

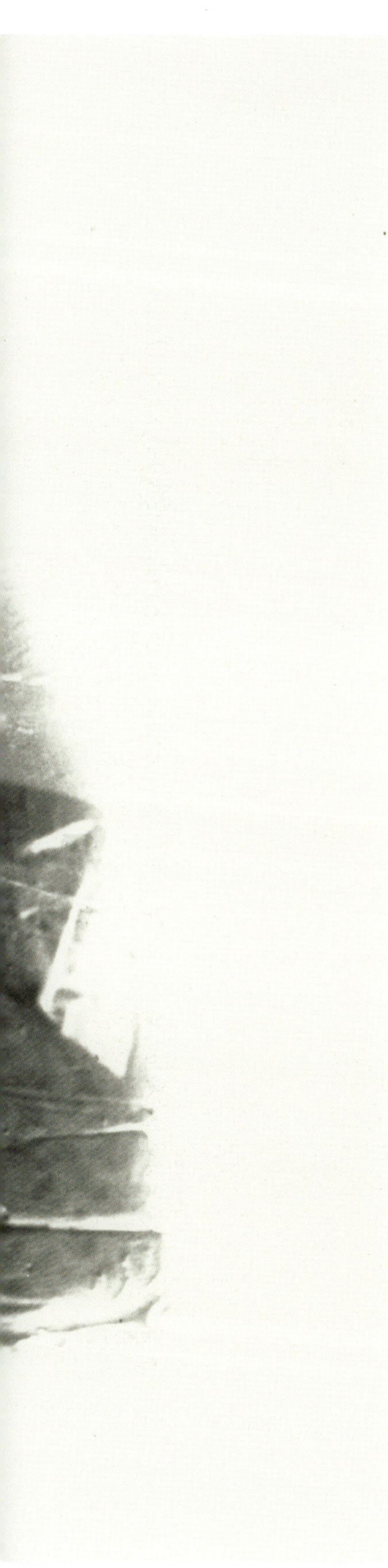

*Untitled* (Mother)
ca. 1989–90
Gelatin silver print
11 × 14 inches

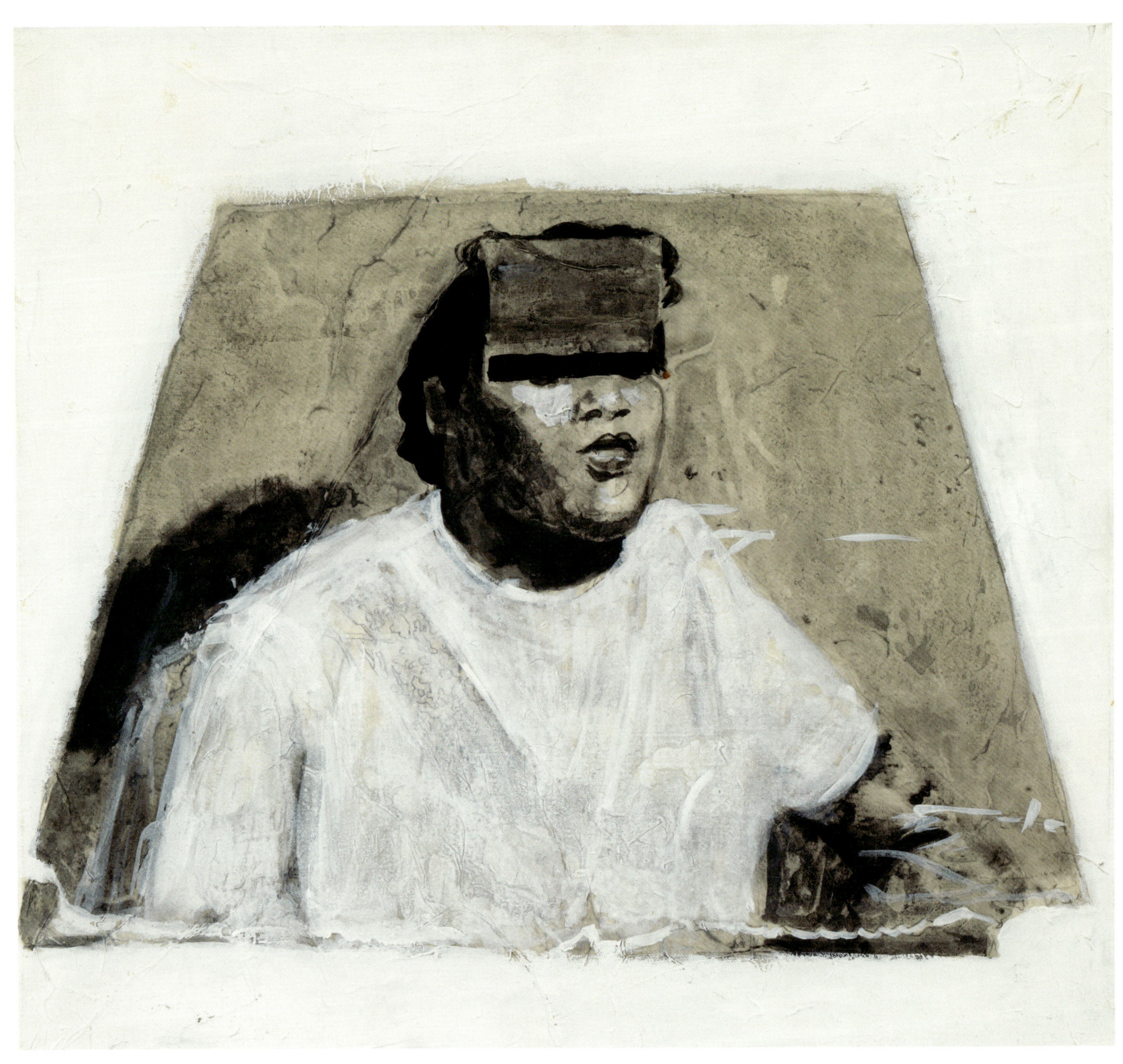

*Untitled* (Mother)
ca. 1989–90
Oil, ink, gouache, and graphite on paper
mounted on canvas
25 × 24 inches

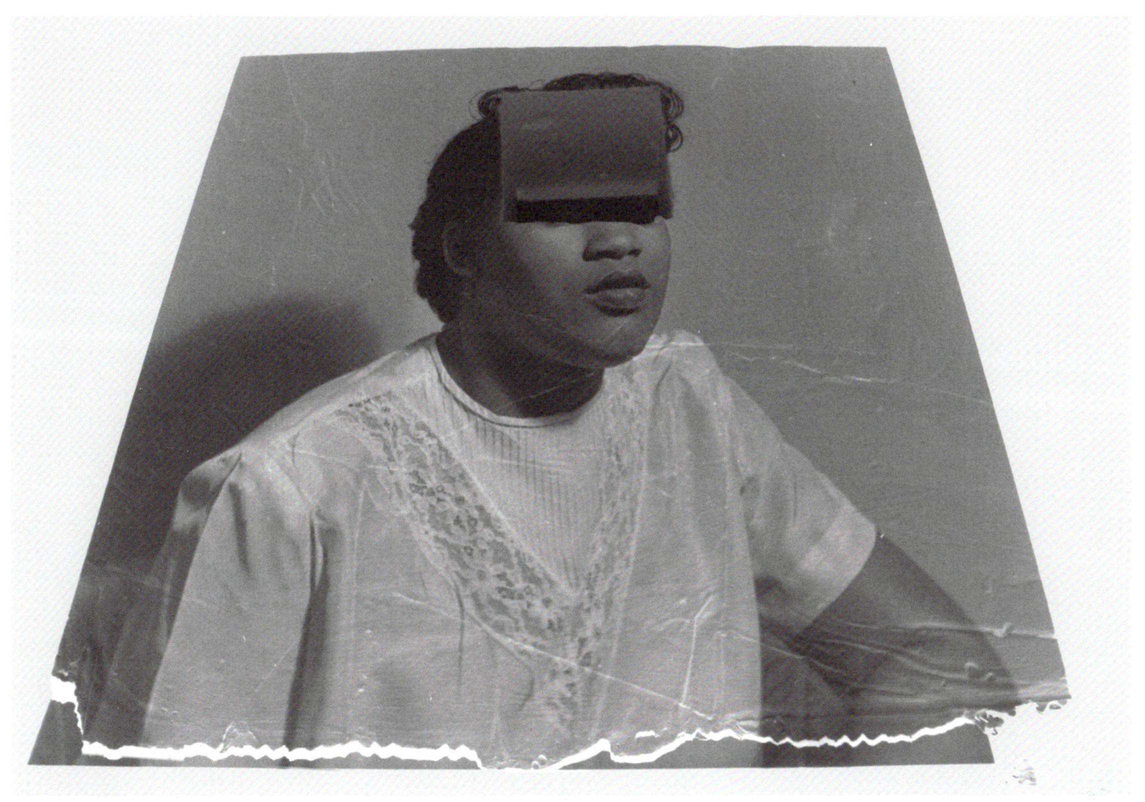

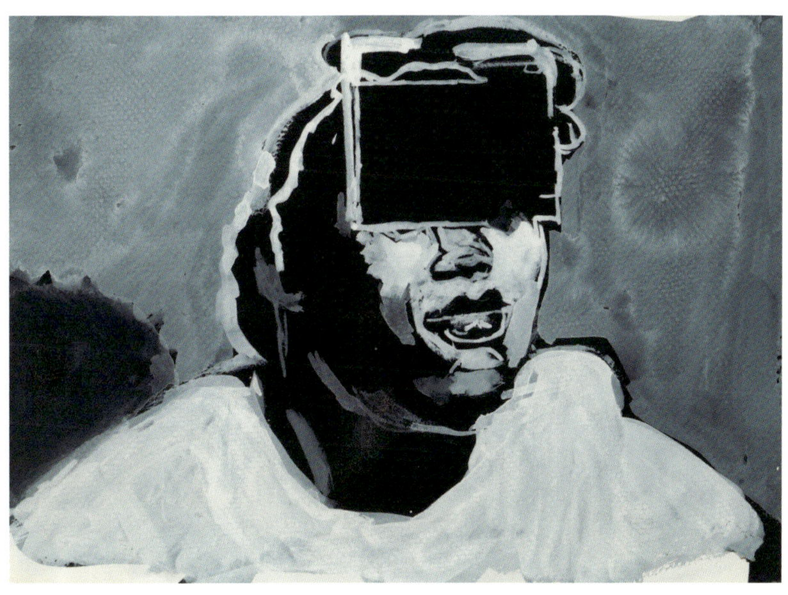

*Untitled* (Mother)
ca. 1989–90
Gelatin silver print
11 × 14 inches

*Untitled* (Mother)
ca. 1989–90
Gouache and ink on paper
8 ¾ × 11 ¾ inches

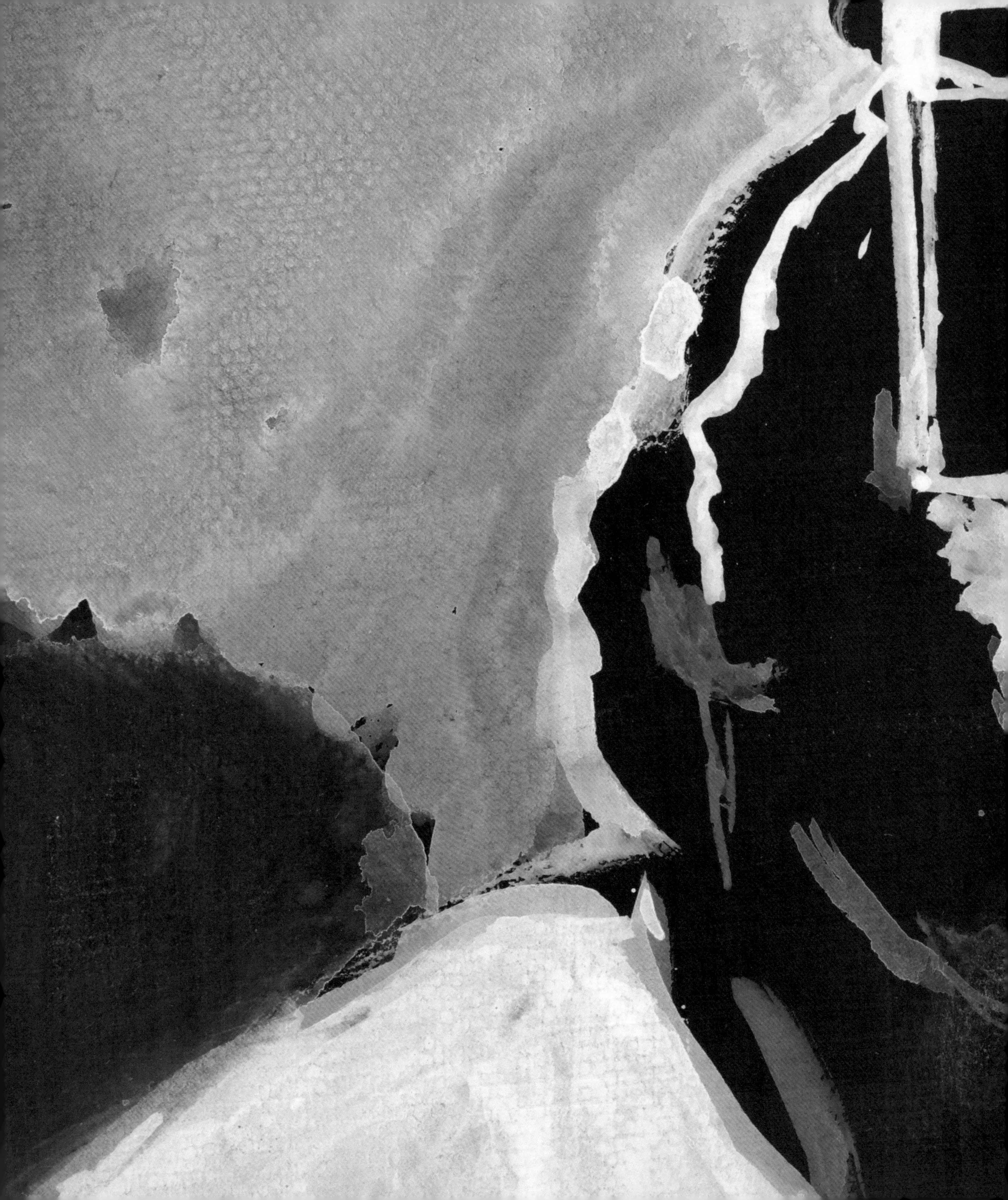

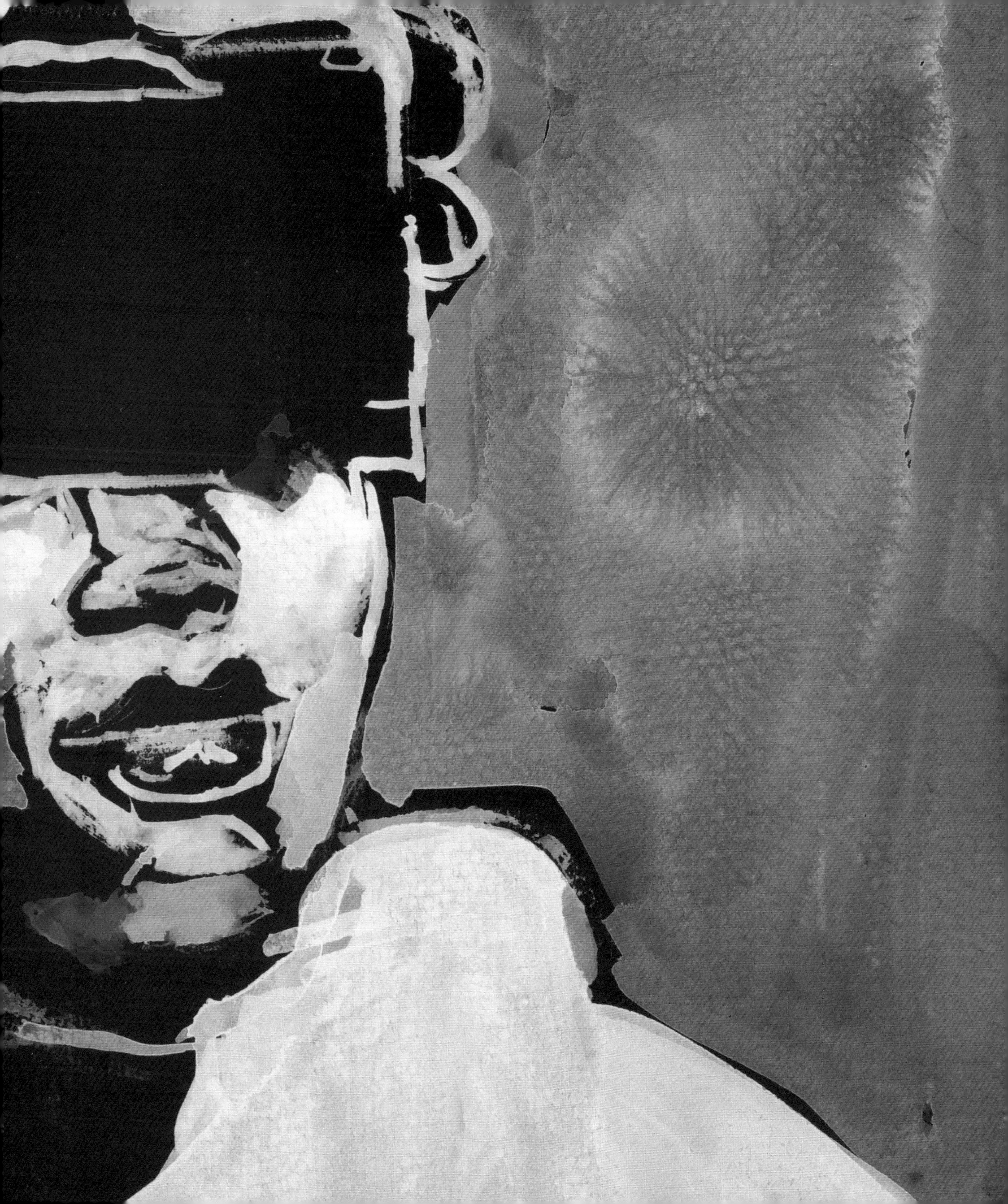

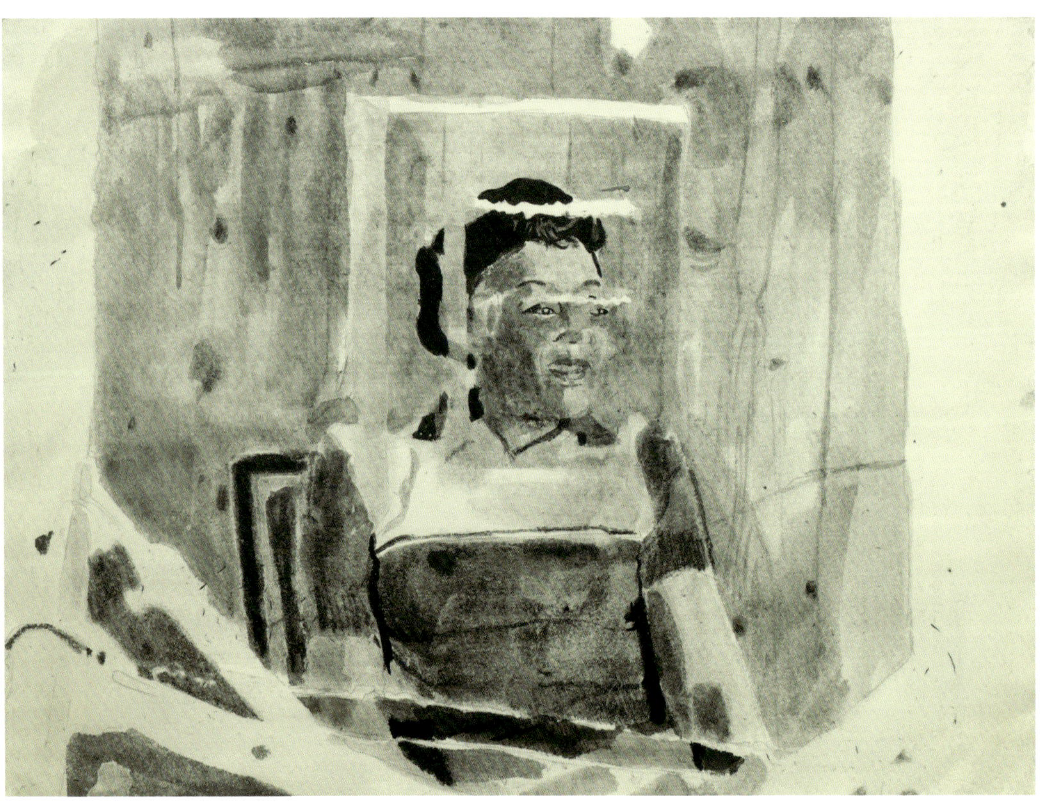

*Untitled* (Grandmother Lillian Ellis)
ca. 1989–92
Ink, wash, and graphite on paper
17 × 19 ⅝ inches

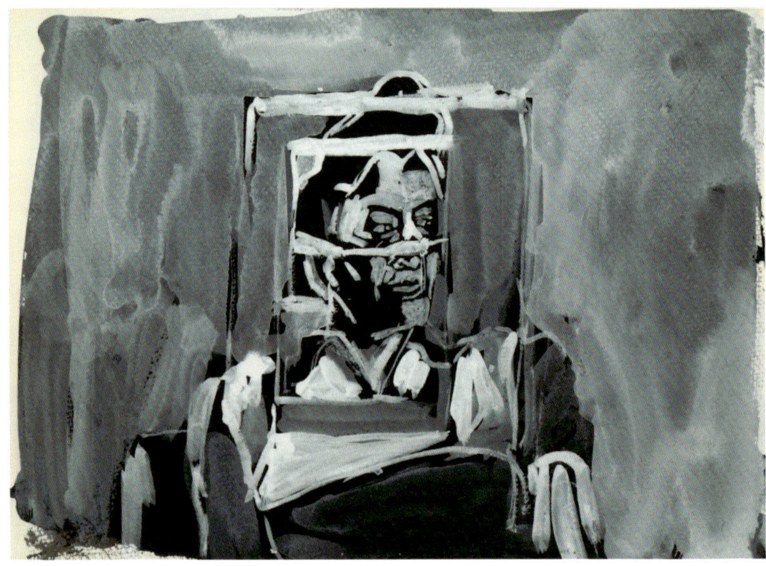

*Untitled* (Grandmother Lillian Ellis)
ca. 1989–92
Gouache and ink on paper
8 ¼ × 11 ¼ inches

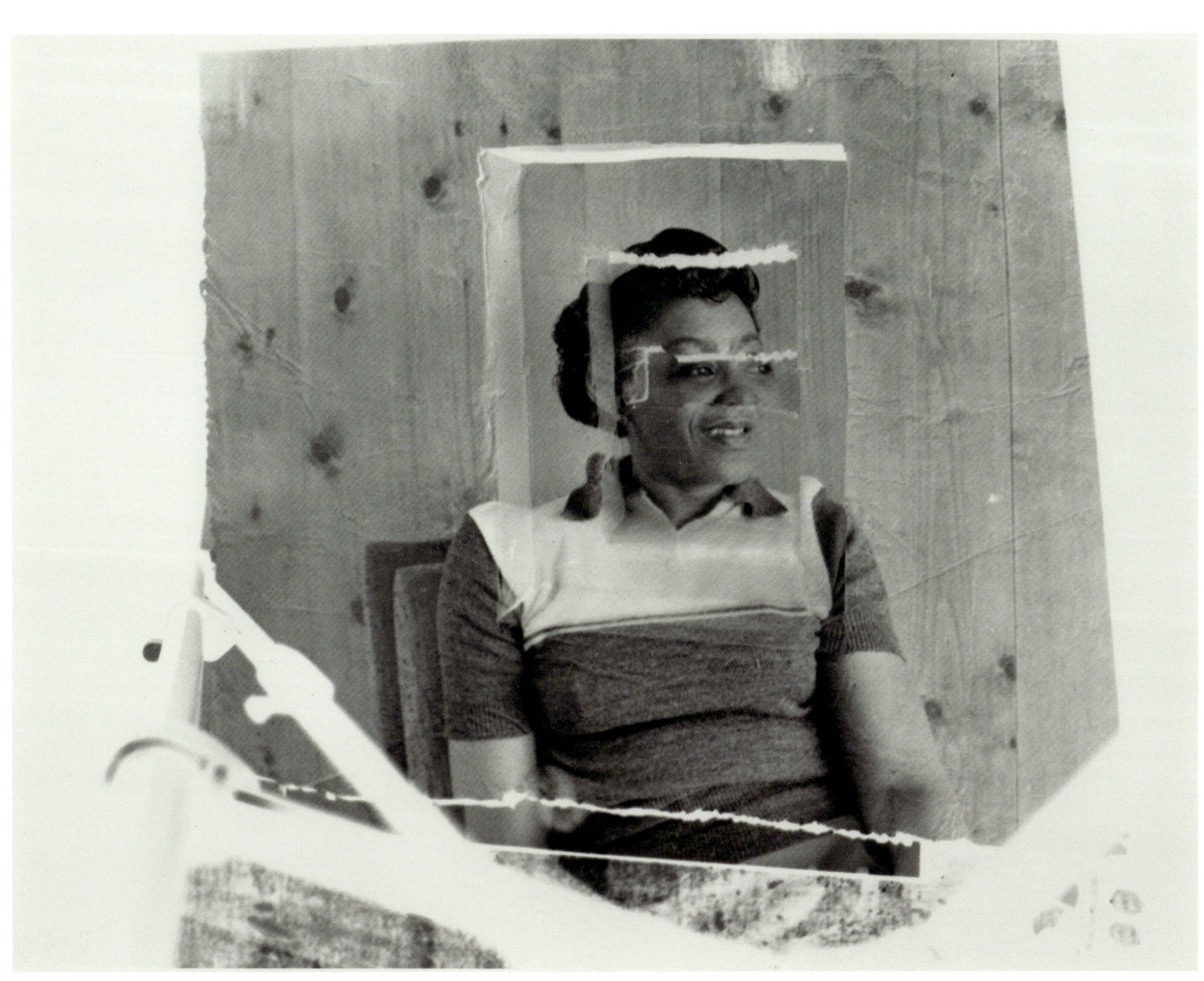

*Untitled* (Grandmother Lillian Ellis)
1989–90
Gelatin silver print
10 × 13 inches

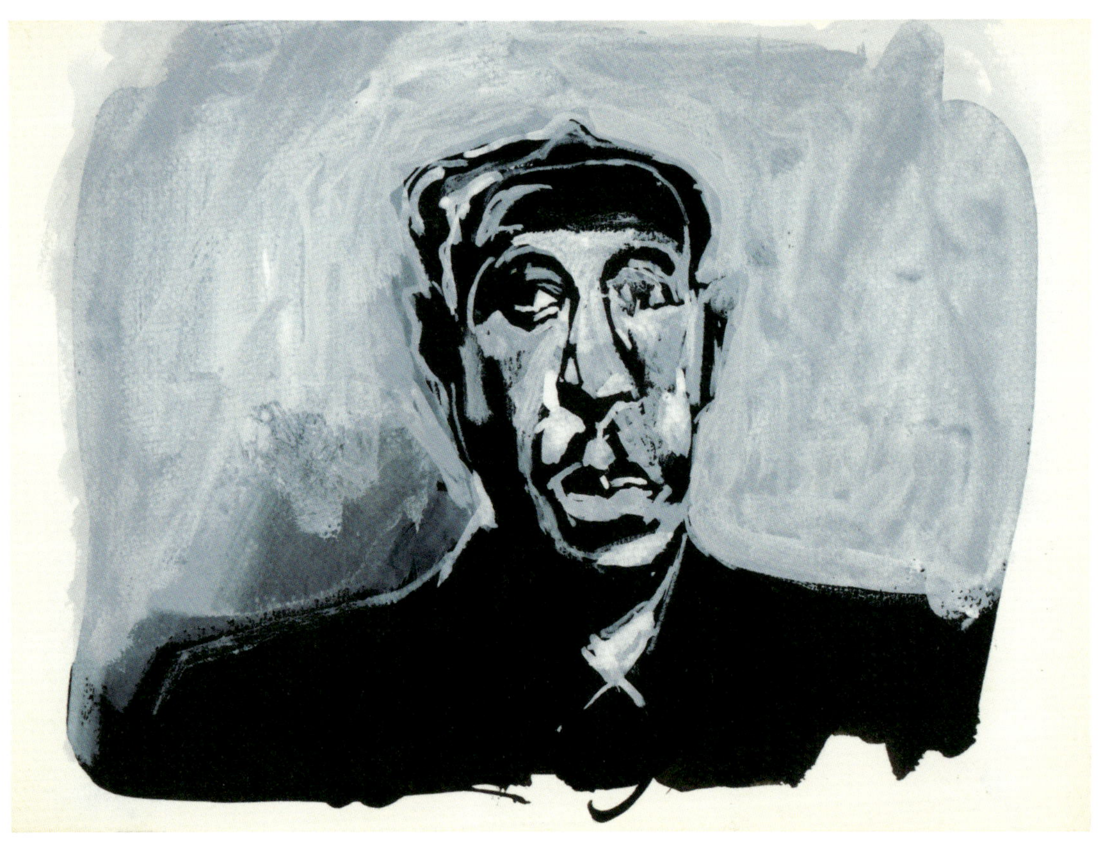

*Untitled* (Great Uncle Joseph Tansle)
ca. 1988–92
Gouache and ink on paper
8 × 10 ½ inches

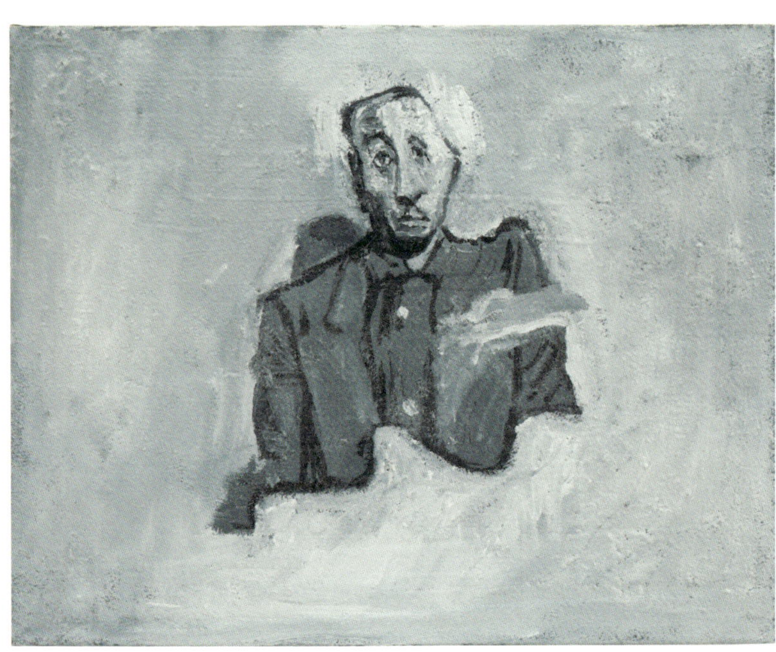

*Untitled* (Great Uncle Joseph Tansle)
ca. 1988–92
Oil on canvas prepared with textured ground
17 × 21 inches

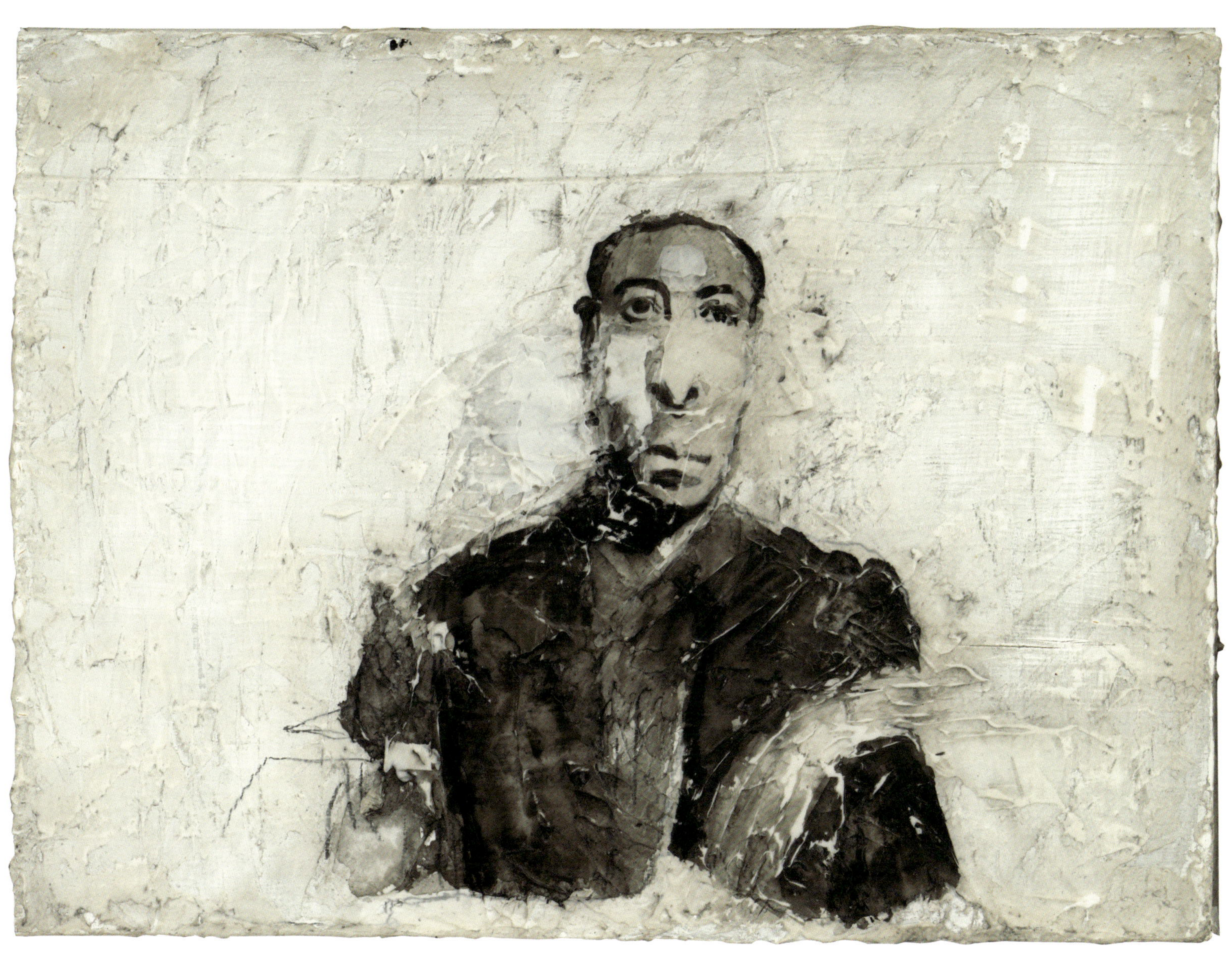

*Untitled* (Great Uncle Joseph Tansle)
ca. 1988–92
Ink and charcoal on wood prepared with
textured ground
12 ¼ × 16 inches
Private Collection

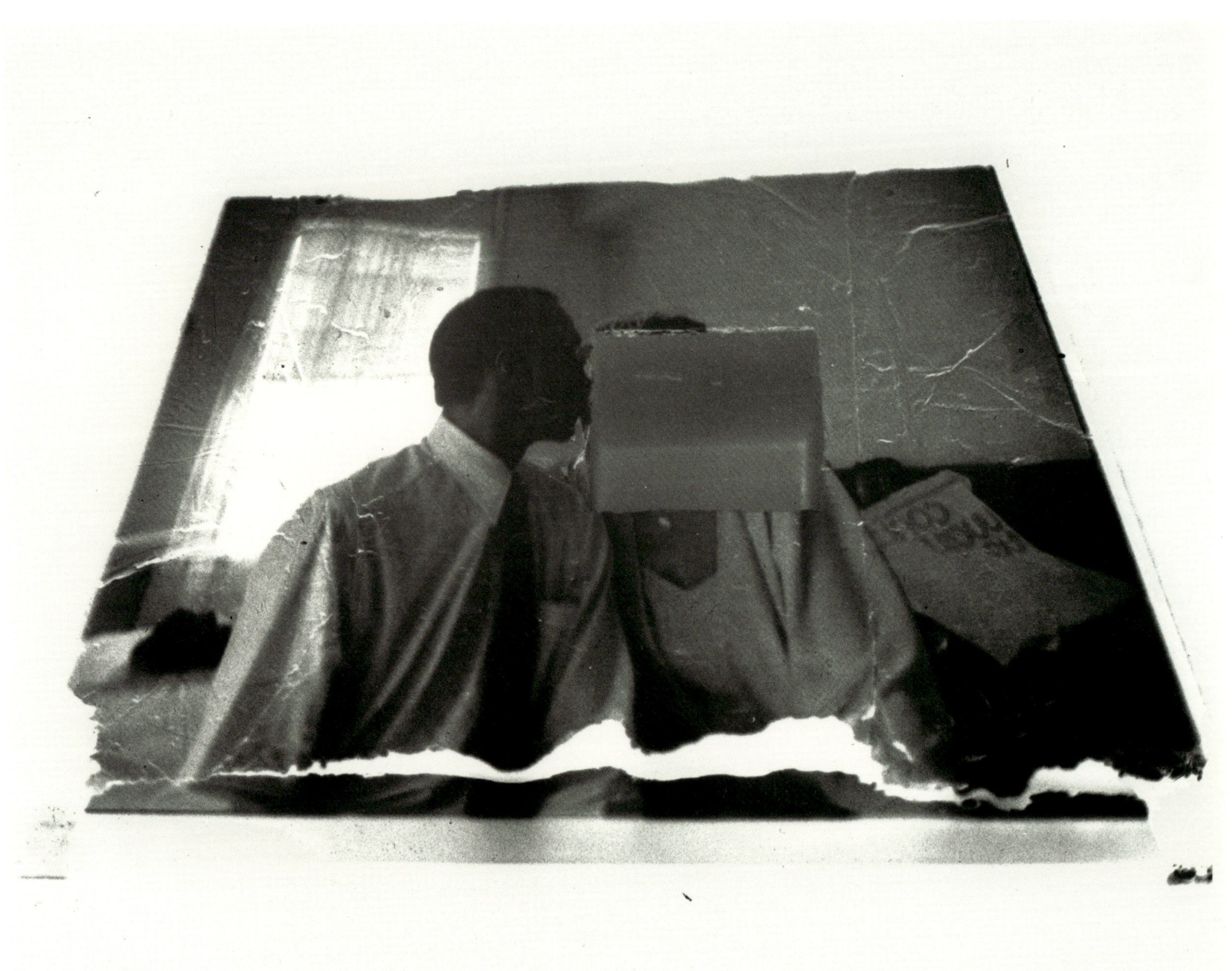

*Untitled* (Couple Kissing)
ca. 1988–92
Gelatin silver print
8 × 10 inches

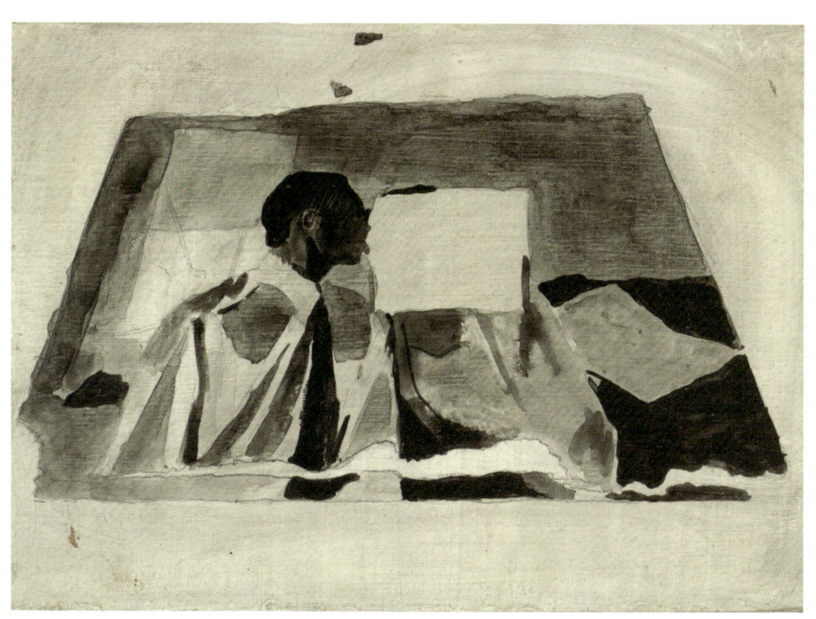

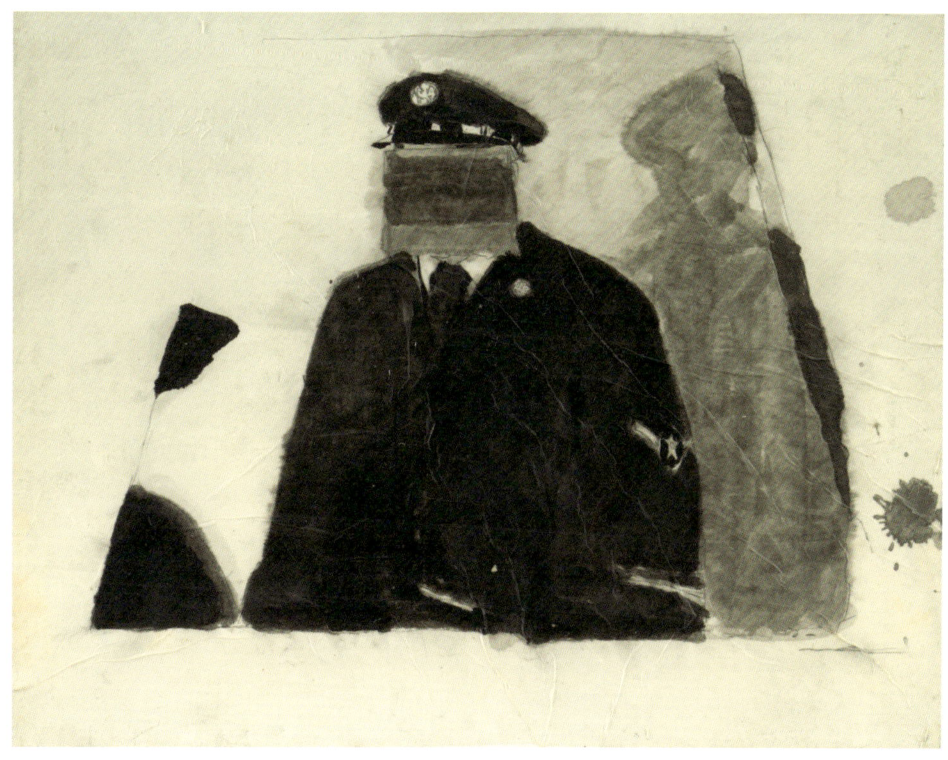


ca. 1988–92
Ink, wash, and graphite on panel with
prepared ground
14 × 17 ½ inches


ca. 1988–92
Ink, wash, and graphite on paper mounted on
panel with prepared ground
19 ¼ × 24 inches

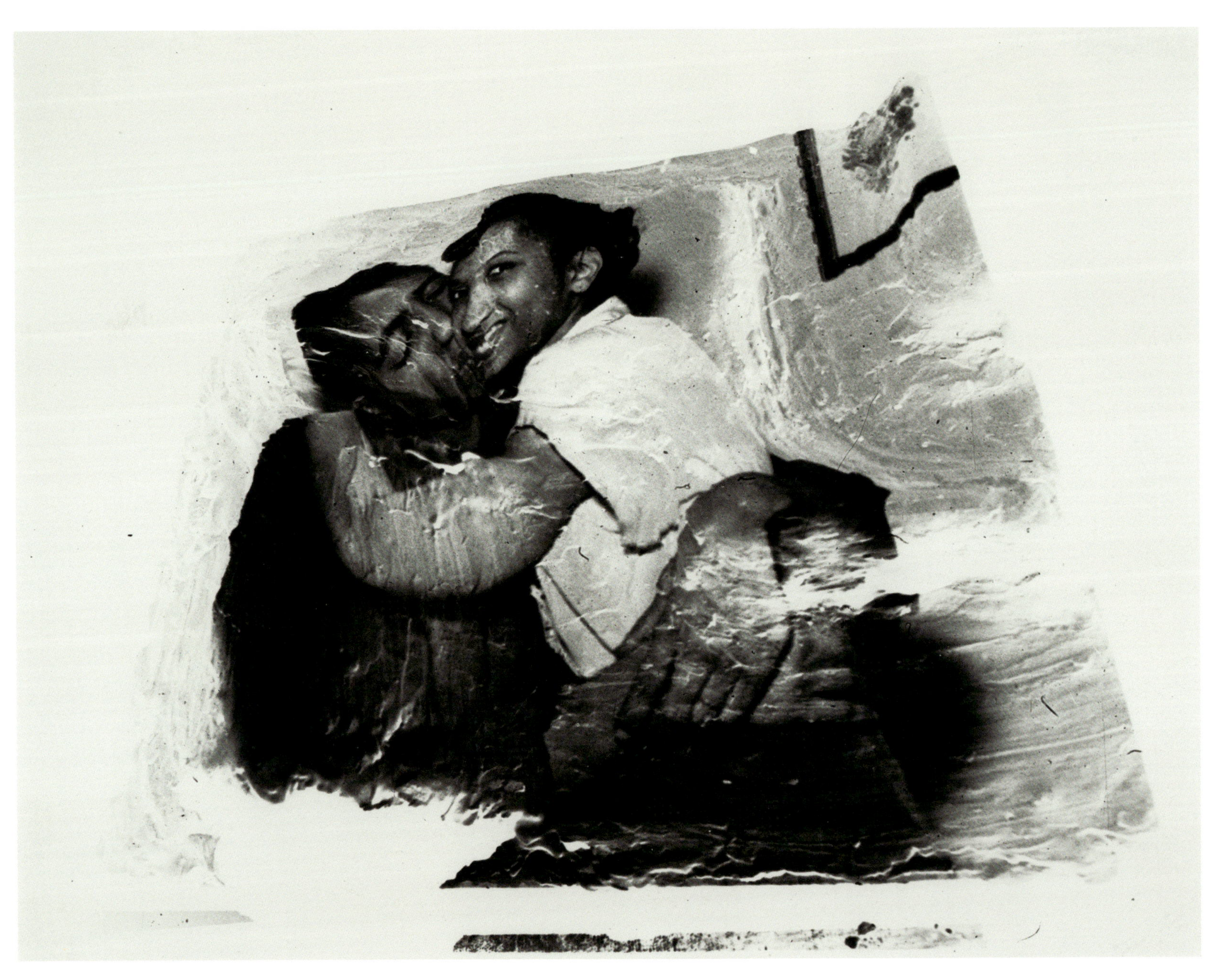

*Untitled* (Aunt Connie and Uncle Richard)
1990
Gelatin silver print
15 ¾ × 19 ¼ inches
Collection of Ebony G. Patterson

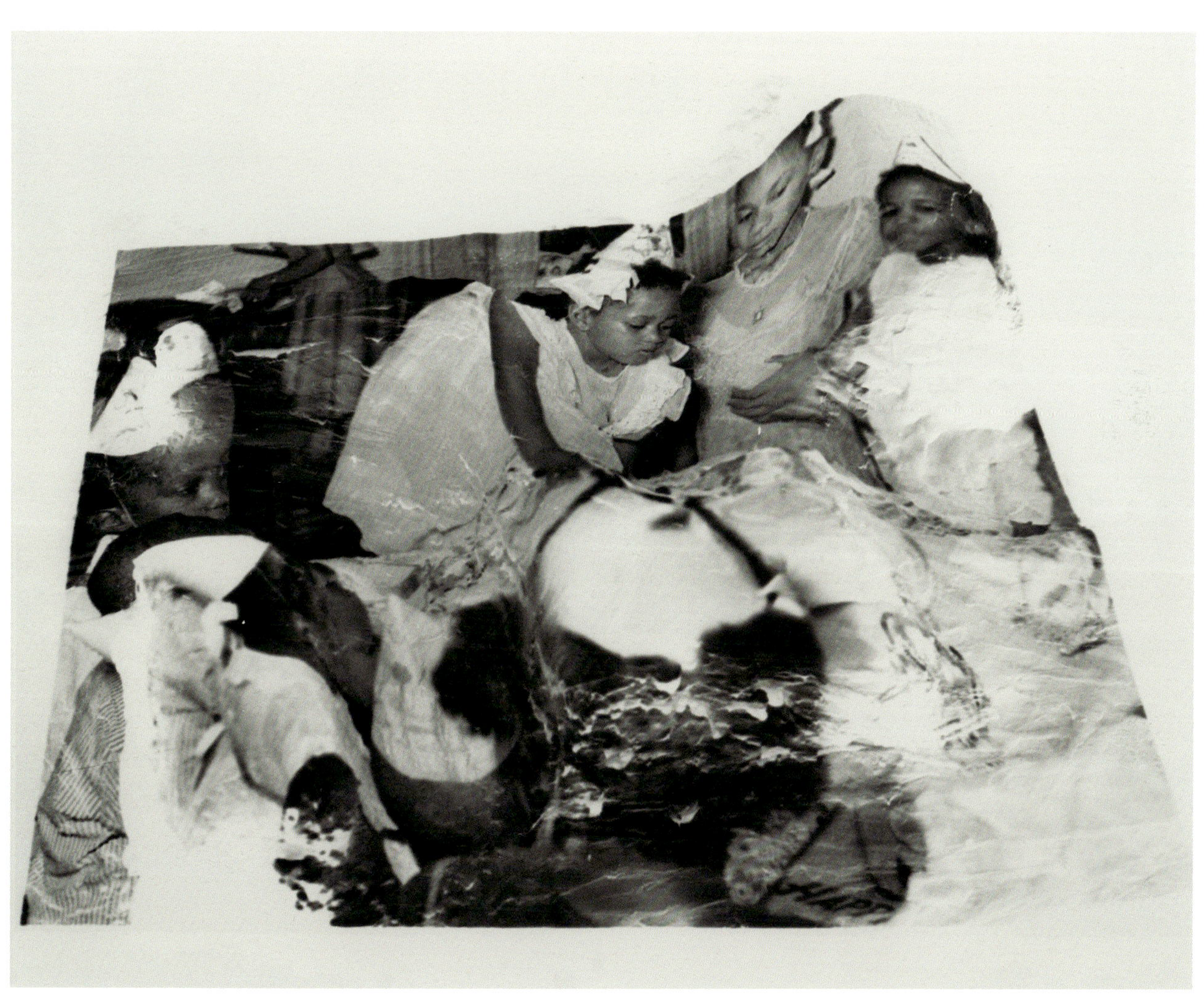

*Untitled* (Birthday Party)
1990
Gelatin silver print
25 × 29 inches

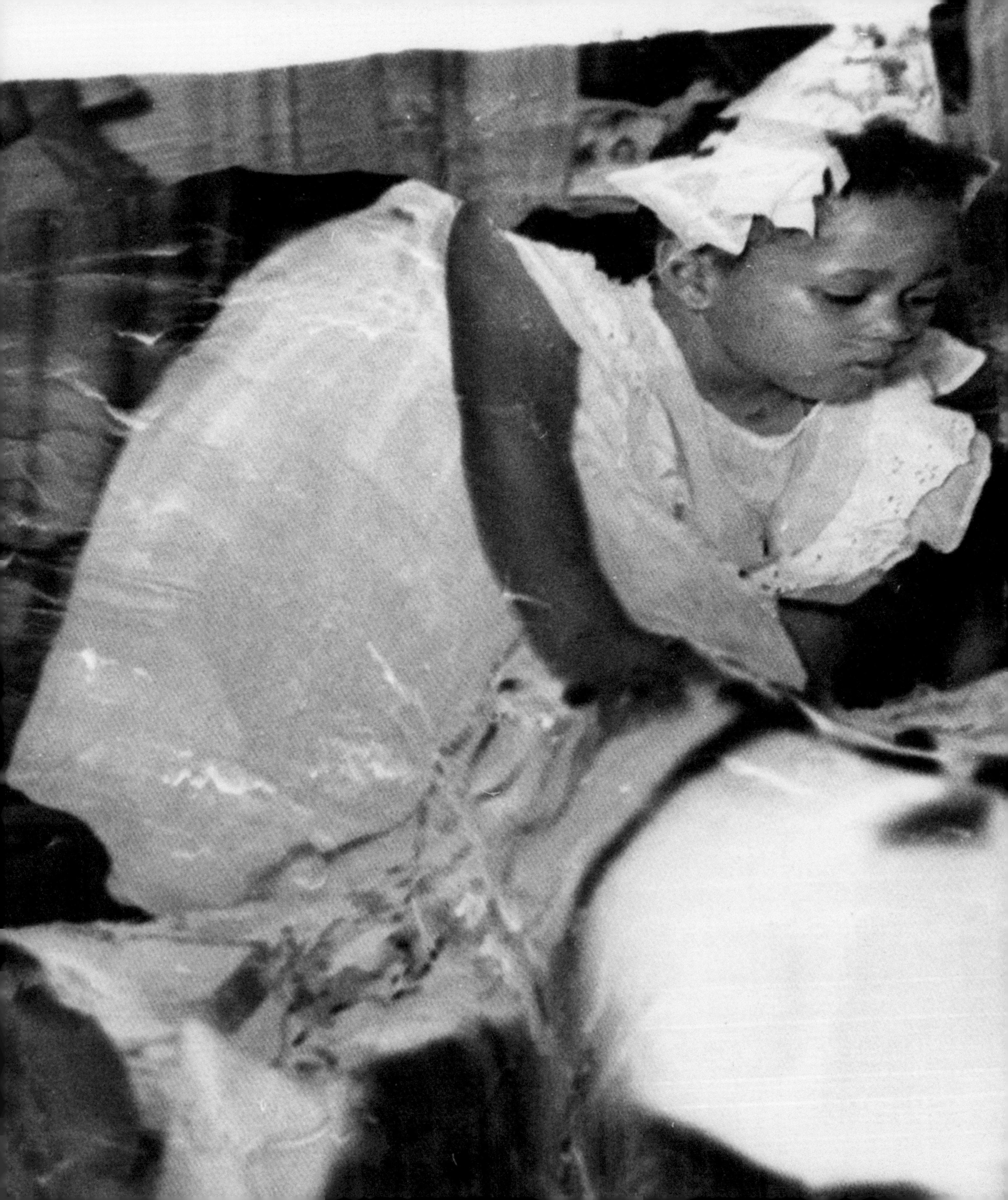

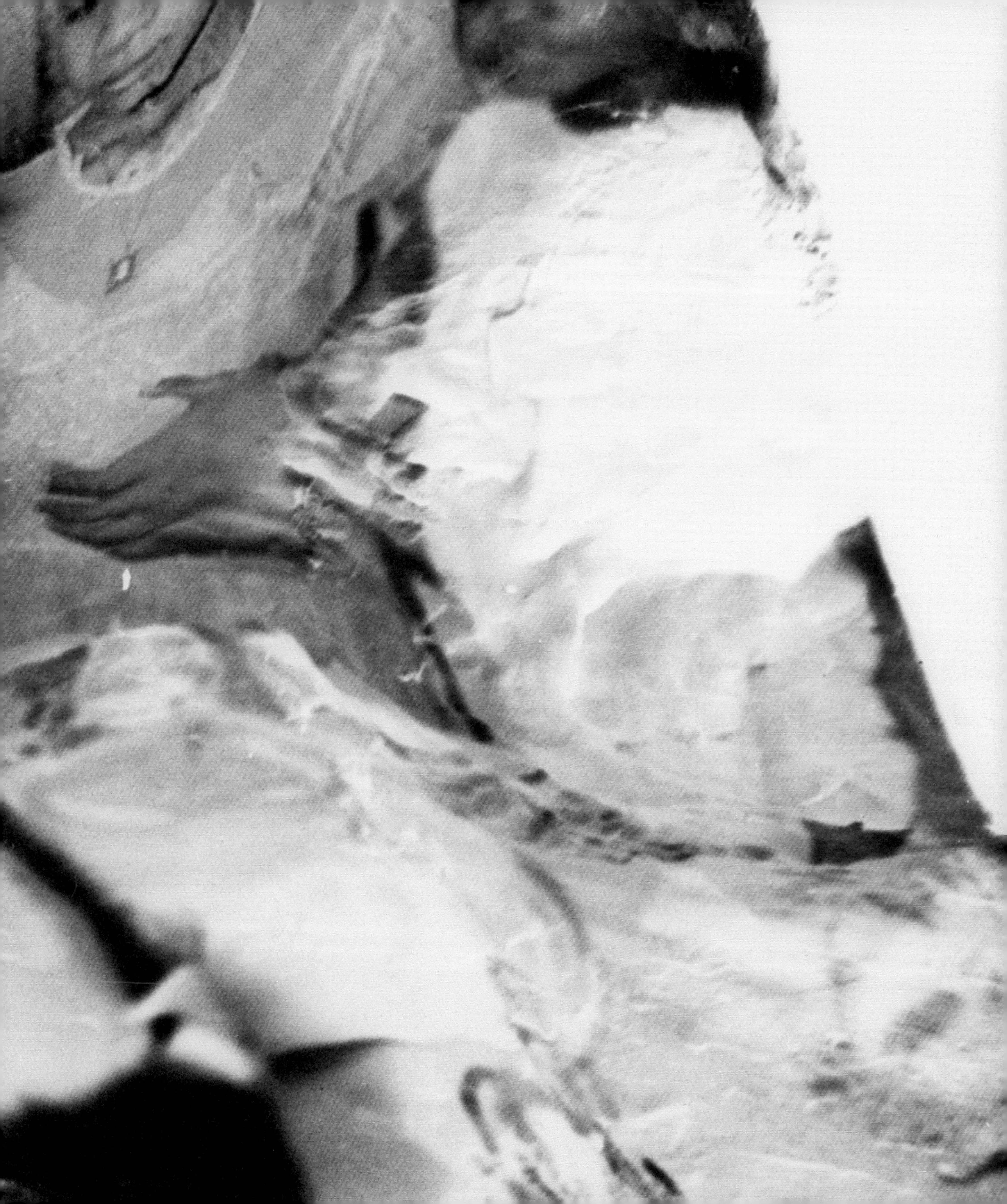

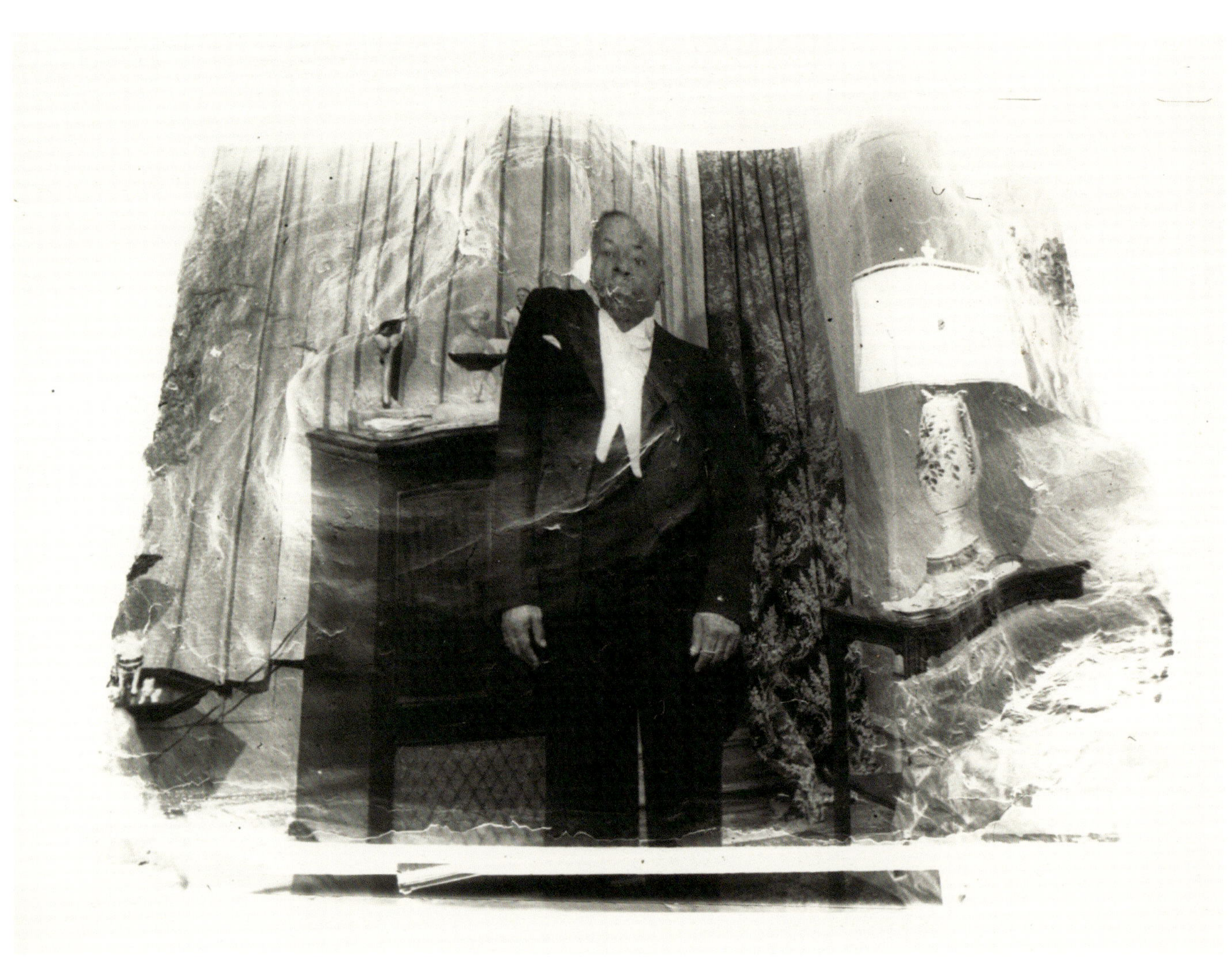

*Untitled* (Grandfather James A. Harrison)
1990
Gelatin silver print
11 × 14 inches
Brooklyn Museum

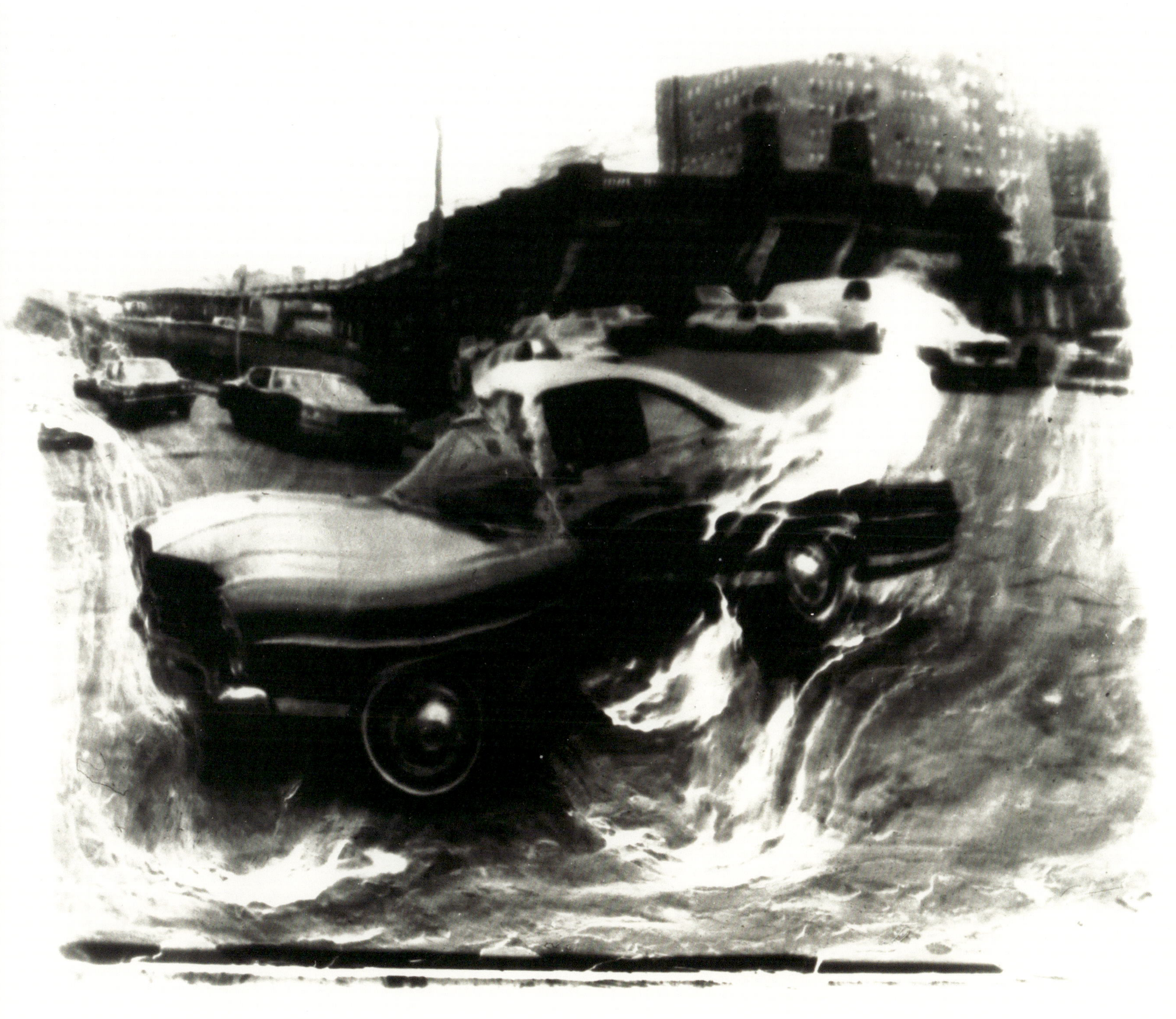

*Untitled* (Car in Street)
ca. 1988–9?
Gelatin silver print
11 × 14 inches

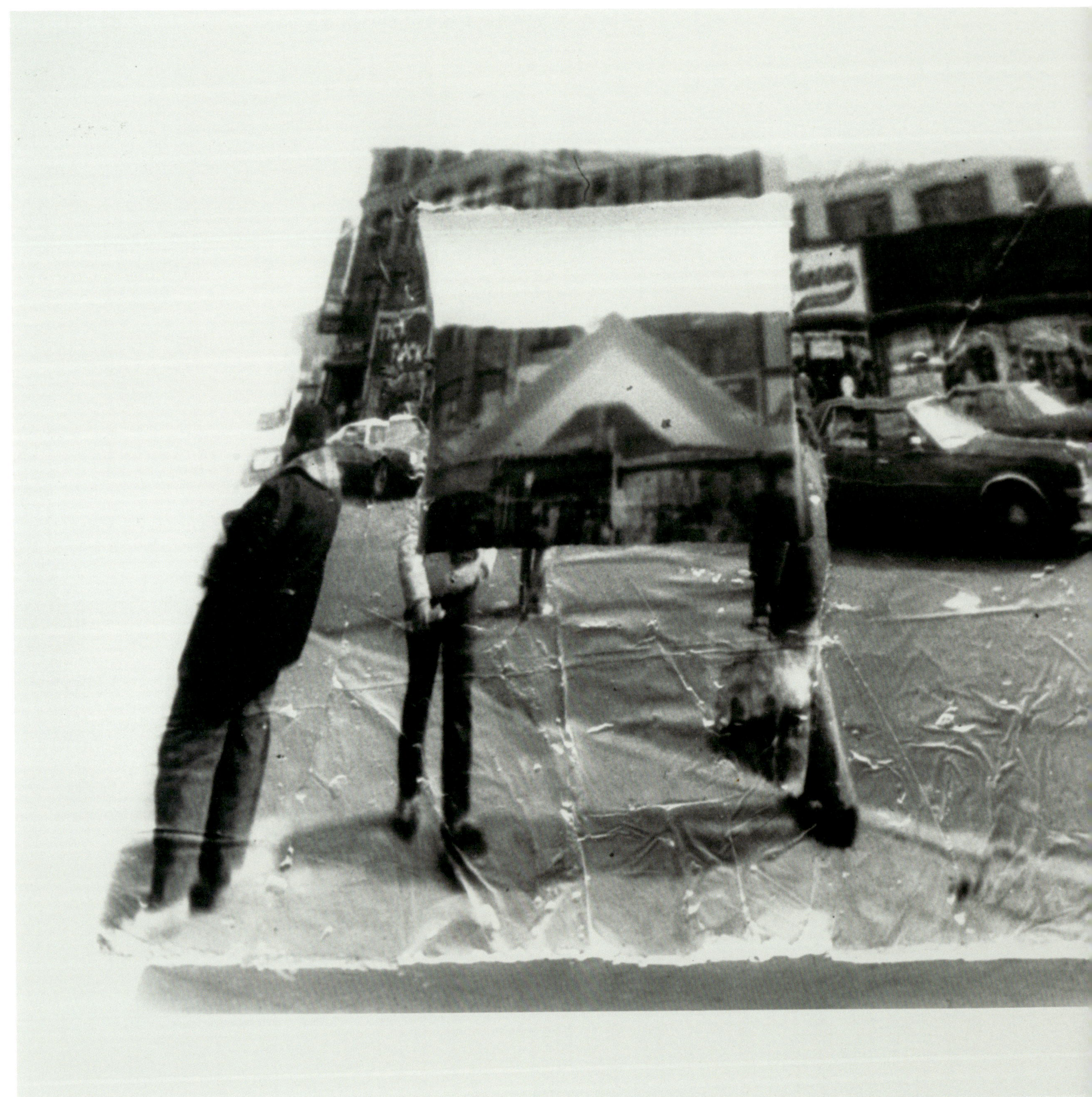

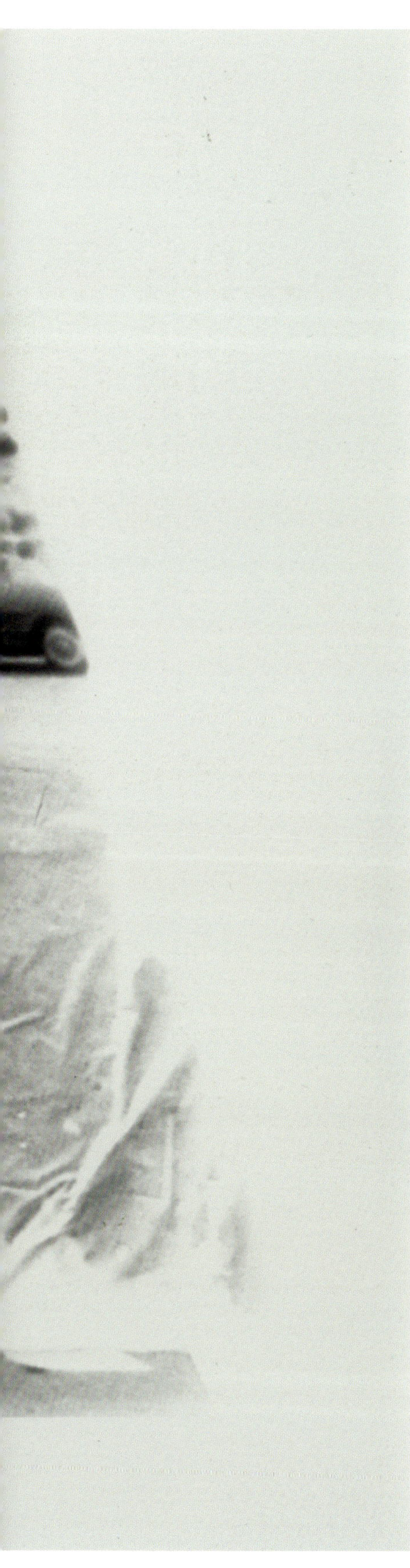

*Untitled* (Street Scene)
1987
Gelatin silver print
11 × 14 inches

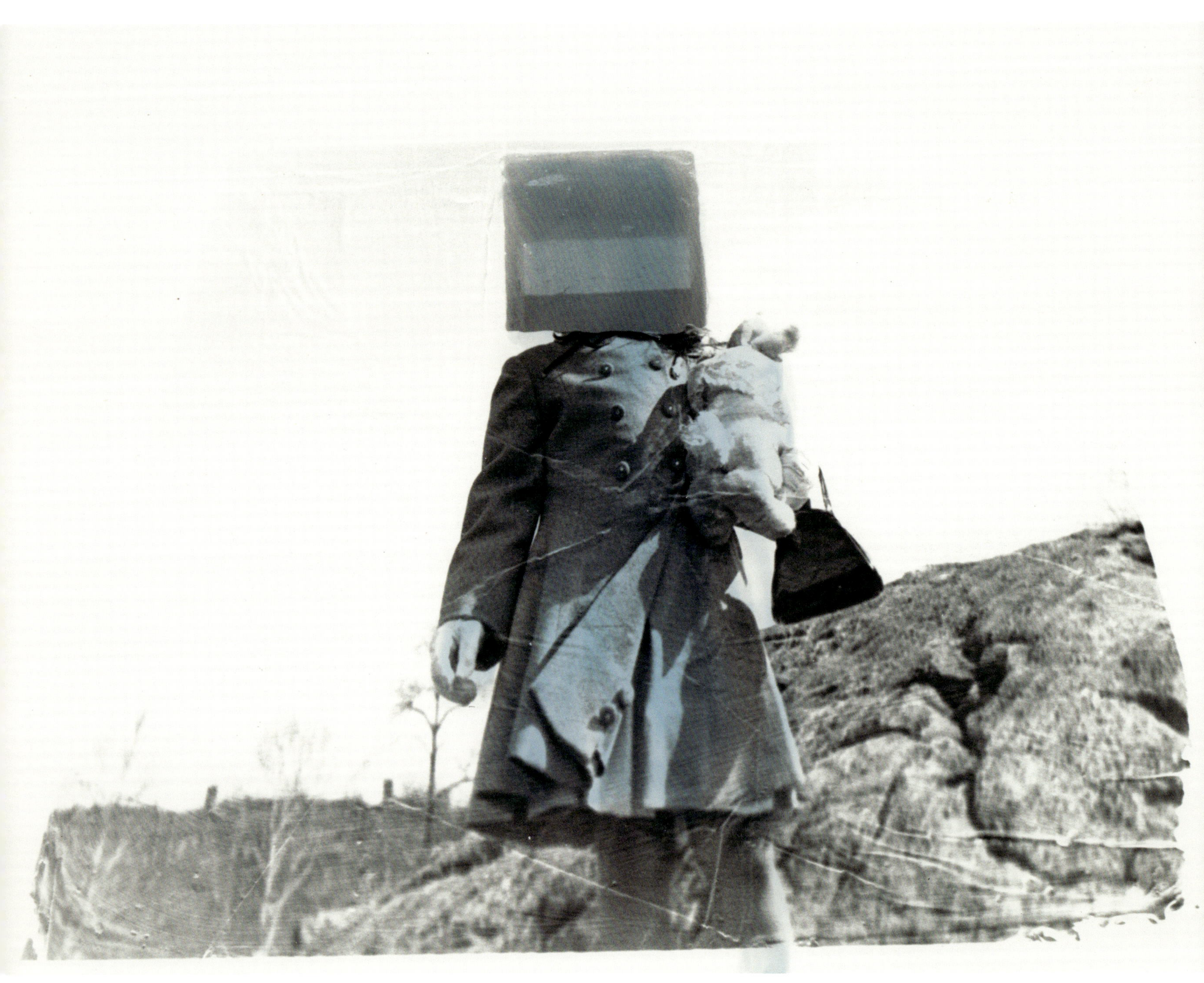

*Untitled* (Laure on Easter Sunday)
ca. 1990
Gelatin silver print with blue ink
11 × 14 inches

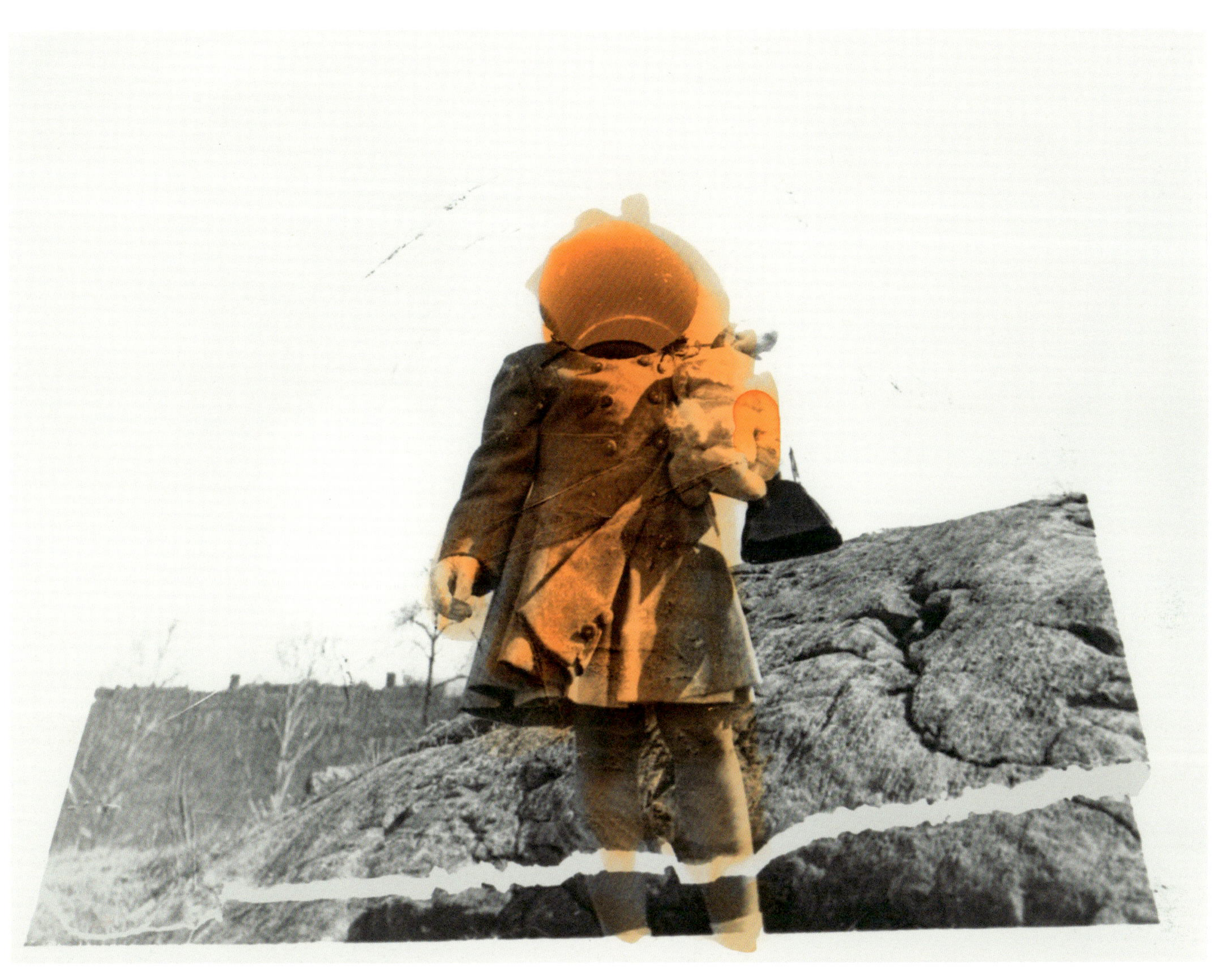


Untitled (Laure on Easter Sunday)
ca. 1990
Gelatin silver print with orange ink
10 ½ × 13 ½ inches

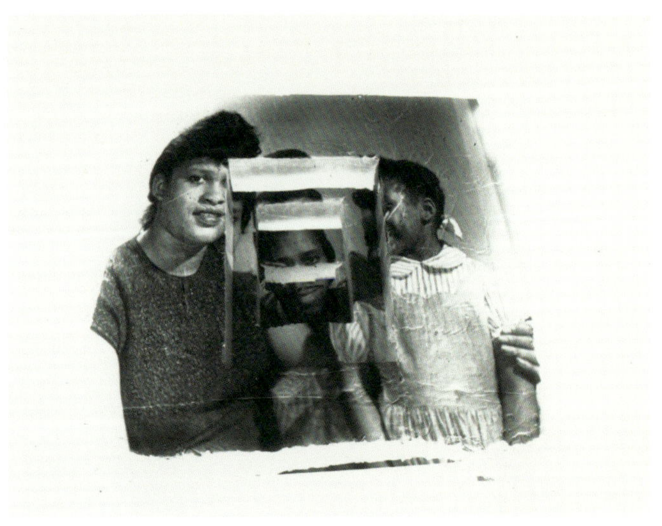

*Untitled* (Mother, Father, and Laure)
1990
Gelatin silver print
11 × 14 inches

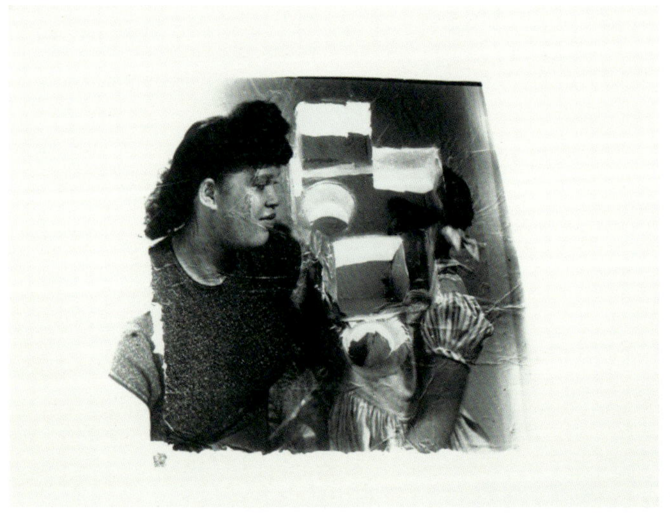

*Untitled* (Mother and Laure)
1990
Gelatin silver print
11 × 14 inches

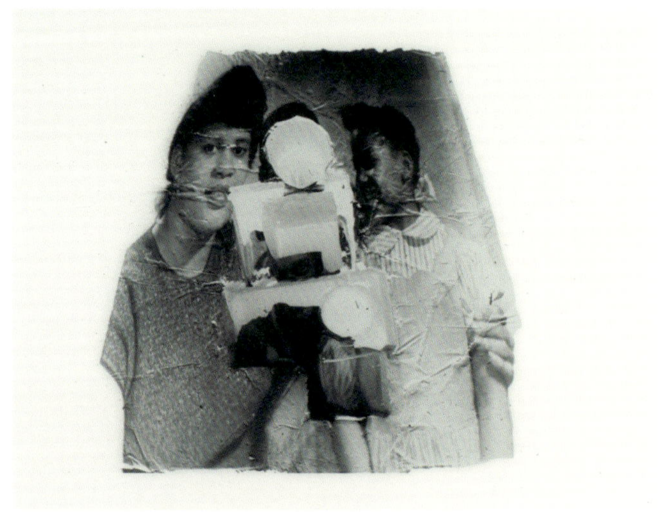

*Untitled* (Mother, Father, and Laure)
1990
Gelatin silver print
11 × 14 inches
Brooklyn Museum

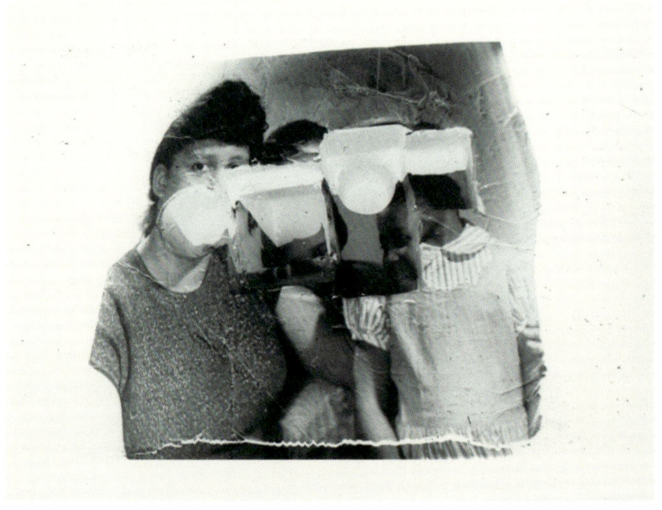

*Untitled* (Mother, Father, and Laure)
1990
Gelatin silver print
11 × 14 inches

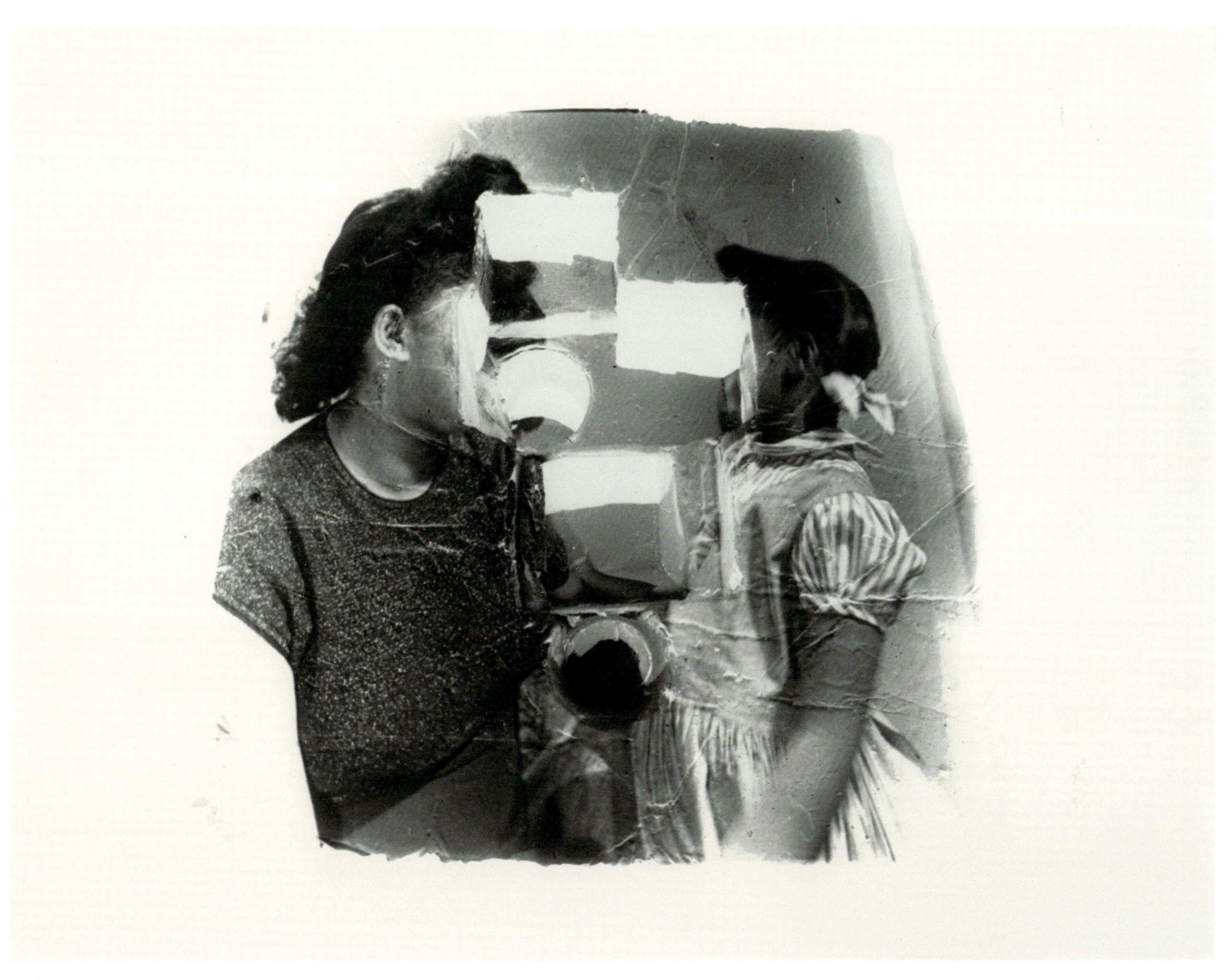

*Untitled* (Mother and Laure)
1990
Gelatin silver print
11 × 14 inches

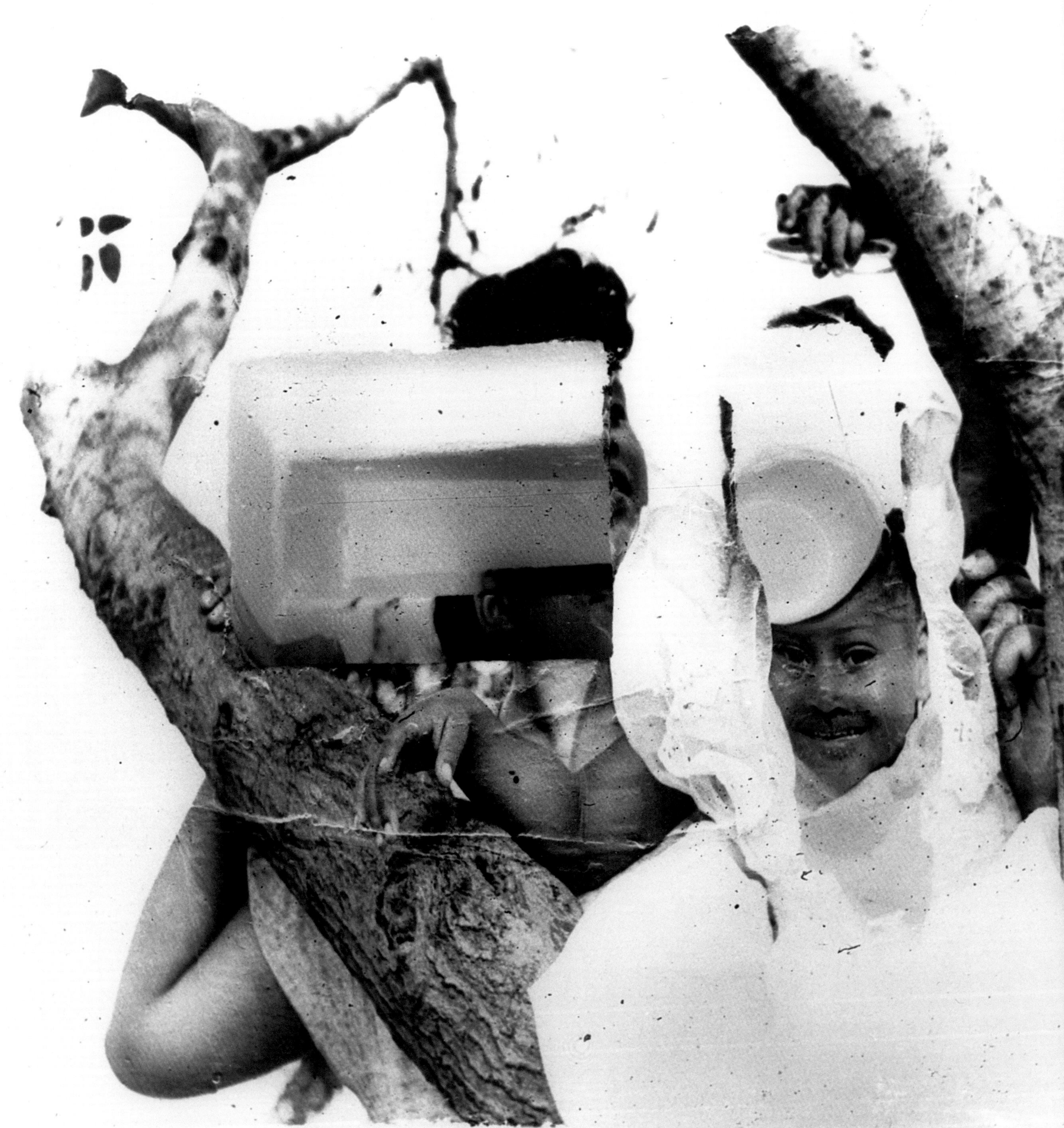

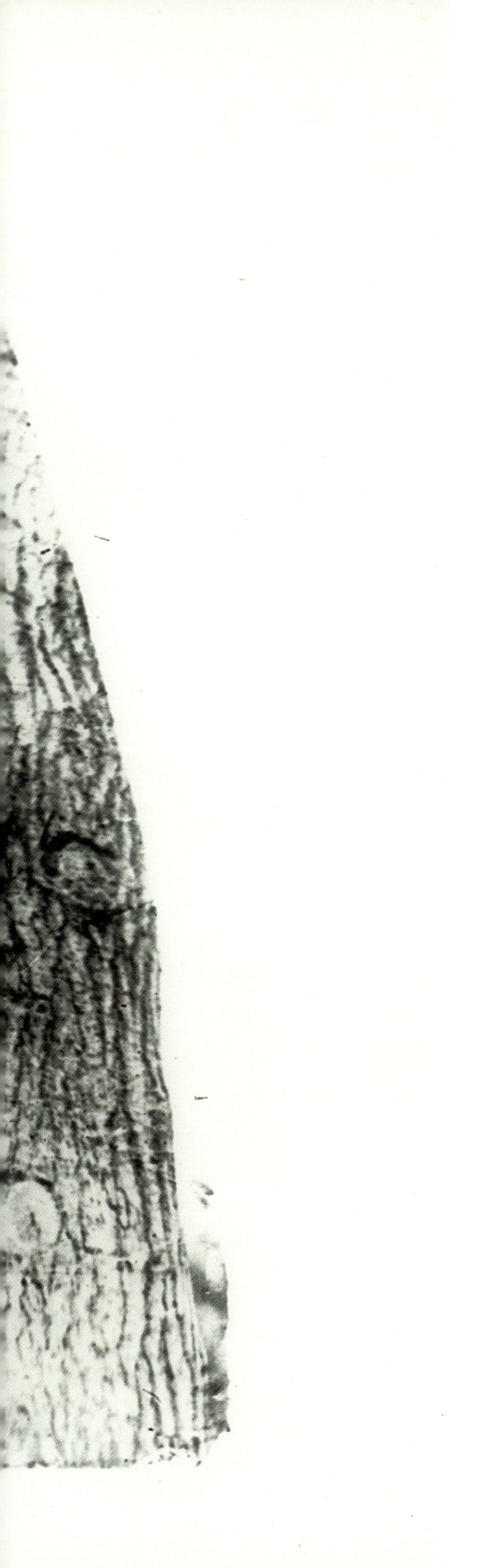

*Untitled* (Mother and Laure in Tree,
Crotona Park)
1990
Gelatin silver print
11 × 14 inches

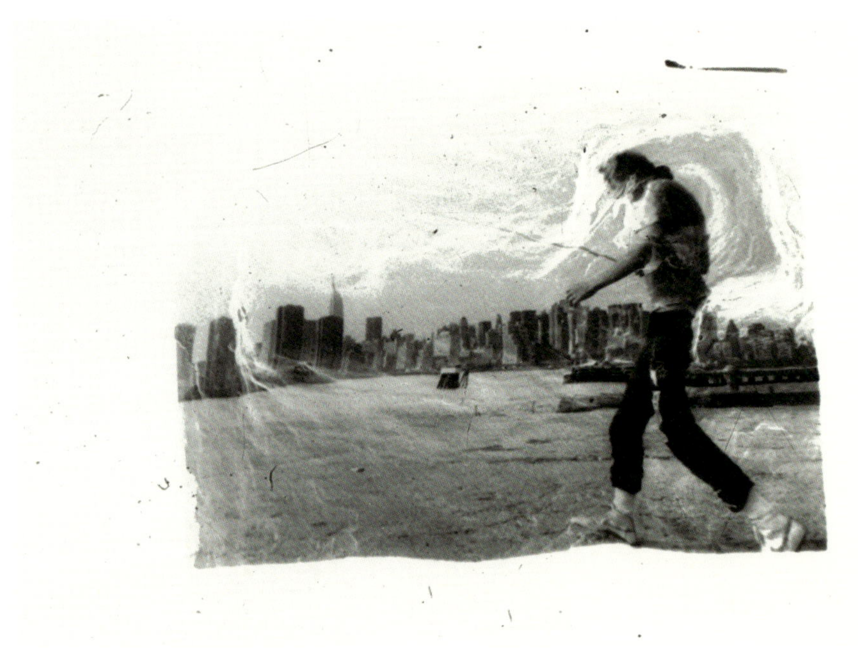

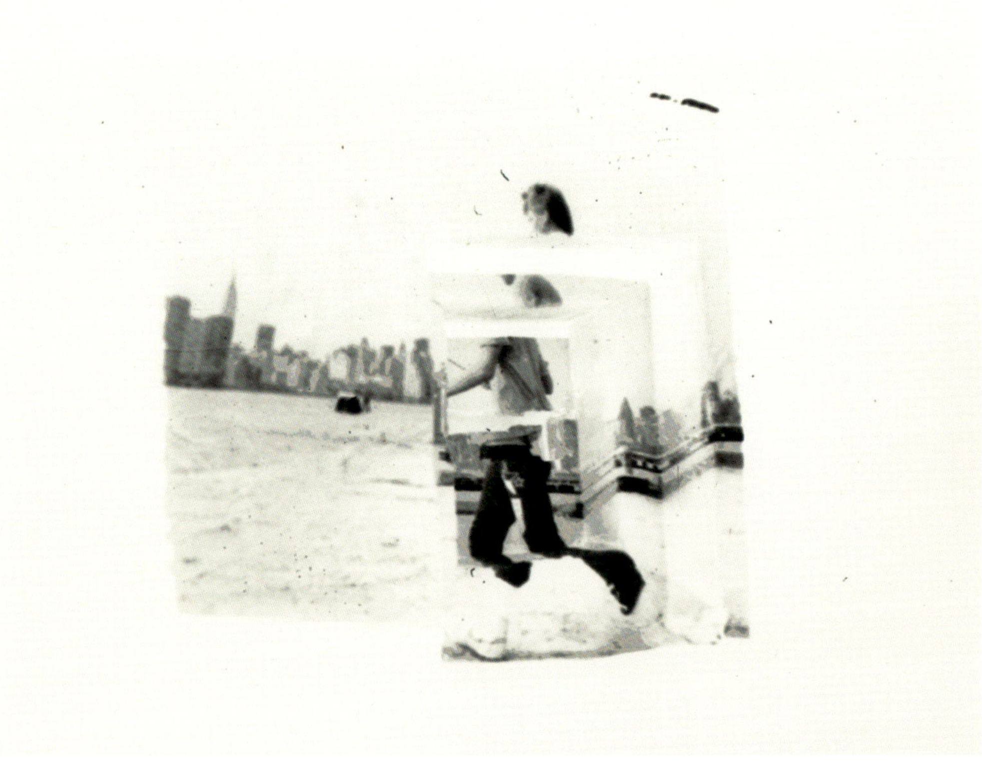

*Untitled* (Figure at Greenpoint Pier)
1991
Gelatin silver print
9 × 13 inches

*Untitled* (Figure at Greenpoint Pier)
1991
Gelatin silver print
11 × 14 inches

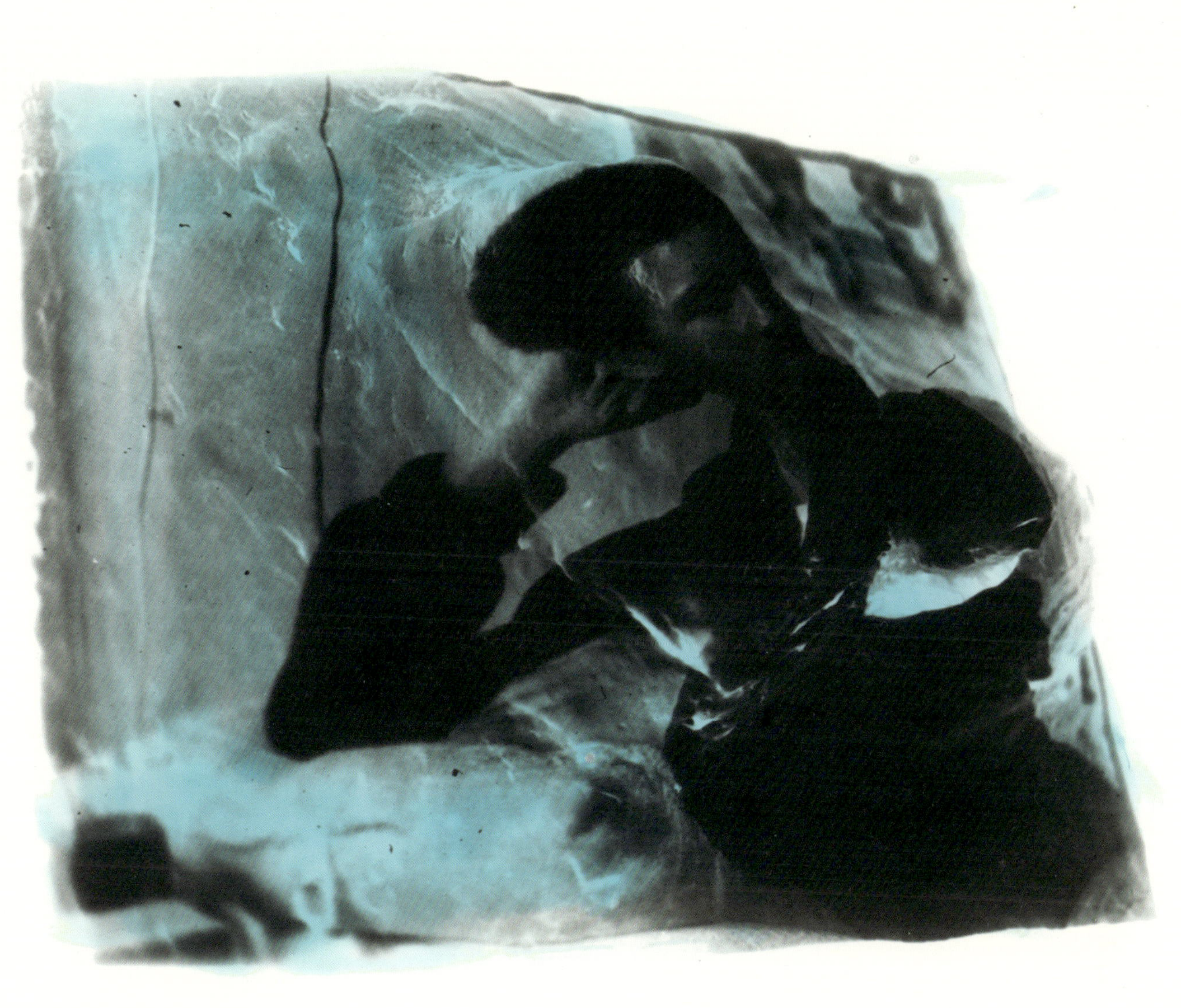

*Untitled* (Self-Portrait after Allen Frame
Photograph)
ca. 1990
Gelatin silver print with blue ink
8 × 10 inches

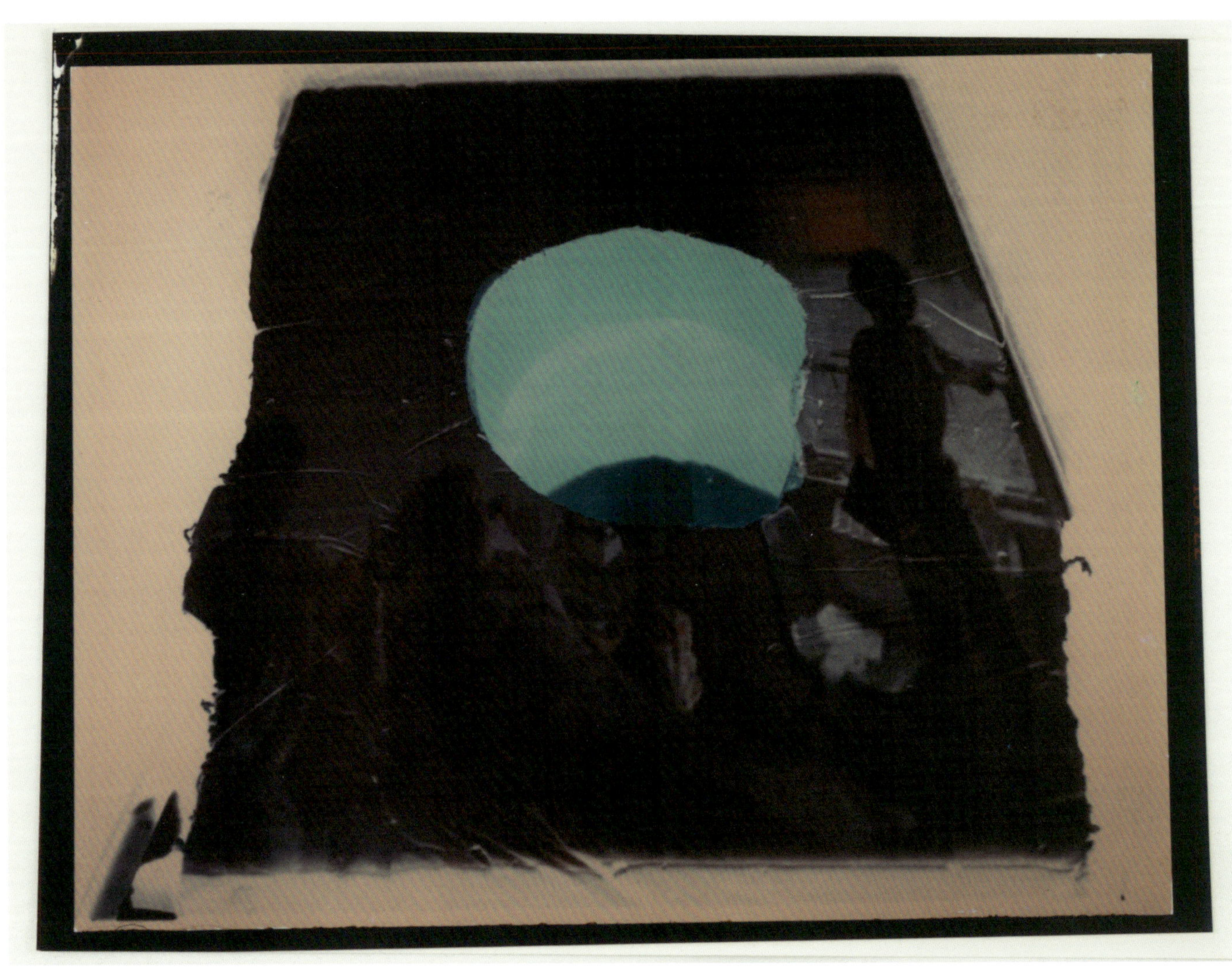

*Untitled* (Figures in Bedroom)
ca. 1988–92
Chromogenic print
8 ½ × 11 inches

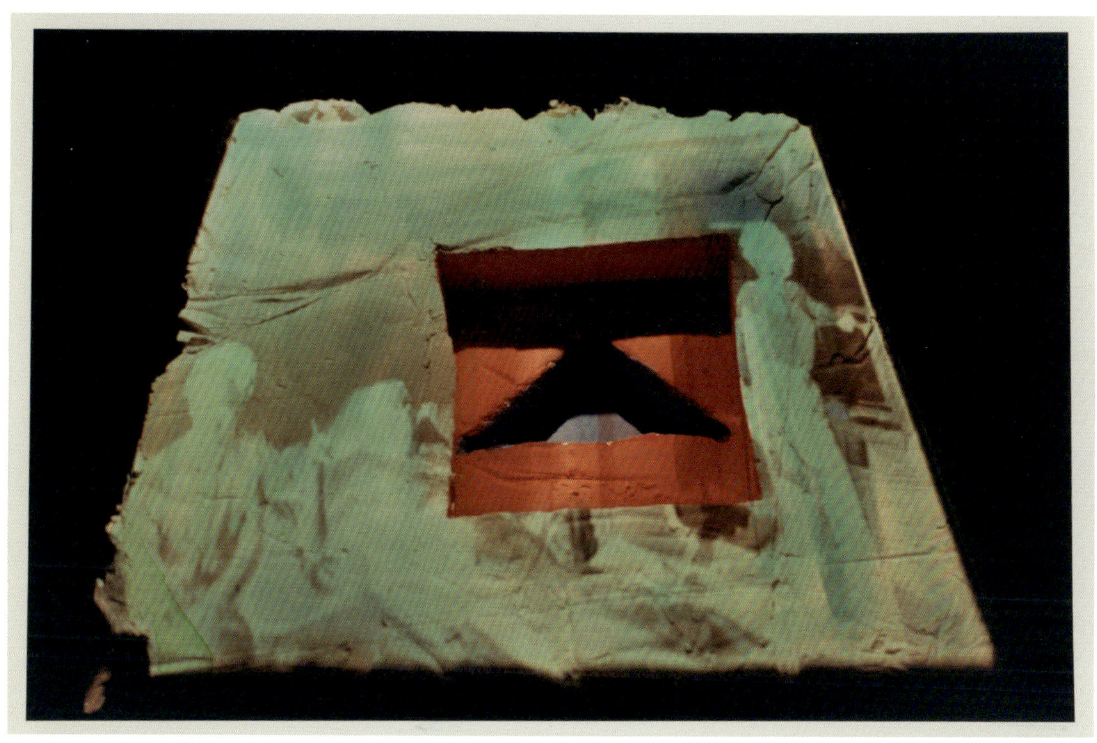

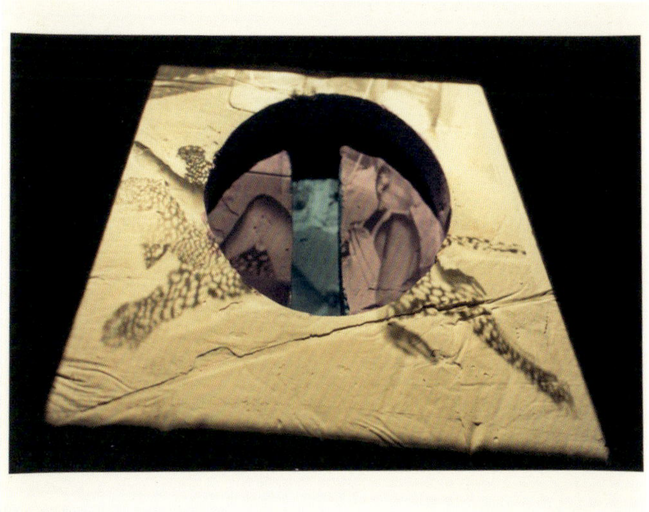

*Untitled* (Figures in Bedroom)
ca. 1988–92
Chromogenic print
11 × 14 inches

*Untitled* (Woman with Leopard Skin)
ca. 1988–92
Chromogenic print
16 × 20 inches

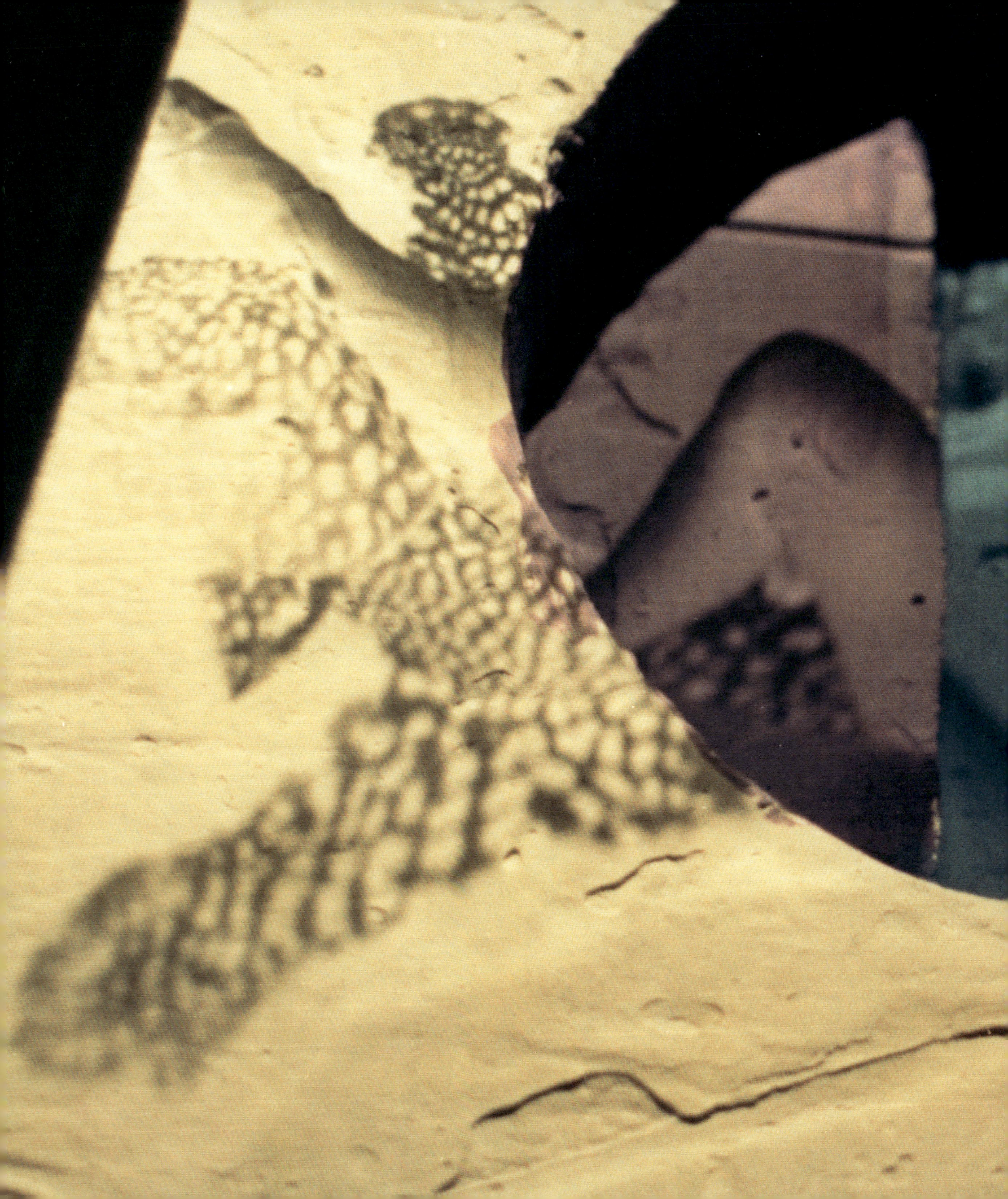

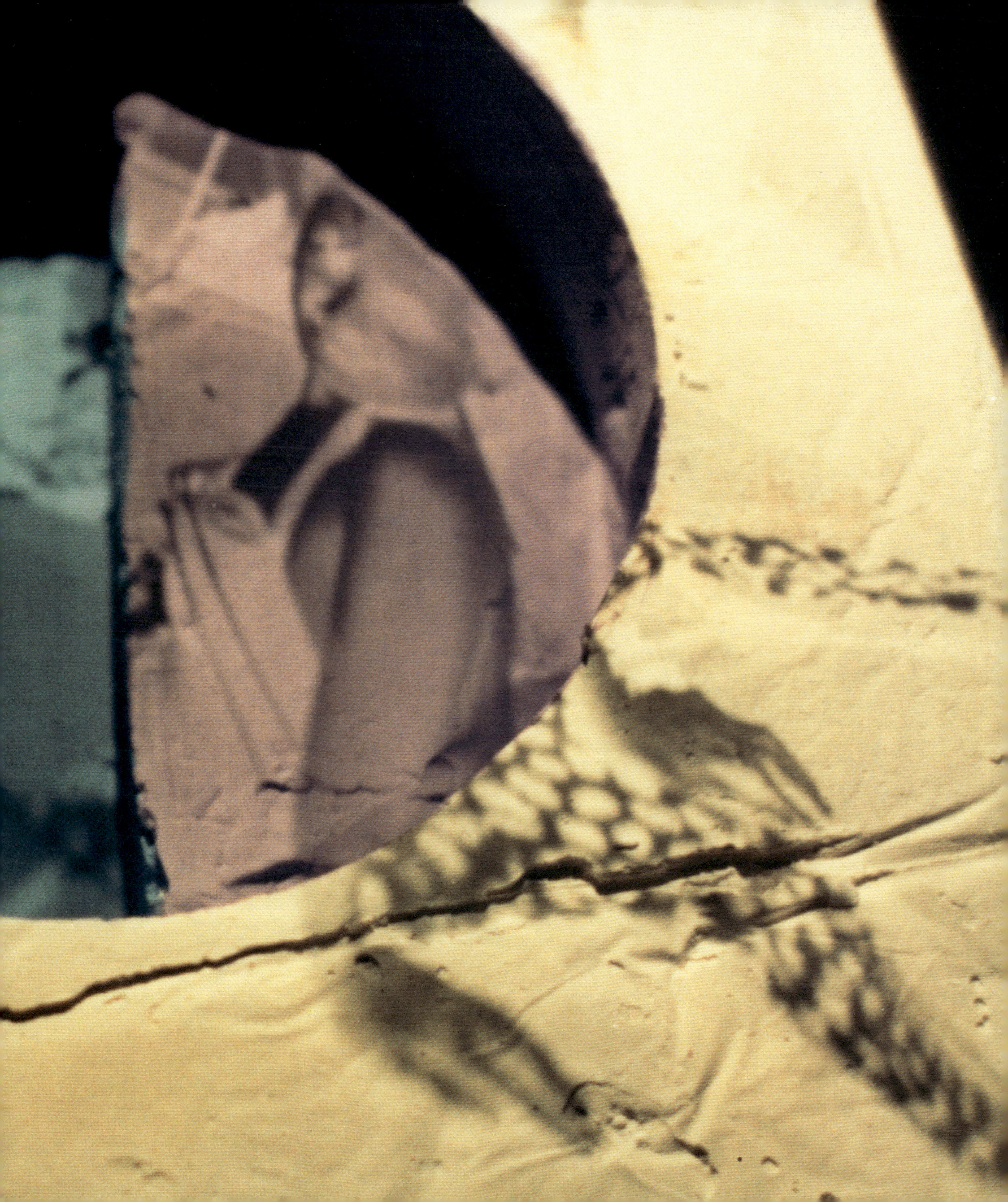

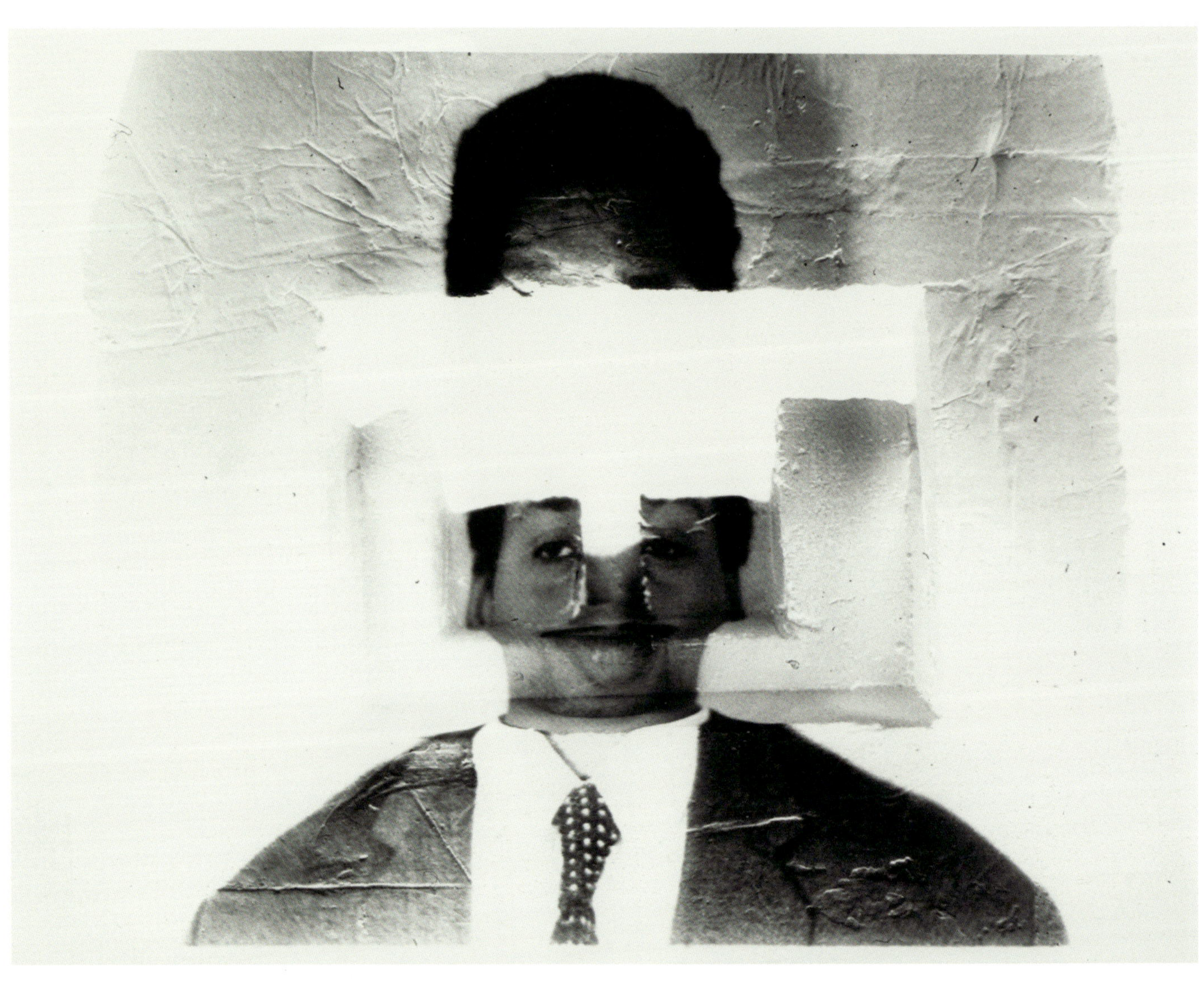

*Untitled* (Self-Portrait after Museum Guard
Photograph)
ca. 1990
Gelatin silver print
8 × 10 inches

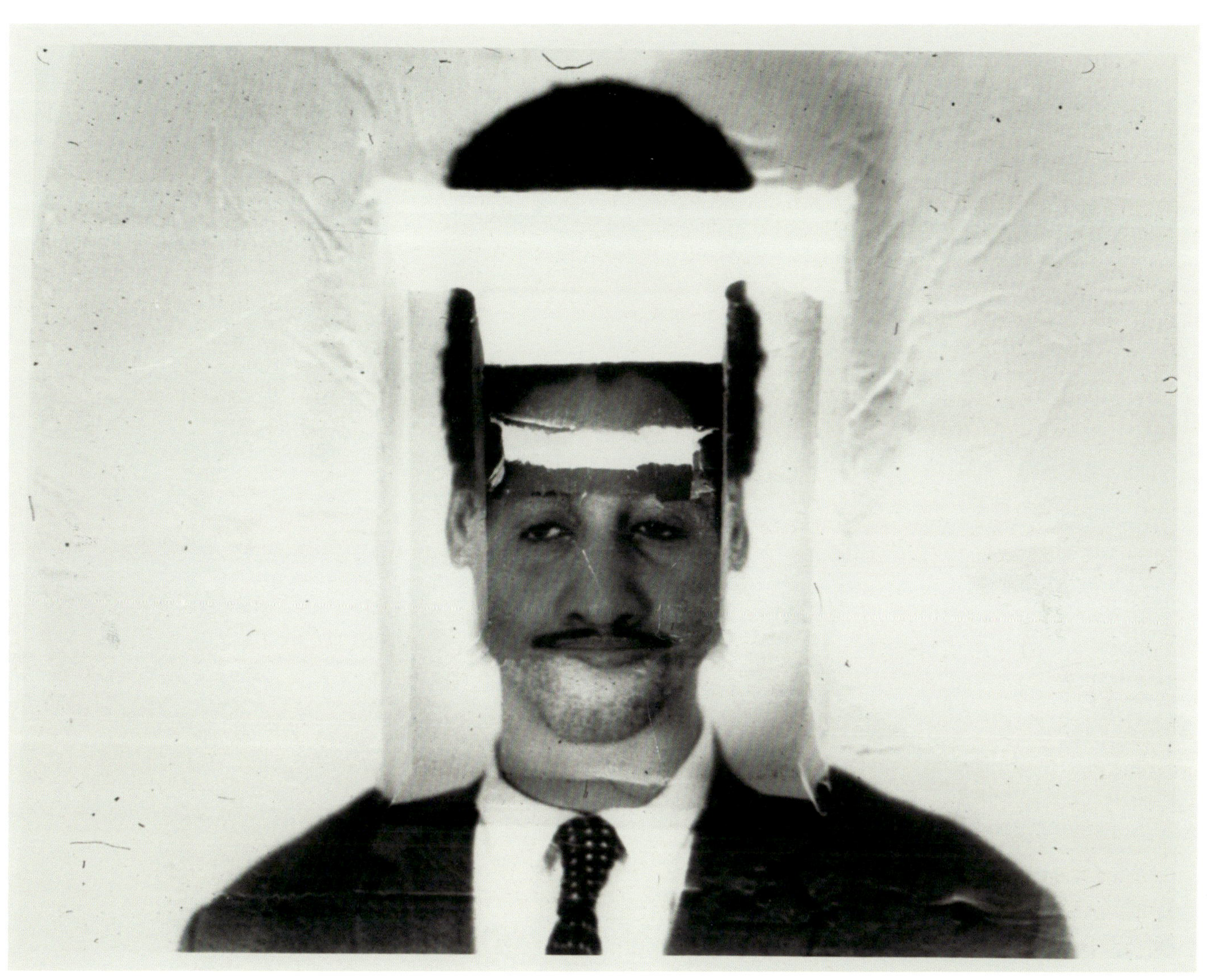

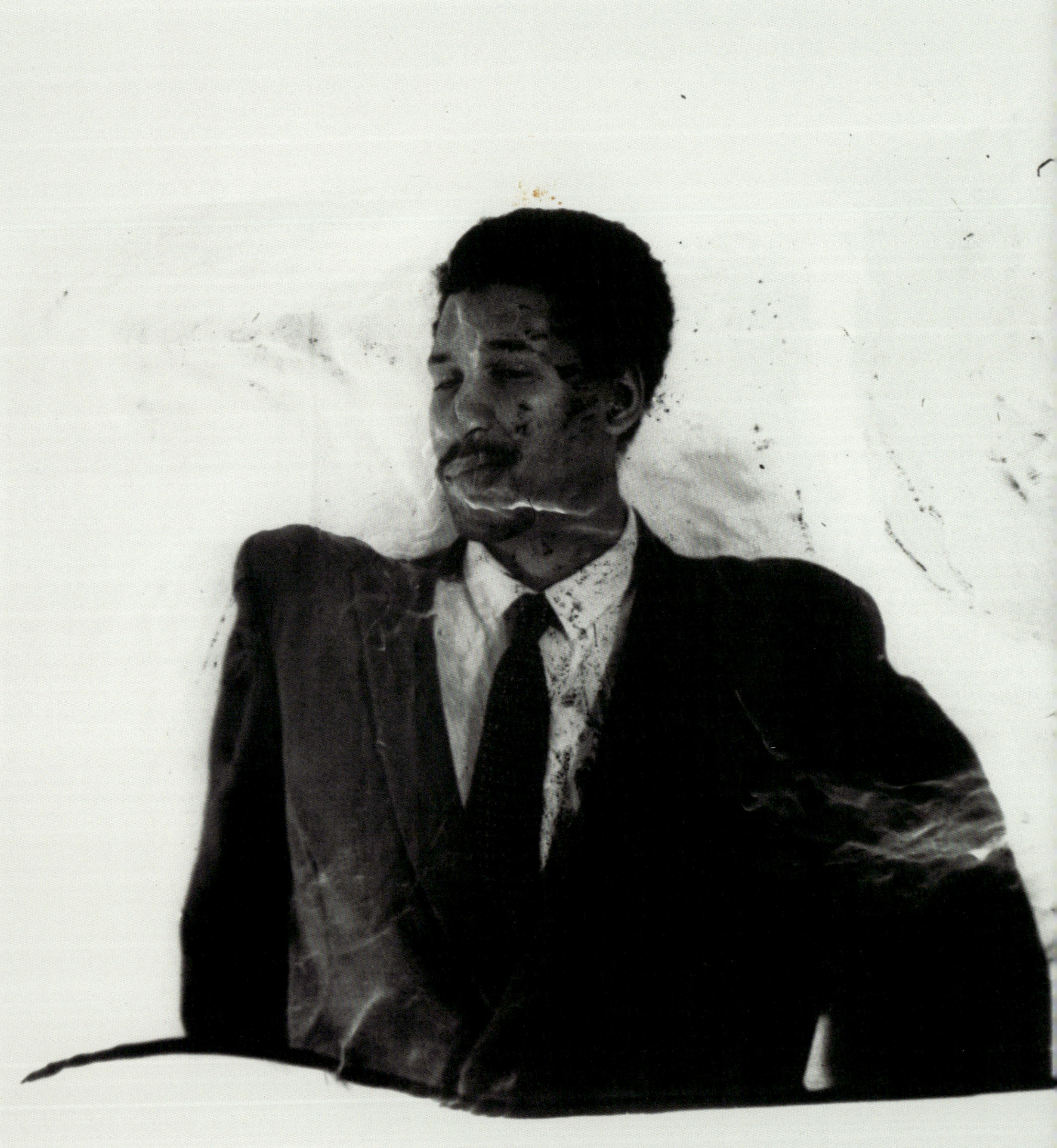

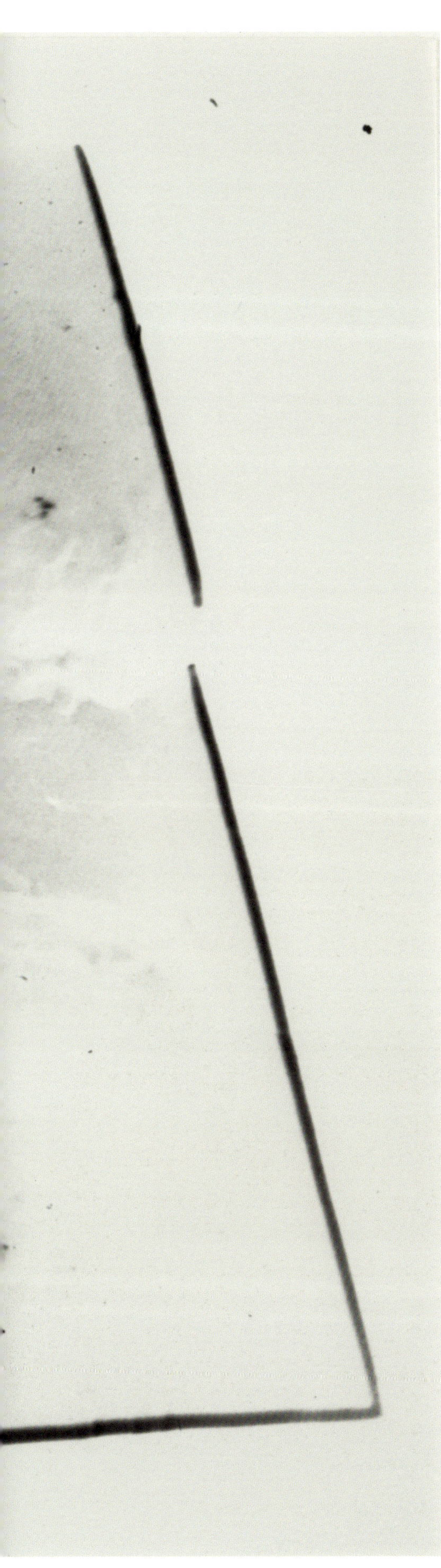

*Untitled* (Self-Portrait after Museum Guard
Photograph)
ca. 1990
Gelatin silver print
8 × 10 inches

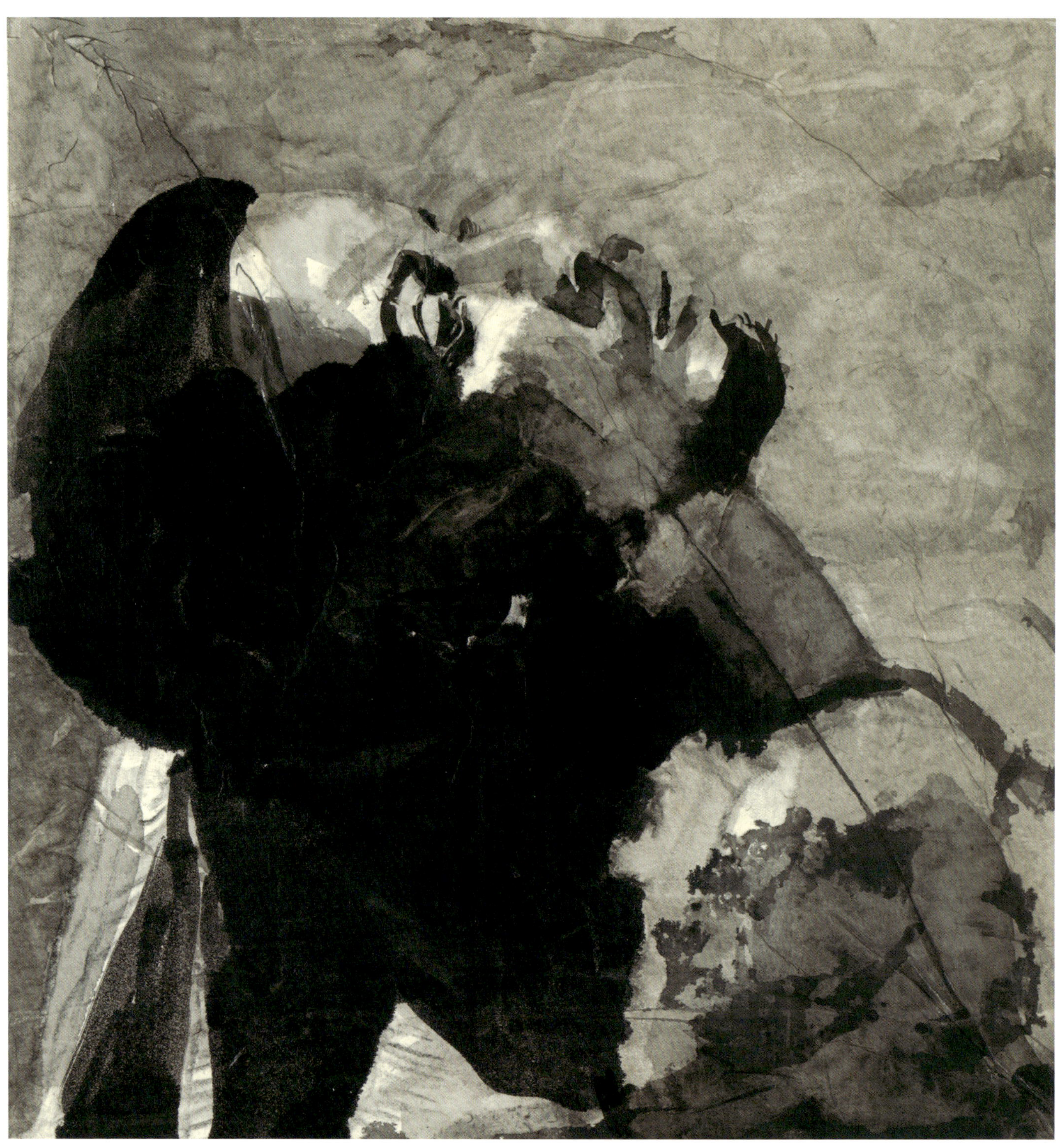

*Self-Portrait after Photograph by Peter Hujar*
1989
Ink, wash, and charcoal on Asian paper mounted
to canvas
24 × 22 inches
The Baltimore Museum of Art

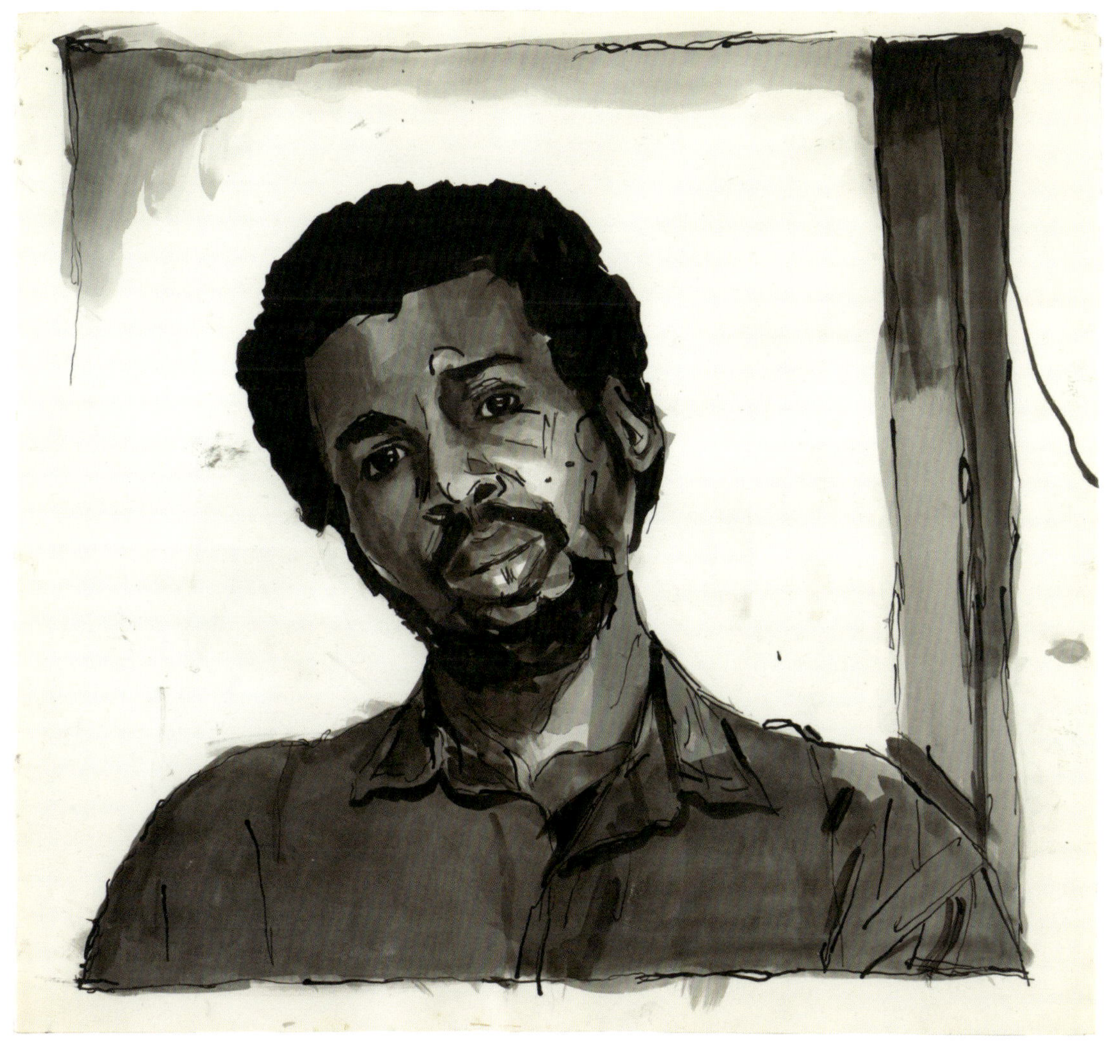

*Untitled* (Self-Portrait)
ca. 1990–92
Ink and wash on paper
25 × 26 inches
Collection of Michael Sherman

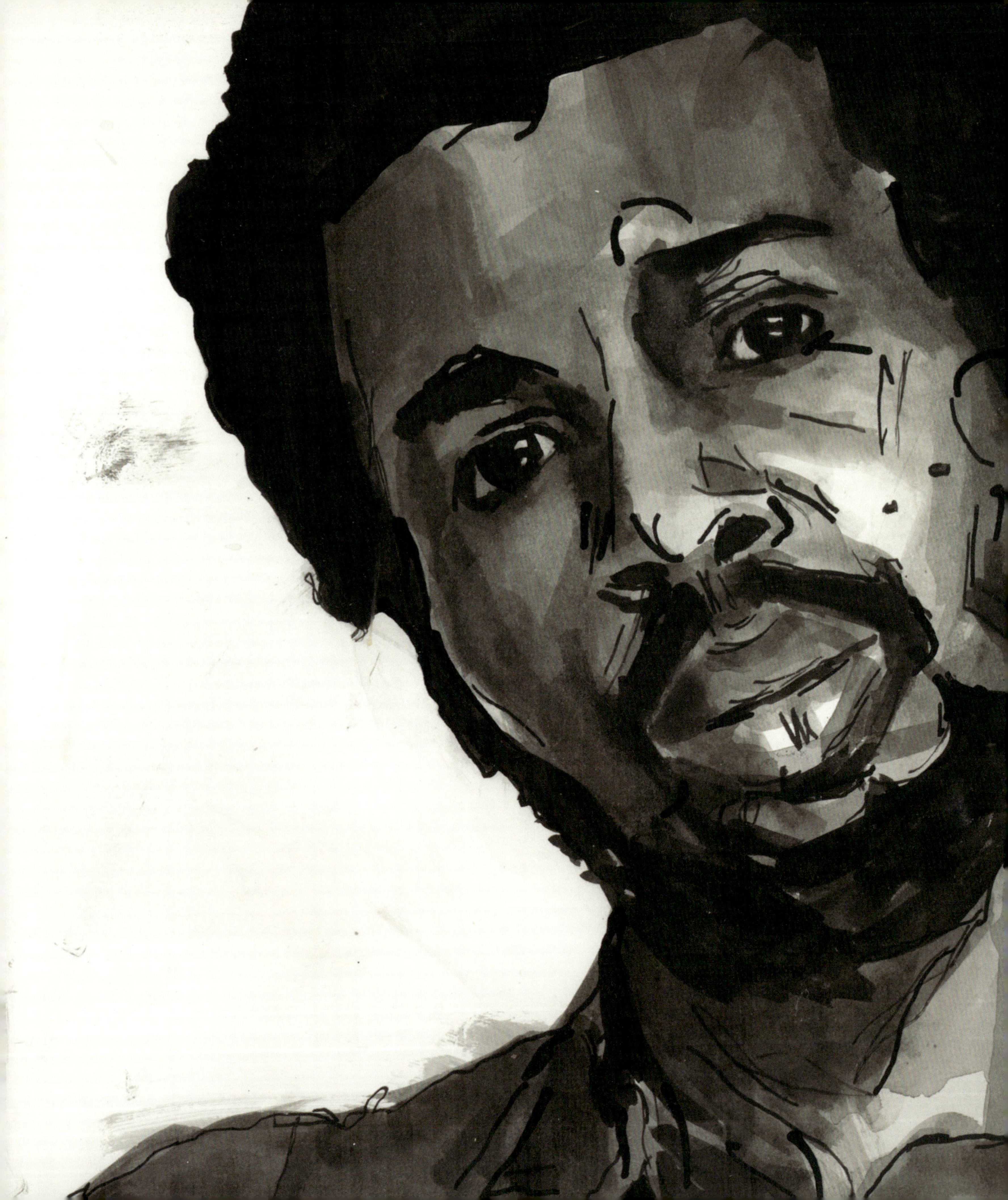

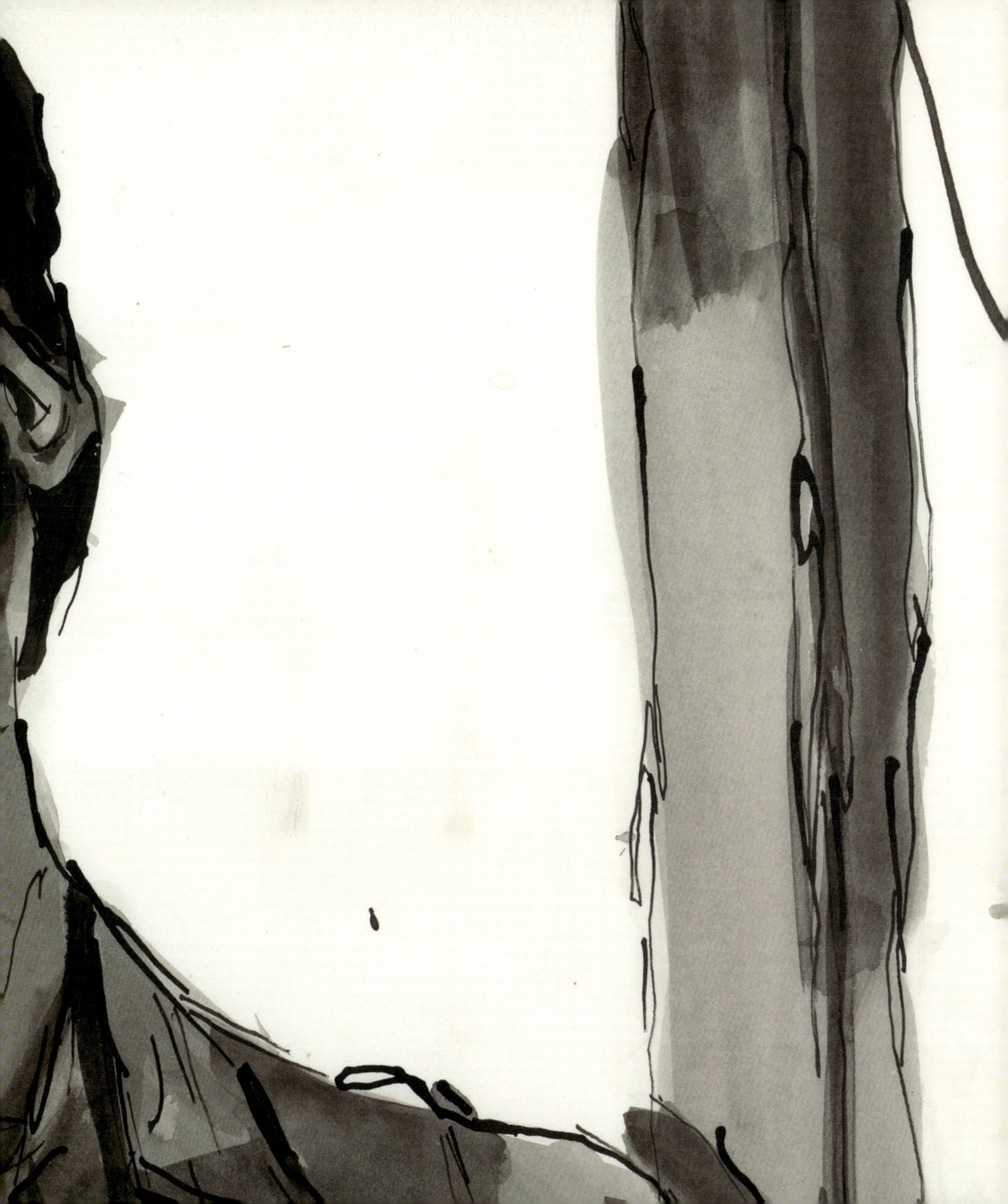

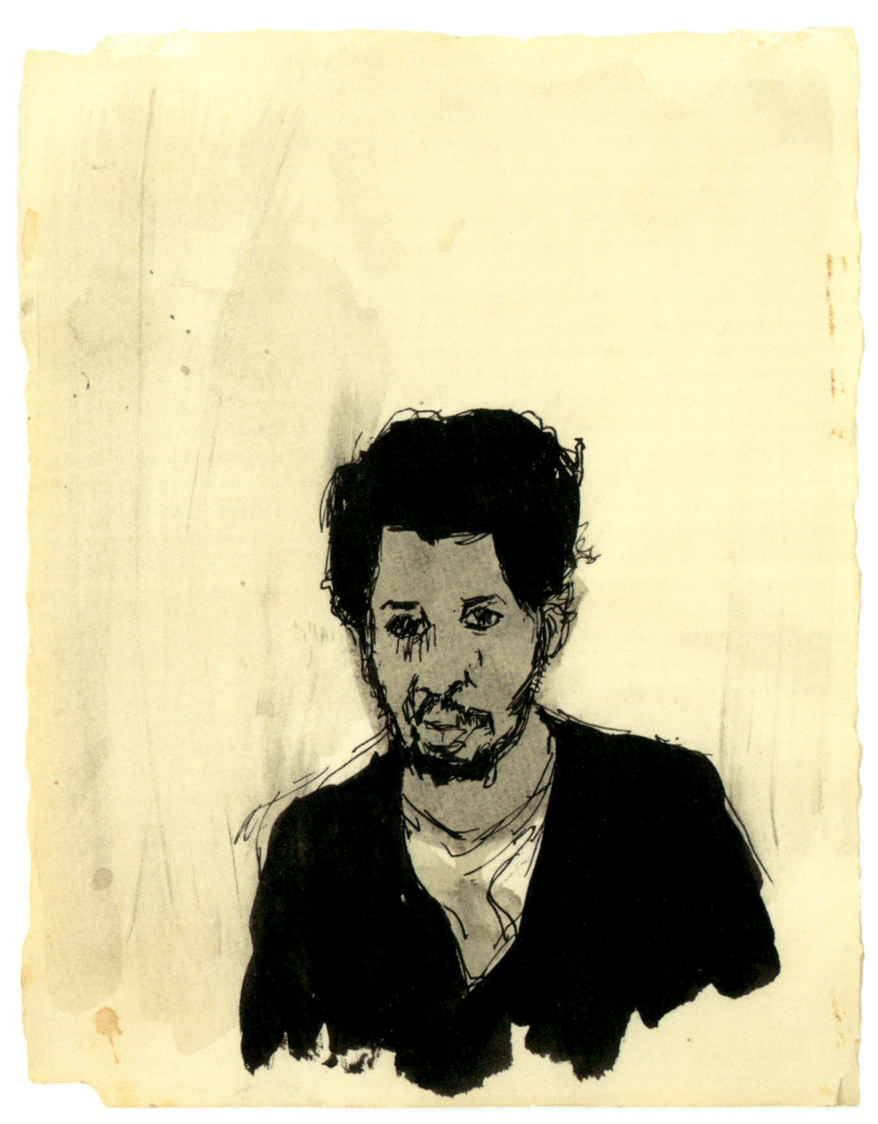

*Untitled* (Self-Portrait)
ca. 1990–92
Ink and wash on paper
11 ½ × 9 inches
Green Family Art Foundation

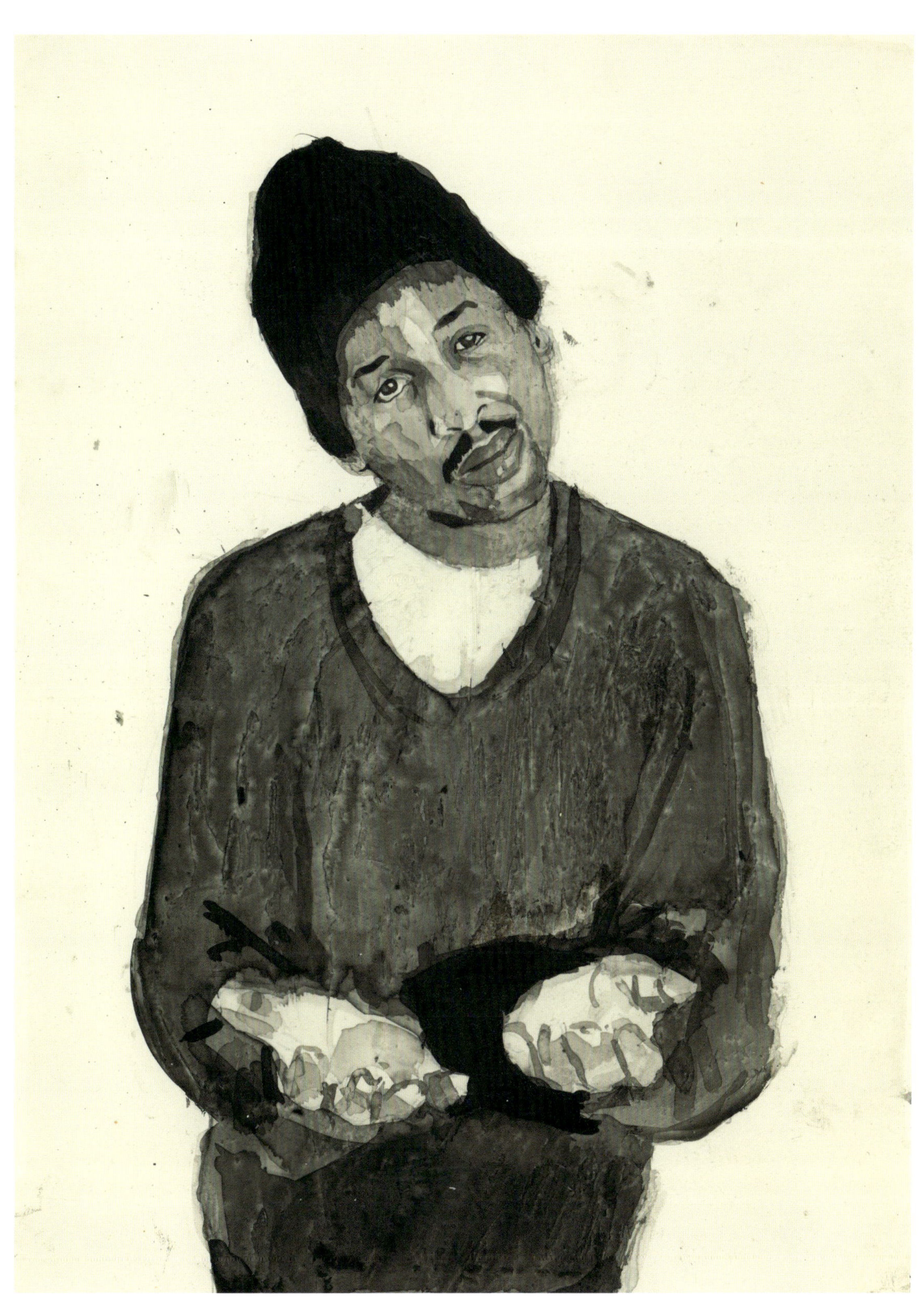

*Untitled* (Self-Portrait)
ca. 1990–92
Ink and wash on paper prepared
with textured ground
24 ½ × 17 inches

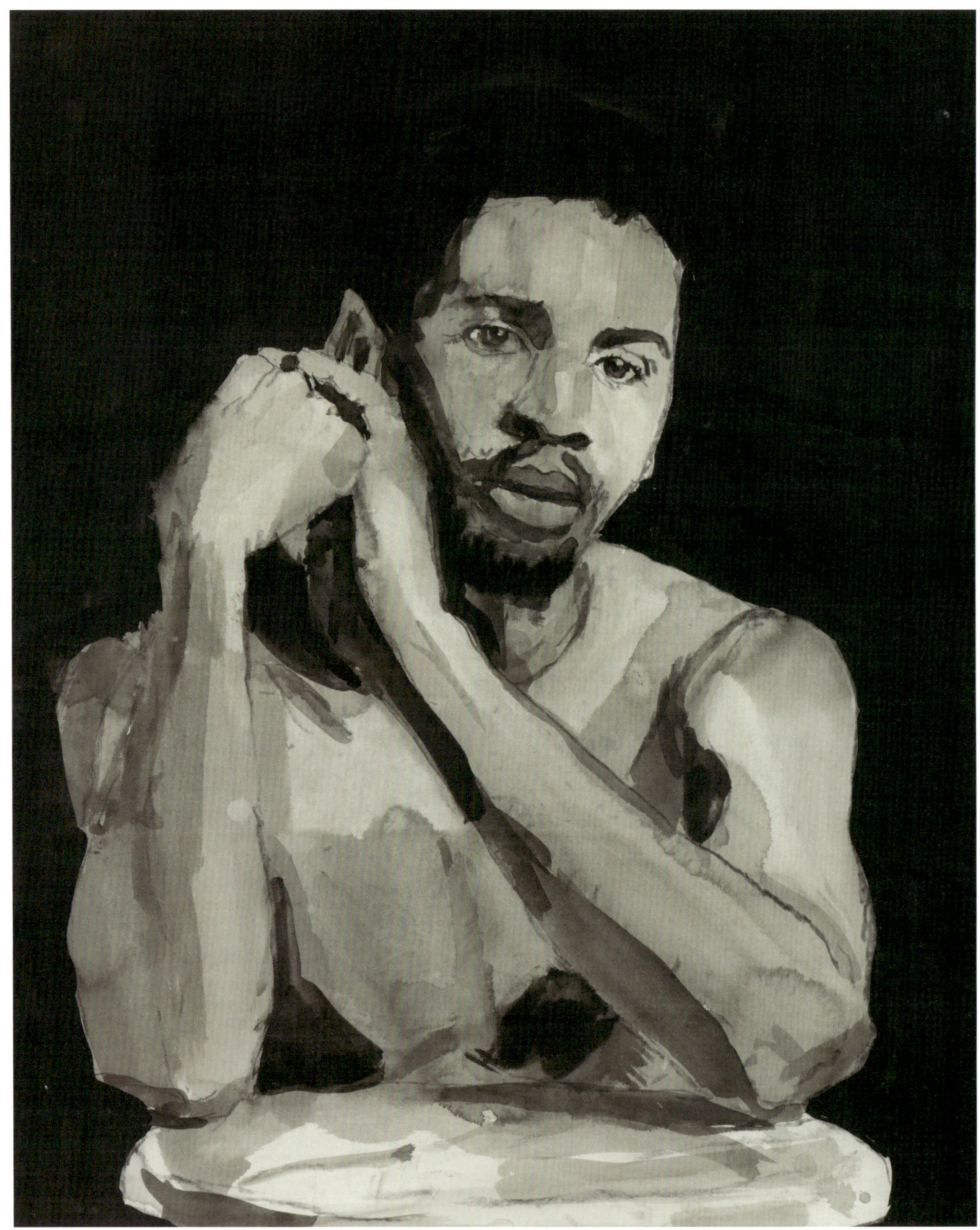

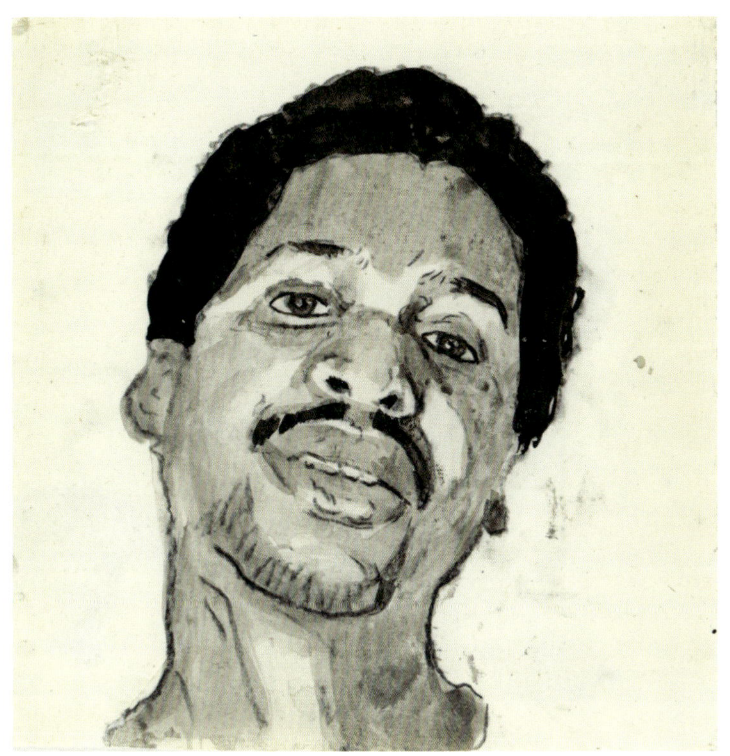

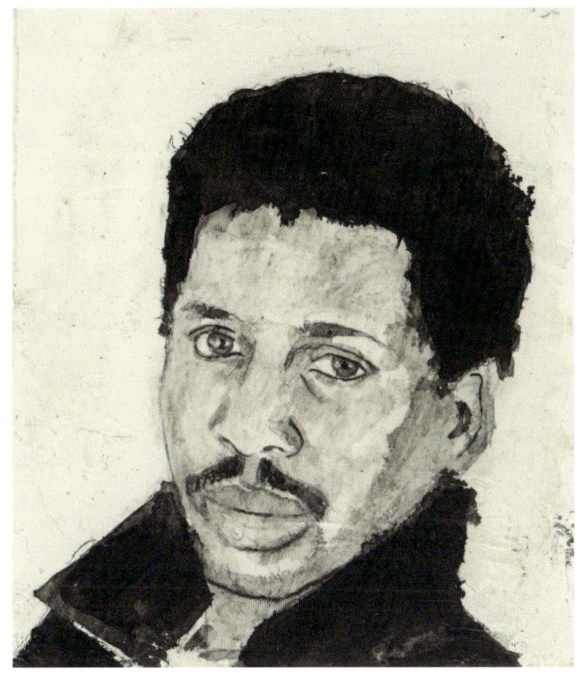

*Self-Portrait after Photograph by*
*Robert Mapplethorpe*
1989
Ink and wash on paper
30 × 23 inches
Collection of George Steinberg

*Untitled* (Self-Portrait)
ca. 1990–92
Ink and charcoal on paper
17 × 16 ¼ inches

*Untitled* (Self-Portrait)
ca. 1990–92
Ink and charcoal on paper with
textured ground
11 ¾ × 10 inches

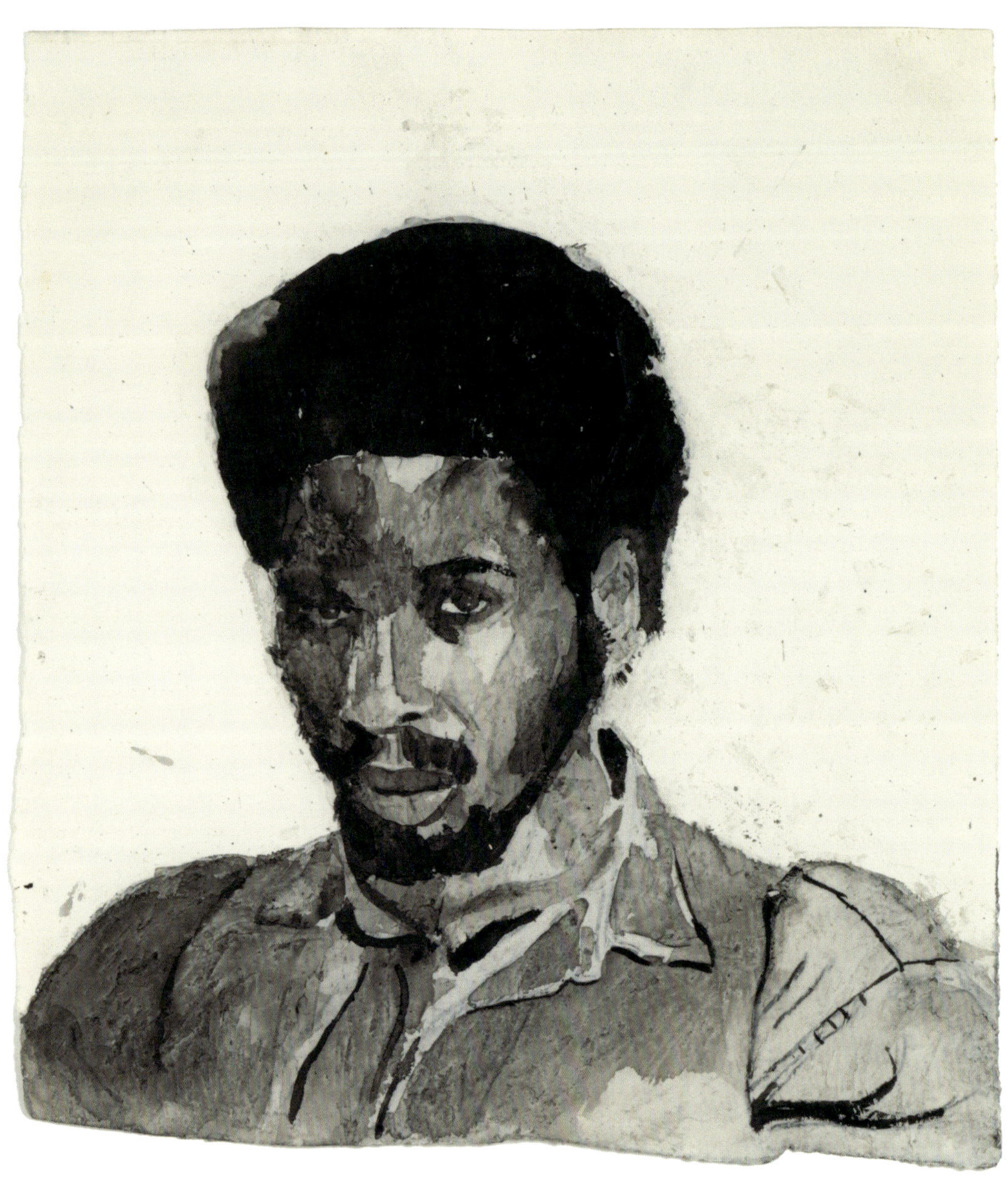

*Untitled* (Self-Portrait)
ca. 1990–92
Ink and wash on paper with prepared ground
16 ½ × 14 inches
Collection of Susan J. Weiler

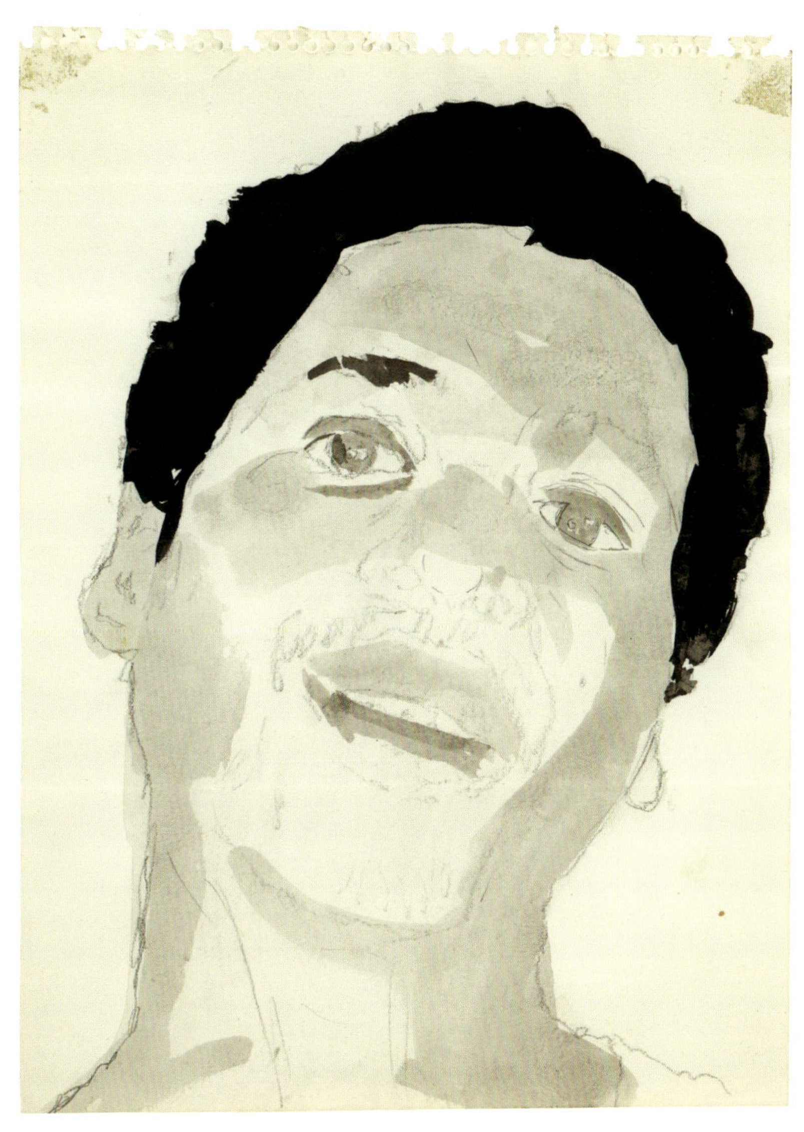

*Untitled* (Self-Portrait)
ca. 1990–92
Ink, wash, and graphite on paper
11 ½ × 8 ¼ inches

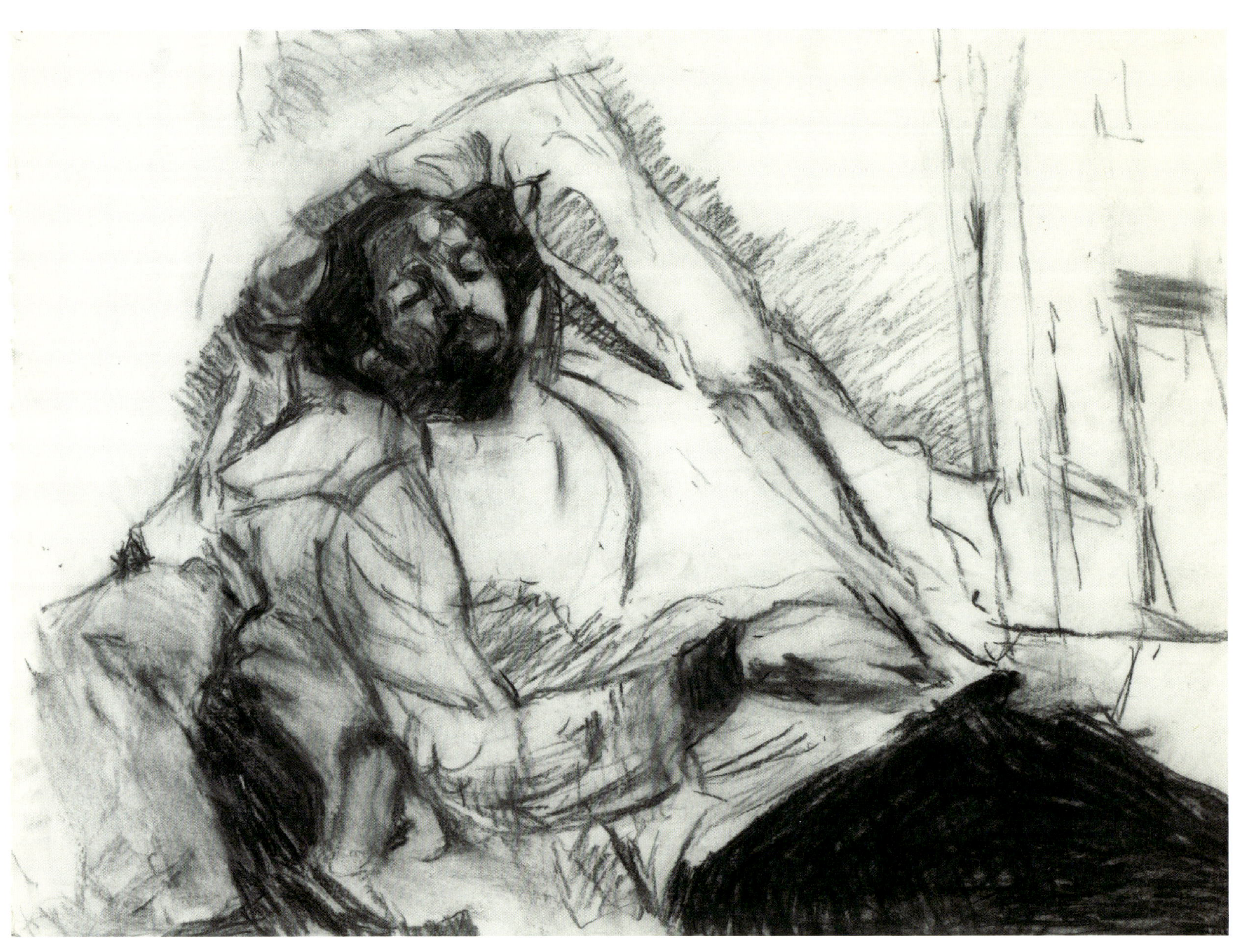

*Untitled* (Reclining Self-Portrait)
1992
Charcoal on paper
22 × 30 inches

To Be
Remembered
/ To Have
Been Real

Sadie Barnette
Alanna Fields
S*an D. Henry-Smith
Paul Mpagi Sepuya
with Ariel Goldberg

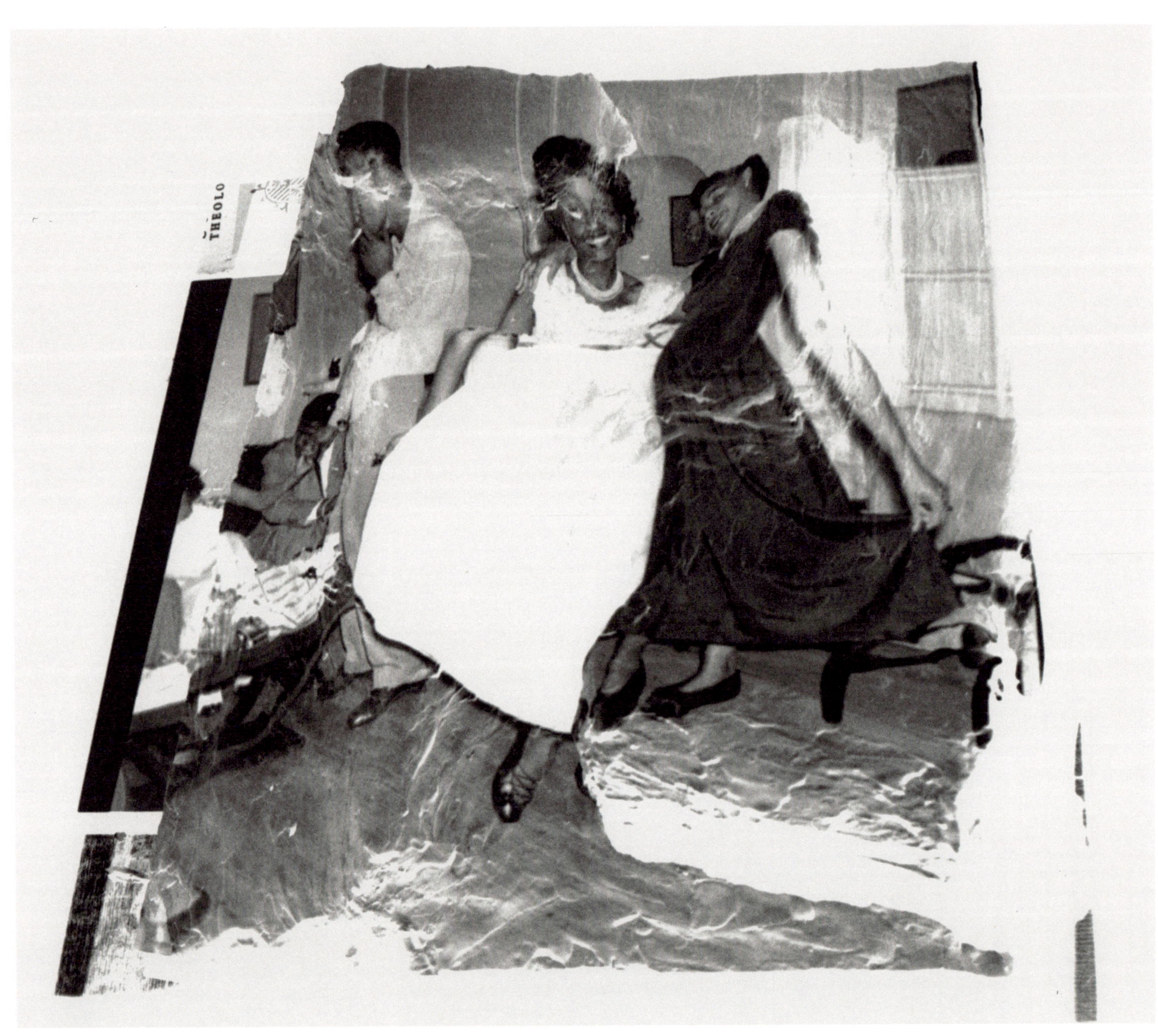



11. *Untitled* (Aunt Lena and Grandmother
Lillian Ellis)
ca. 1988–92
Gelatin silver print
11 × 14 inches

In the summer of 2020, writer and scholar Ariel Goldberg, in collaboration with Visual AIDS, organized and moderated two virtual meetings with artists Sadie Barnette, Alanna Fields, S*an D. Henry-Smith, and Paul Mpagi Sepuya to discuss selected works of Darrel Ellis. Inspired by Ellis's observations toward the end of his life that maybe, at age thirty-two, he was finally moving into his own time, our intent was to bring together a coterie of Black artists whose approach to their own image-making practices shares some kinship with Ellis's. How would these artists, some of whom were experiencing Ellis's work for the first time, relate to his artistic vision and process, and how would their looking further illuminate Ellis's work and legacy? By bringing Ellis into conversation with a younger generation of artists, our hope is to foster a lineage of influence and inspiration that was interrupted by Ellis's early death.

### Ariel Goldberg

What resonates with you when engaging with Darrel Ellis's images, from his photographs, drawings, and paintings?

### Sadie Barnette

I'm quite moved by the work. It's not lost on me how tender I want to be in handling this oeuvre by someone who really should be here to talk about it themselves. One word that comes to mind when spending time with these images is *inheritance*. Darrel Ellis has inherited this beautiful, tender, intimate archive of family photographs by a dad that he never got to meet— that's his inheritance, as well as this really complicated relationship to state violence.

### Alanna Fields

Ellis's abstract approach to re-representing his father's photographs is a way of visually speaking about the complications of memory, right? Photographs of photographs are serving as proof of existence, or that something happened. What are the ways in which people who are in that space, that moment, view the original event? If we take a photograph, put it up, abstract it, and interrupt it, and layer it and really shift that opacity, I think we start to get how complicated memory and photographs are when we have to recollect our experiences.

### Paul Mpagi Sepuya

When I started looking more at Ellis's works I got really into the perspectival space in them. These images allow us to think about how a viewer encounters an image as a reader of a family album. The forced perspective implies the reciprocal relationship to looking and viewing and reading, more so than what I think we often do in archival work, which tries to present an "objective" view of a work. In Darrel's work, we're always looking at the images being read and reread. Think about the queer artist going through their own family photo album. Is that act about excavating a possible suppressed queer history? There are so many ways in which I think we queer people enter into that archive.

### S*an D. Henry-Smith

Often I'm thinking about the role of photography in relation to Black representation and visibility, and the thing that is so rich about all Black family archives is that we're in control of these narratives. Regardless of skill or technique, these kinds of images are important because they affirm, *This is what we look like and this is what we look like to each other*. They show ourselves to ourselves.

What images are you drawn to that speak to Ellis's relationship to family archives?



What drew me to this image (fig. 11) of the party scene was that there are all of these domestic and social cues that the original family photo snapshot captures, and freezes, almost like a fossil. The original image, taken by Darrel's father, Thomas Ellis, preserves this moment, whereas Darrel, through his process, undoes this moment. The resulting image is melting rather than freezing, and in a way, it's capturing how fragile that moment always is. In letting it melt, it's maybe even more of a real depiction of the always fleeting moments and gestures, like the two fingers holding up the corner of the skirt, the pose of a high-heeled shoe, the cigarette. In my work, I'm always trying to capture and save those family photos where it's all right there.



Formally, I really loved how some of these prints get this sort of slanted look. I don't necessarily understand the perspective from which they're printed, but it happens in a few of these images where it looks as though the negative has been crumpled first and then it's printed at a tilt. I'm really drawn to the way that the final image warps the memory of the original photograph. Even on the floor of the image, it almost looks like it's printed on or projected onto the wall of a cave. It's so earthly in form.



The tilt actually comes from the act of projecting and rephotographing his father's negatives, which Darrel kept in pristine condition. The combined angle of the projector and Darrel's camera create the skewed perspective we see.



I love the joy in this photograph also. The way these figures are embracing and posing, you can see how much fun they're having in those dresses. I don't know what the party is, but I just love the gestures that these people are making with their bodies, alongside that man casually smoking behind them. It all feels so familiar and unfamiliar, like when you revisit a family album, and you're like, "Oh, man, who *is* that? Is that my great-aunt so-and-so?" These distortions seem to mirror how memory works.



I'm attracted to the various modes of movement in this photograph. The fluid movement in the figures' bodies while dancing, gesturing, and swaying their dresses mimics water that is seemingly crumbling, as you said, S*an. It feels transcendent.



What interests me in this image is that the scene feels very much like a house party, as opposed to a hall or restaurant. There's a certain type of intimacy and groove that happens in this space. There's also a certain kind of dancing that happens that's different in the living room as opposed to when you're out in public among strangers, like at a bar or club. To go back to the joy that Paul mentioned, I see in this image the joy of peacocking that you feel when you get dressed up for the party. Darrel must have been interested in that joy, alongside the decay, because he lets that smile shine really bright in his version.



So much of Darrel's work is set in the home, places he lived, both with his family in the Bronx and, at the end of his life, alone in Greenpoint, which makes me think about how important these intimate and interior spaces are to our understanding of his work. What do you notice in Darrel's images based on his father's photos taken in parks?



Those pictures do something so different than they did in the originals taken by Thomas Ellis. Darrel's images seem less at ease or peaceful than the original photos, especially since they're in spaces of leisure, play, and safety. The projection process adds a layer that feels fraught, and a little less safe.



I think those experiments are in line with the process of a photographer working through his family archives— it's kind of like you're there and you're not there because you're in the role of re-witnessing and additionally as a kind of editor.



Sitting with these works in person, I was immediately drawn to Ellis's manipulation of the surface and how that changed my understanding of his photographs contrasted against the originals. I've been thinking about multiplicity and what it must have meant for him to recreate these moments over and over again, each nuanced. These manipulations to the surface,

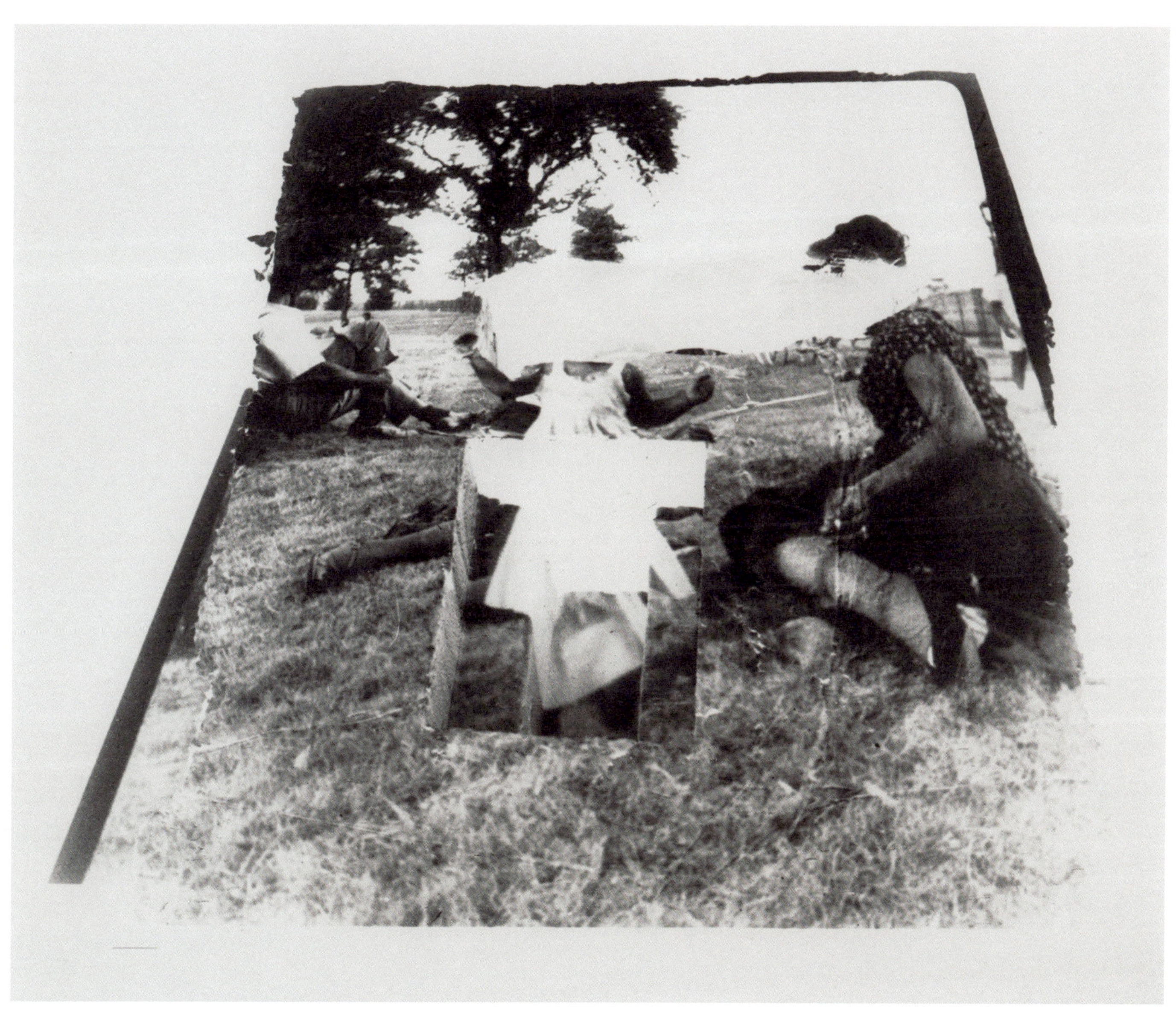

12. *Untitled* (Laure and Mother in Crotona Park)
ca. 1988–92
Gelatin silver print
10 ½ × 13 ½ inches
Metropolitan Museum of Art

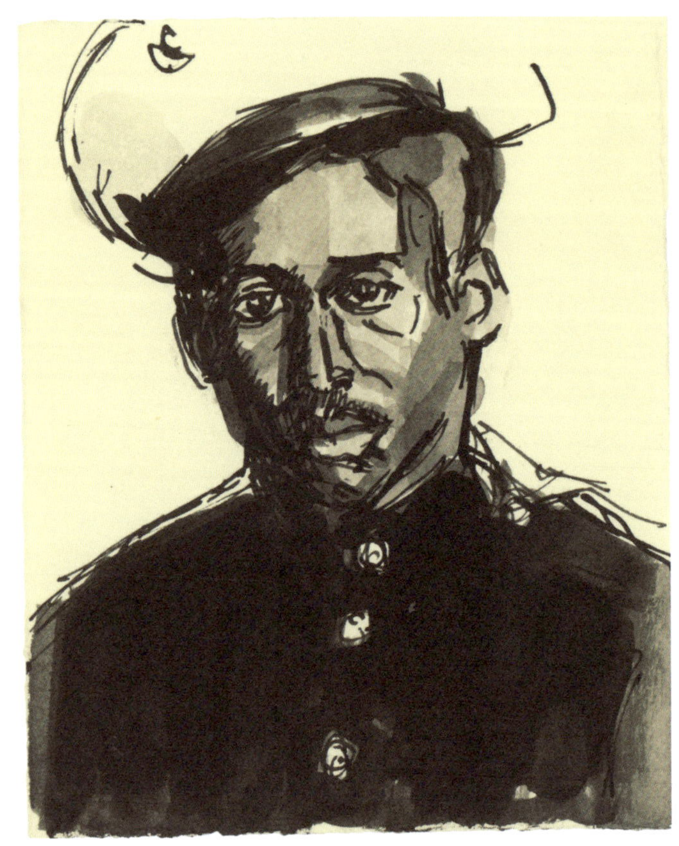

13. *Untitled* (Father in Marine Uniform)
ca. 1981–85
Ink and wash on paper
6 ½ × 5 inches

the uneasiness, introduce a complexity absent from his father's images, which, to me, speaks to Ellis's relationship with his family members.



I'm still really fixated on this ink wash (fig. 13) of his father. I'm drawn to the incompletion of the cap, as well as the lines of his uniform not being complete. I feel the tenderness in his eyes—there's a sort of sadness there that runs across several of Darrel's works.

Alanna

Yes, I too was drawn to this gaze and apparent sadness. Traditionally, portraits of men in uniform exude a pride that I find strikingly absent here. There's a sense of knowing or foreshadowing in his eyes that his uniform will not complete or protect him. It's punctuated in his eyes, the tension in his lips, and the shadowing of the ink falling over his face.

S*an

Yes, that sadness is present in more than the eyes—it comes through in the shadow on his cheek. I'm also noticing there are no insignia, badges, or flags. This is an image absent of pride. In some ways, Darrel is looking to his ancestors to understand his present and future, in addition to understanding his own place within the family, a family that he has been robbed of. There's a certain kind of understanding of himself that is interrupted through losing his father to police violence.

Ariel

I wonder if Darrel's remaking of images of his father, in particular, is a way to commune with him. How do you think the photographs Darrel worked with from his family archive relate to his self-portraiture work?

Paul

I like that these self-portraits (fig. 14) are all out of focus, but the one that draws me to it is the image on the lower left, in which the sofa is incredibly in focus. Out of all these photographs, it's the only thing that's in focus. I was thinking about this sequence of images of Darrel because we can tell from the way his body is in these that he's not holding the camera he's set up—it could be on a stack of books on a nightstand, or on a tripod, and he just set it up, put on a timer, walks in . . . However, the one on the bottom gives me the impression that maybe he stood up and then focused the camera, thinking, OK, I'm going to focus on the plant and then I'll try to sit where it was . . .

So, yes, I am drawn to the working process, and the idea of him being with himself, looking and experimenting. I also like that he looks kind of content, and a little inquisitive.

Ariel

These self-portraits you draw our attention to, Paul, are from the same roll of film, although we don't know how Darrel would have edited these images.

Sadie

What I wrote down while looking at these images was "to be remembered to have been real." I experience these as a moment of Darrel dealing with his own mortality while he was alive to process it.

S*an

His face doesn't feel like the face that you necessarily offer to someone else, or maybe it's only after you realize that you offer this face to someone else that it's the face that you wear all the time. I've been sitting with some self-portraits I made recently and I've had that realization of, Oh, I always look like this? I like that, with this series, we see how the photographer appears to himself when he's just sitting with himself. I also really love the way he employs blur and that, even in his own stillness, he is full of potential. He's not necessarily going anywhere, and yet there's this dreaminess because it operates in the way memory tends to, where it's the pose in transition.

Alanna

Yes, there's this feeling that we've dropped in on a moment of vulnerability that we wouldn't usually have access to.

Ariel

These were taken at the end of Ellis's life. I think they were part of his focus on self-portraiture in the early nineties, in his Greenpoint apartment, post-HIV diagnosis.

Alanna

I wondered that.

Ariel

It's hard to tell if these straight photographic self-portraits are more of his archive and reflect his process, and were taken with the intent to base drawings or paintings on, or if they are photographs that stand on their own. Let's talk about the self-portrait of Darrel sitting, perhaps at the edge of a couch leaning his head on his hand; the image appears liquefied almost through one of his projection techniques.

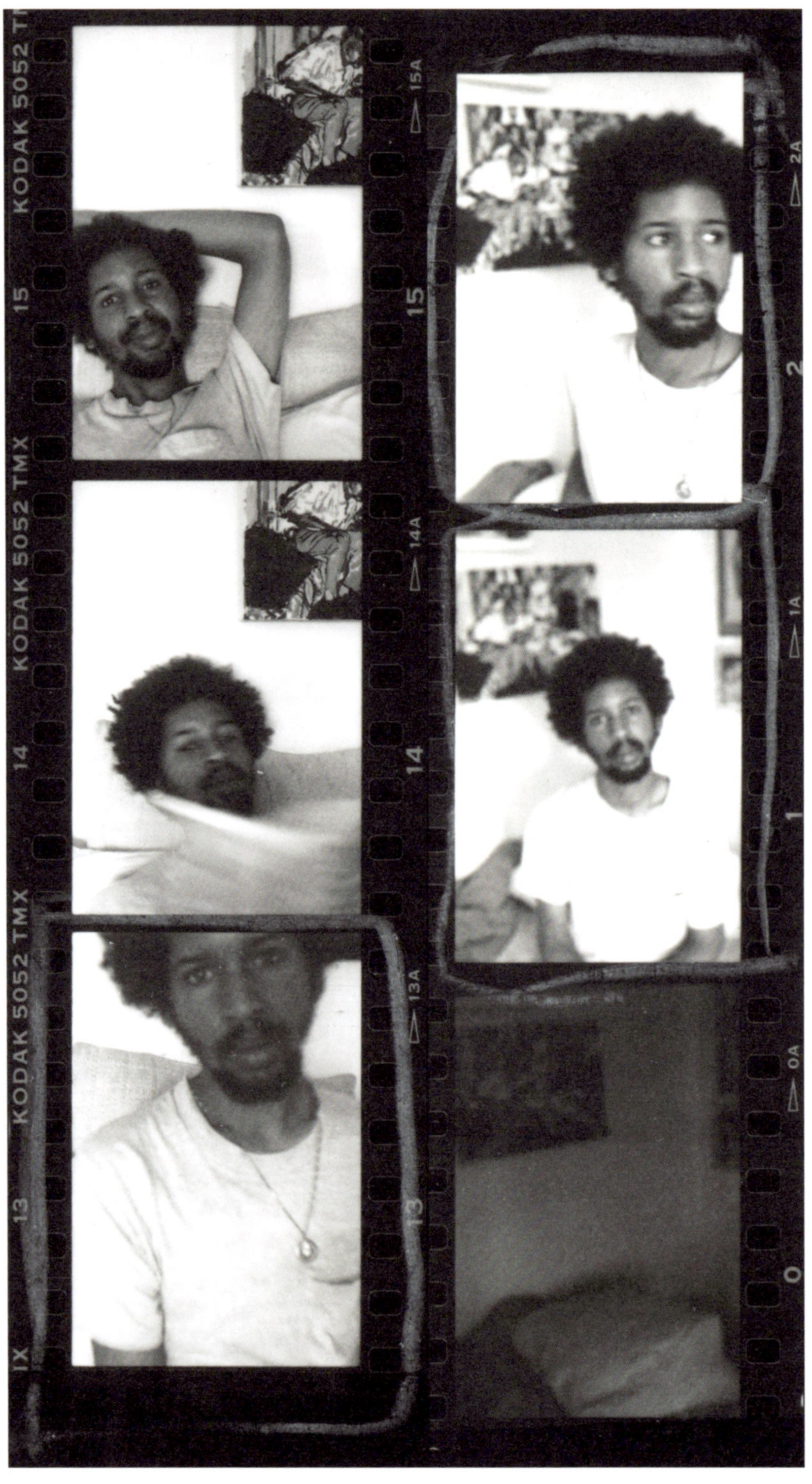

14. Contact sheet of self-portraits taken by Ellis as material for later paintings and photographs, ca. 1991–92

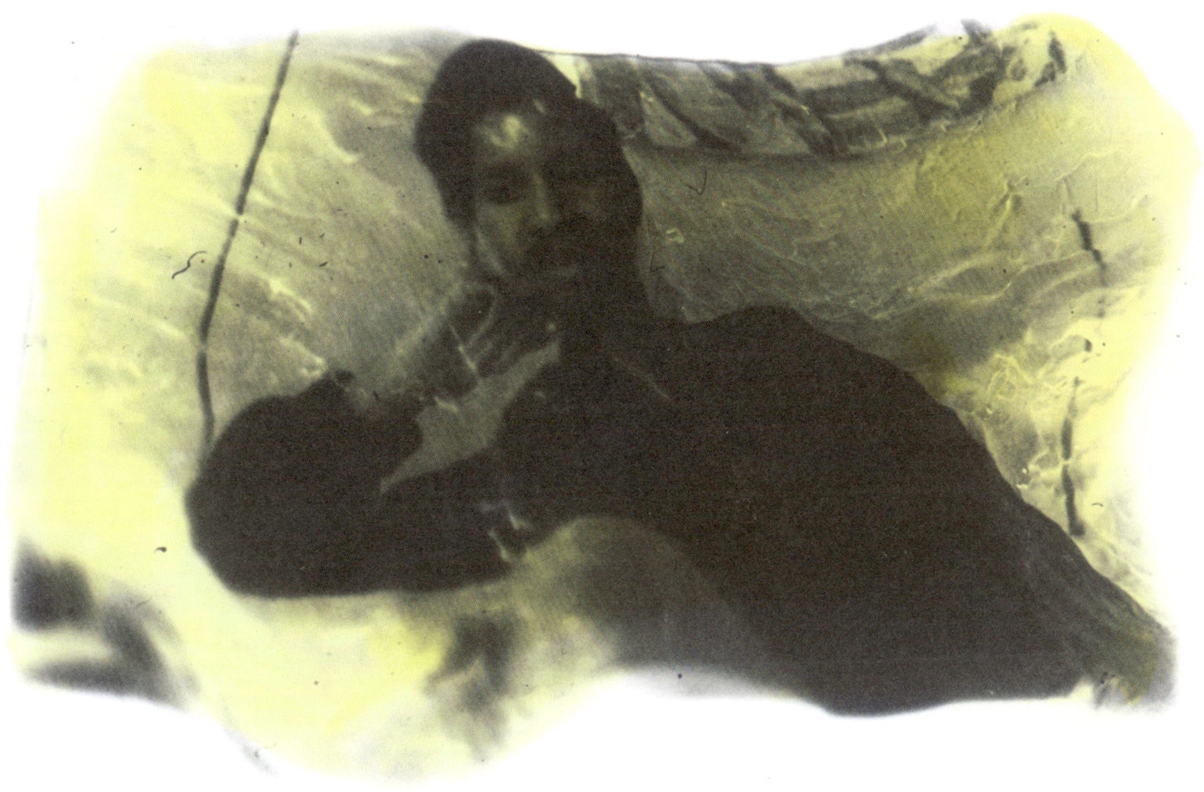

15. *Untitled* (Self-Portrait after Allen Frame
Photograph)
ca. 1990
Gelatin silver print with yellow ink
8 × 10 inches

### Alanna

I love this piece (fig. 15). Initially, I was intrigued by Ellis's choice to not block his face, as he did in another iteration of this photograph. This blocking and abstracting of the face shows up a lot in his work, but I appreciate that we're given access to his full face, his gaze, his expression. And yet it still has an element of obscurity. This movement, which I think of as foiling or watering, isn't composed of hard lines but rounded edges that are uneven. It's unclear whether there is a flowing into or out of, but Darrel is at rest. I appreciate the softness of his figure, and the comfort that seems to be there. It feels like he's in a safe space. Still, with his gaze off to the side, there's something that feels unresolved, or perpetually contemplative.

### Sadie

It reminds me of the way an insect or a plant might get caught in amber. Yeah, I love this image; I hadn't spent a lot of time with it before, but now I feel like I could look at it forever.

### S*an

This one actually does offer me a lot of joy because it's such a sweet picture and it's really playful in the way that it warps. Even as I understand that it's rendered in 2D, I still feel like I can dip myself into it.

### Ariel

This is an unusual self-portrait because it's not rendered in gray scale; it's a gelatin silver print with ink. So, some post-production experiments there.

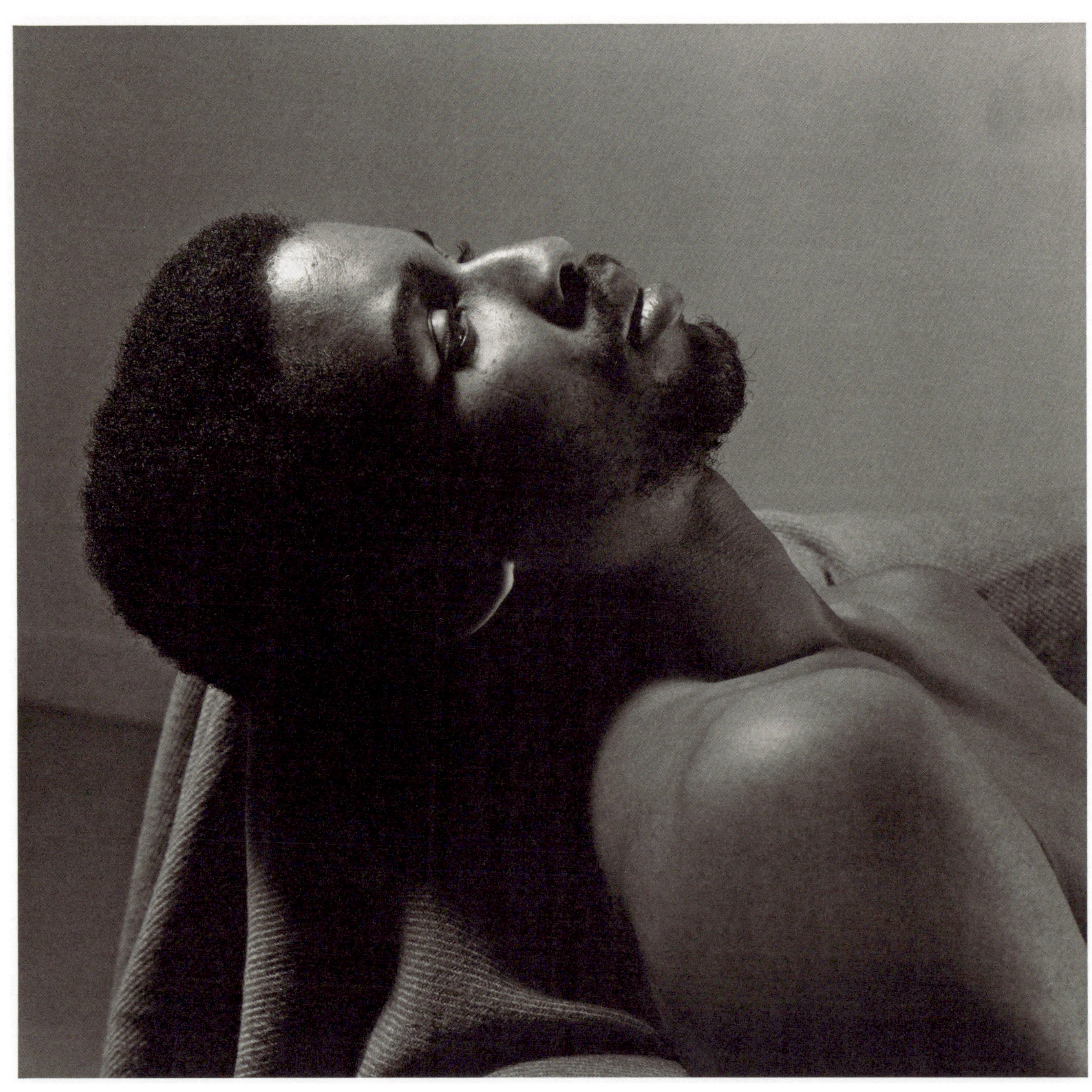

16. Peter Hujar, *Darrel Ellis (II)*, 1981
Gelatin silver print
20 × 16 inches

Alanna

I value having this record of him in repose, capturing a really, really, really quiet moment in his body . . . Ellis's self-portraits open a lens on not only how others saw him, but also how he saw himself. In the interview with David Hirsh, Ellis doesn't really speak a lot about how he sees himself as a Black gay man.[1] Maybe it was a place that he felt better going to visually than verbally.

Ariel

While Ellis was making self-portraits throughout his life, he focused on self-portraiture in earnest directly after media circulation of a self-portrait featured in the exhibition *Witnesses: Against Our Vanishing*, in 1989. This self-portrait was captioned, "I struggle to resist the frozen images of myself taken by Robert Mapplethorpe and Peter Hujar. They haunt me."[2] What do you think about this painting of Darrel in profile (p.112), which he based on the photograph Hujar took of him?

Paul

Hujar made the photograph (fig. 16) in 1981. When was the painting made?

Ariel

1989.

Paul

OK. Perhaps it's a nostalgic image. Let's think about where Darrel was in his life, toward the end of his life.

S*an

Had he been diagnosed at this point?

Ariel

Yeah, I think he had been, but he wasn't public about it. I don't think he was, ever.

Paul

Yeah, and Hujar had passed away by 1989, so there's a conversation there.

It seems like Ellis is looking both forward and back. People tend to look back to an idealized image of themselves in their youth, but by this point we already know the end of Hujar's life. So many people had passed away that there's sadly a road map ahead. The nostalgia goes both ways, and the fear.

Alanna

That painting is really seductive. It makes me wonder, Who was this man? There are these moments where he appears kind of shy and quiet or serious, but I like that he was able to see and envision himself in so many different ways. I think even that is repetition, right? How many ways can I see myself? How many levels of what I am can I tap into? And I think that's really brave to just not have one idea of yourself, and to push up against that.

Ariel

I also feel like the brushwork in this late self-portrait has such a varied texture and it reminds me of the jagged and liquidlike surfaces in the photographs that he made through projections onto sculptural objects.

Paul

I was really drawn to his reclaiming of the photographs of him by Hujar and particularly Mapplethorpe.

Black gay men are so involved in this complicated back-and-forth between the white male gaze and all of those power structures. His frustration and repeated revisiting of these portraits feels like it has something to do with the idea of mastery. It's related to the way Ellis discusses his experiences working as a museum guard and being really frustrated with this Frank Stella exhibition.[3] The frustration pushed him to think about how sculpture and image can work together. I really connected to that sense of looking out at the art world and finding a frustration that demands you as an artist to ask more questions. There's also something really interesting about that unique position as a Black gay man and having to contend with the white-authored images of Black men, the position they may have held relative to his, and perhaps a complicated desire to be a part of that, but also the need to reclaim it. And then the way that might extend to his father's archive of being able to connect to this father who he didn't know.

## S*an

The labor of sorting through family archives and self-portraits is usually done alone. There is this self-investigation always at the forefront of this labor. I think what we witness afterward in the images are a kind of answer or kind of resolve that happens in the repetition. It's like all these images are all different answers to the same set of questions. The thing about portraiture is that one's body, rather than the camera, is the primary medium for interpretation, and all art forms emerge from being embodied. The fact that there is an embodied presence reinterpreted involves going inside to then externalize what you as the artist see. That cyclical process is really interesting to me.

## Sadie

A lot of the abstraction in Ellis's photographs is unearthing the plane that exists just beyond reality, just beyond the photograph, just beyond language, and I felt this quite deeply when looking at this work.


Notes

1 Darrel Ellis, interview by David Hirsh, January 21, 1991, Visual AIDS Archive Project, New York.

2 Nan Goldin, ed., *Witnesses: Against Our Vanishing* (New York: Artists Space, 1989), 20.

3 Ellis, interview by Hirsh, 1991.

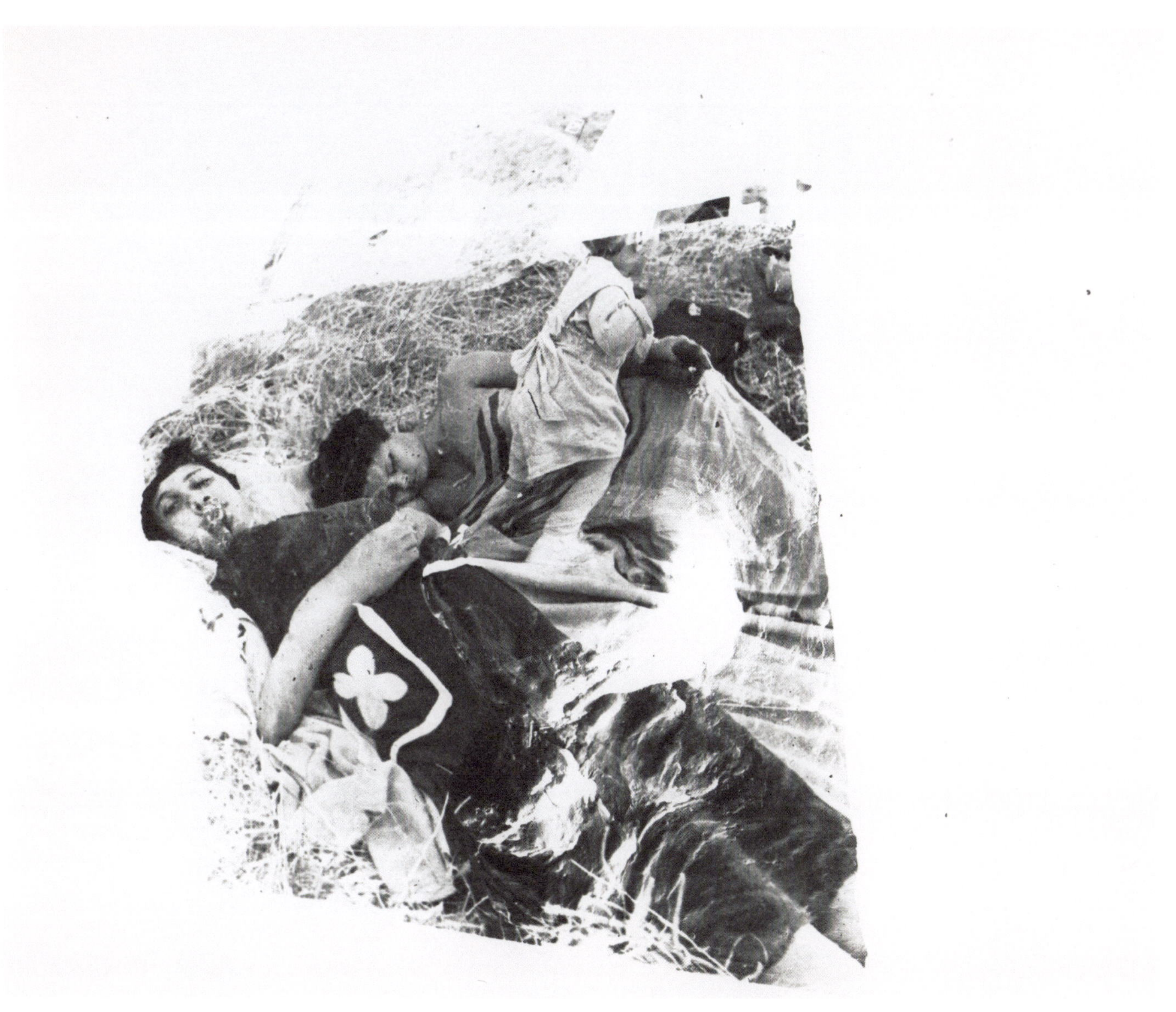

17. *Untitled* (Mother and Laure in the Grass)
 ca. 1988–92
Gelatin silver print
16 × 20 inches

# Process

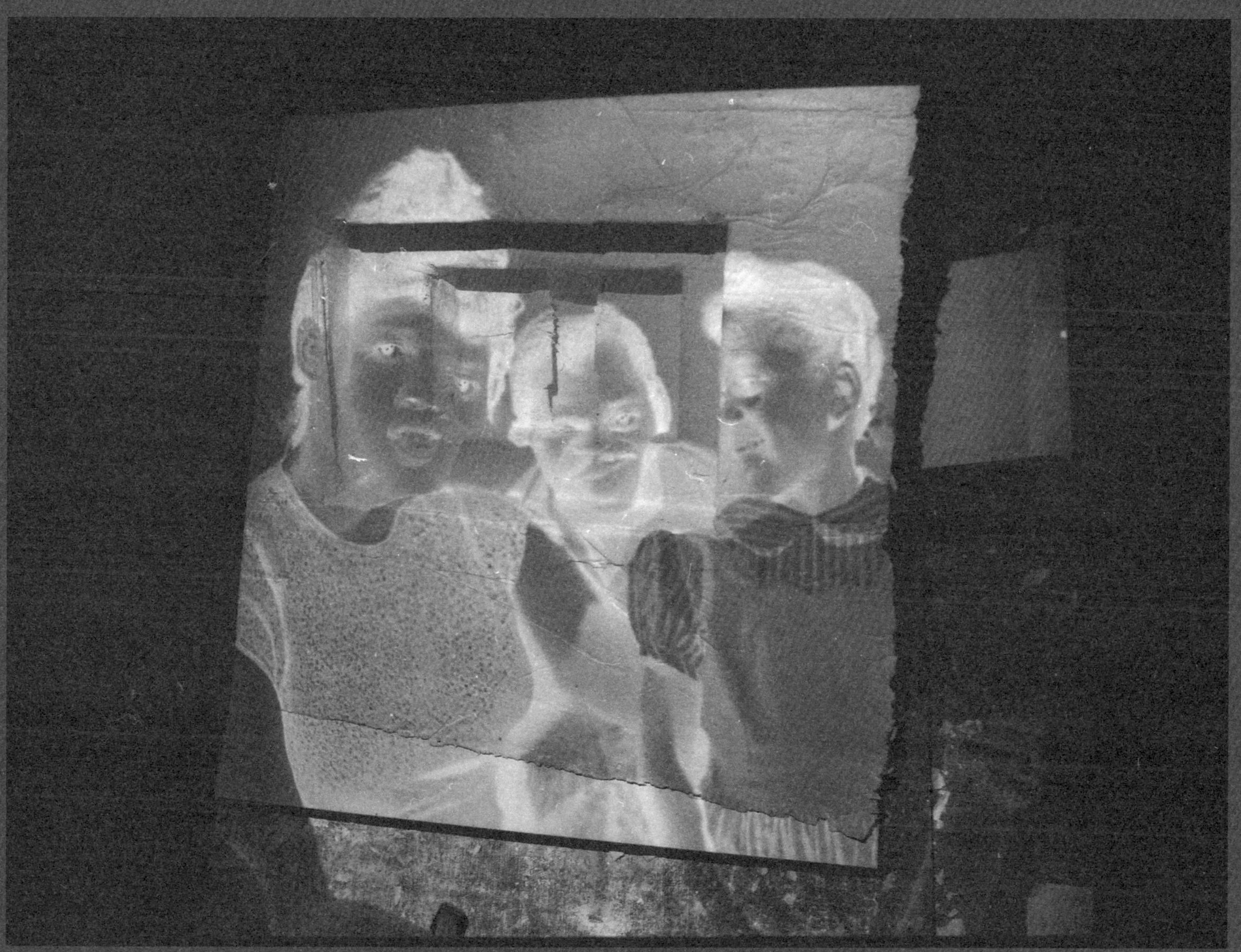

A negative from Ellis's archive, shown inverted here, offers a look into the artist's process

Darrel Ellis's experimental photographs are perhaps the most haunting aspect of his oeuvre. He began exploring his interest in photography alongside the artist James Wentzy, while the two were living in a shared studio space at PS1 from 1979 to 1980. Ellis brought a painterly interest in perspective, depth, and dimensionality to photography, leading him and Wentzy to experiment with projecting photographs onto disposable sculptural forms and then rephotographing the resulting distortions. This early collaboration pushed Ellis to consider the relationship between matter, perception, and revivification, as photographs took on a three-dimensional quality when projected in his studio, only to be flattened again when recaptured on film. During this time, Ellis mainly used his own 35 mm negatives as source material—snapshots of cars, friends, and figures on the street.

After finishing his residency at PS1 and beginning the Whitney Independent Study Program in 1981, Ellis began painting and drawing from his father's printed photographs. When he showed these works to his mother, she gave Ellis a trove of hundreds of negatives shot by his father, mostly on medium format film. Inspired by this intimate collection of never-before-seen images, Ellis made use of the darkroom at the ISP to produce contact sheets and work prints of his father's photographs, immersing himself in his family's visual archive. In contrast to his father's meticulously printed photographs, Ellis's work prints were mostly quick and utilitarian, used as reference material for his early paintings.

Ellis focused on painting from his father's photographs for several years, only returning to his rephotography technique in 1987, after he had moved into his own apartment. Using money he set aside from his security job at MoMA, Ellis purchased a photographic enlarger, a special projector usually used to print negatives onto photo paper.

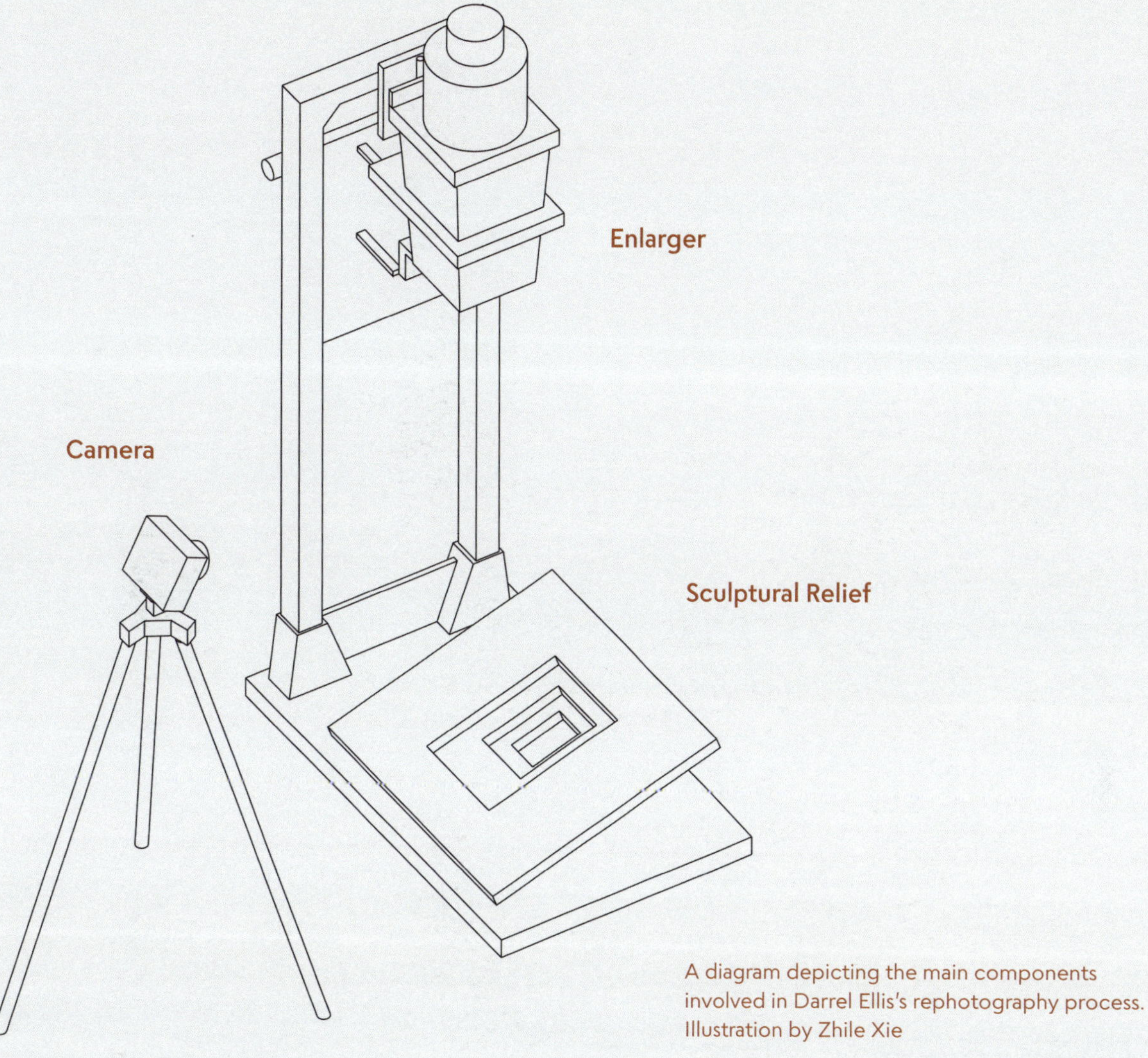


A diagram depicting the main components involved in Darrel Ellis's rephotography process. Illustration by Zhile Xie

To create his distorted photographs, Ellis constructed rudimentary sculptural reliefs out of cardboard, foam, and plaster bandages, which he would then place on the floor beneath his enlarger to use as a projection surface. After placing one of his father's negatives into the enlarger, he could change the position of the relief to adjust the interaction between the projected photograph and the relief's sculptural qualities.

He then used a standard 35 mm camera to photograph the distorted projection from various positions. The angle of his camera relative to the relief introduced an additional form of perspectival distortion, creating the striking trapezoidal shape that frames many of his works. The open play between these elements— enlarger, relief, and camera—offered Ellis a way to bring the gestural looseness and intuition of his painting practice to photography. Although the resulting images often looked collaged or chemically treated, the process was entirely nondestructive, leaving his father's negatives intact and allowing Ellis to produce endless iterations from a single image.

In his notebooks, Ellis differentiated between "organic" and "geometric" sculptural reliefs. The more organic surfaces produced warped effects, as figures stretch and bend over a mountainlike topology. Ellis conveyed that these distortions "give the image a heightened sense of life." The more geometric reliefs featured rectangular and circular indents, sometimes nested within each other to create multiple levels of depth. When a negative was projected onto these forms, the geometric indentations created shadows, producing

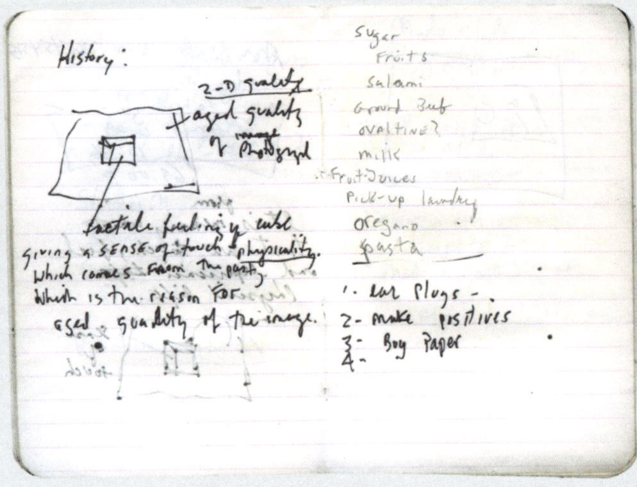

Process notes and a shopping list from one of Ellis's notebooks, ca. 1988

He would take his film to a photo lab for processing, where his negatives would be inverted once more into an internegative, which was then used for printing the work onto photo paper.

Ellis described the rephotography process as a reverse form of anamorphosis, a perspectival technique developed by Renaissance painters to create the illusion of depth from a single viewing angle. The technique produces images that appear skewed when viewed head-on, but assume a three-dimensional quality when viewed from a specific position (such as the skull in Hans Holbein the Younger's *The Ambassadors*, 1533). Ellis's works, however, confound our sense of depth from every angle, in part because the shadows cast by the projection are inverted and appear white in the printed image.

When Ellis reflected on the ephemeral and performative nature of this technique, he considered himself as an artist documenting a private performance. As he observed in conversation with David Hirsh, his father's photographs and his sculptural surfaces "come together and . . . marry for a while, then they split up." Ellis explained that he returned to the rephotography process in 1987, when he realized that it aligned with his interest in spirituality and transcending physical forms. In his words, the images were "photographs of sculpture, but they had no physical reality."

It is remarkable that from the hundreds of negatives Ellis had access to, he chose to rework a small set of his father's photographs, primarily portraits of family members with whom he had grown up. After rephotographing these portraits, Ellis continued to "disrupt the sacredness" of any imagined photographic objectivity by creating drawings, ink washes, and paintings on canvas, further abstracting the source photograph. This iterative and serial process produced a large body of work that has come to define Ellis's legacy.

the abrupt blockages and holes seen in Ellis's final works. According to Ellis, the geometric reliefs "function as a way to enter the 2-d[imensionality] of the photograph."

The rephotography process required a series of translations between negative and positive images. In traditional photography, a camera captures a negative image on film, which is then projected with an enlarger onto photosensitive paper, producing a positive image. When Ellis worked with his father's photographs, he was rephotographing a projected negative image, thereby inverting it again and capturing a positive image on his 35 mm negatives. This is why the shadows produced by the projection process appear inverted (white) in Ellis's final print, while his father's photograph appears as a recognizable positive image. Although he owned an enlarger, Ellis did not have a darkroom in his apartment.

1   This internegative shows what Ellis would have seen while making the work. A sliver of printed text is visible from the cover of a book lying near the relief.

2   The relief casts a shadow onto the base of the enlarger. When the negative is printed, the dark shadow becomes white, slicing through the image.

3   This relief creates continuous, warped distortions instead of sharp breaks. The handmade surface adds texture to the plain walls and floor captured in the original photograph by Thomas Ellis.

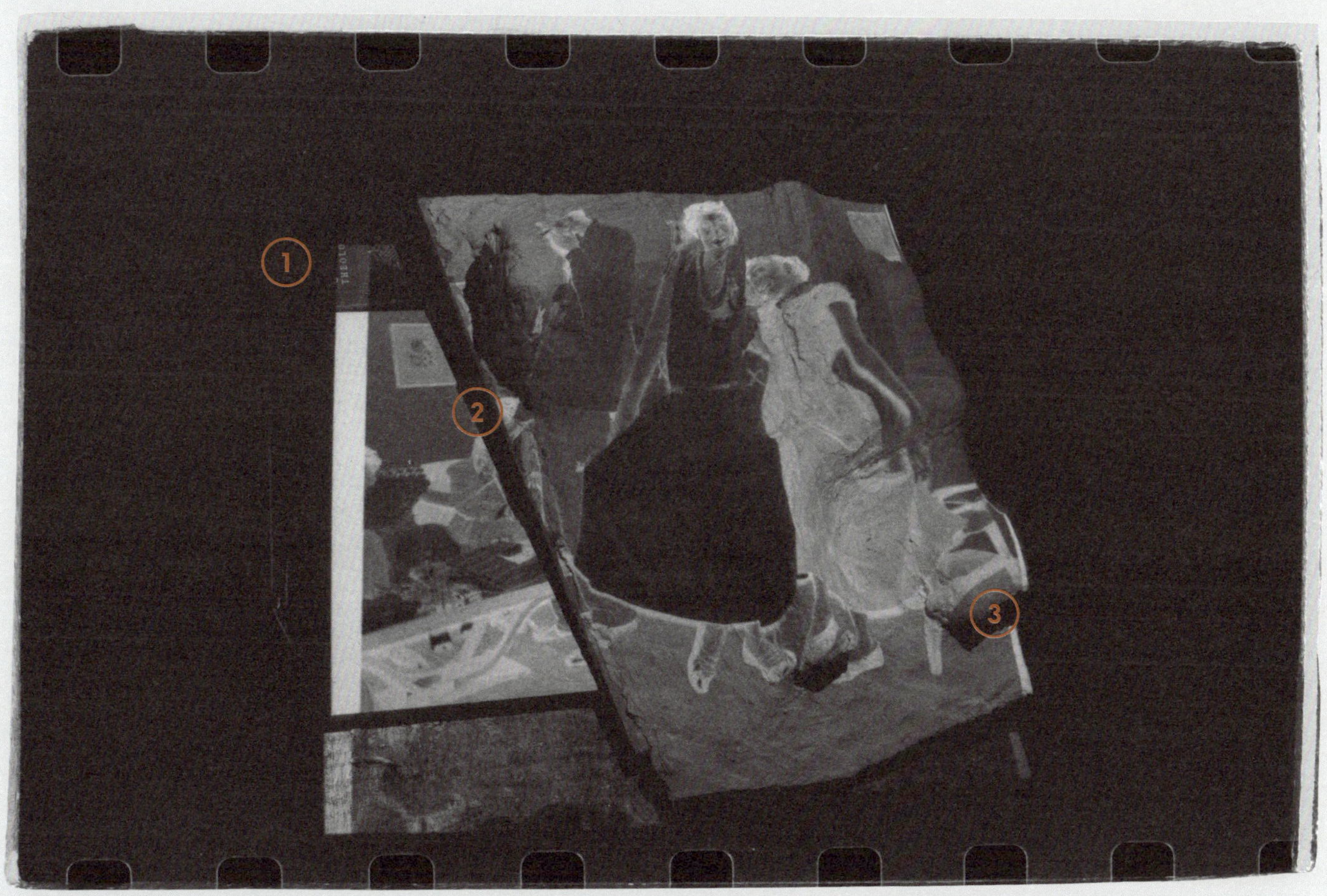

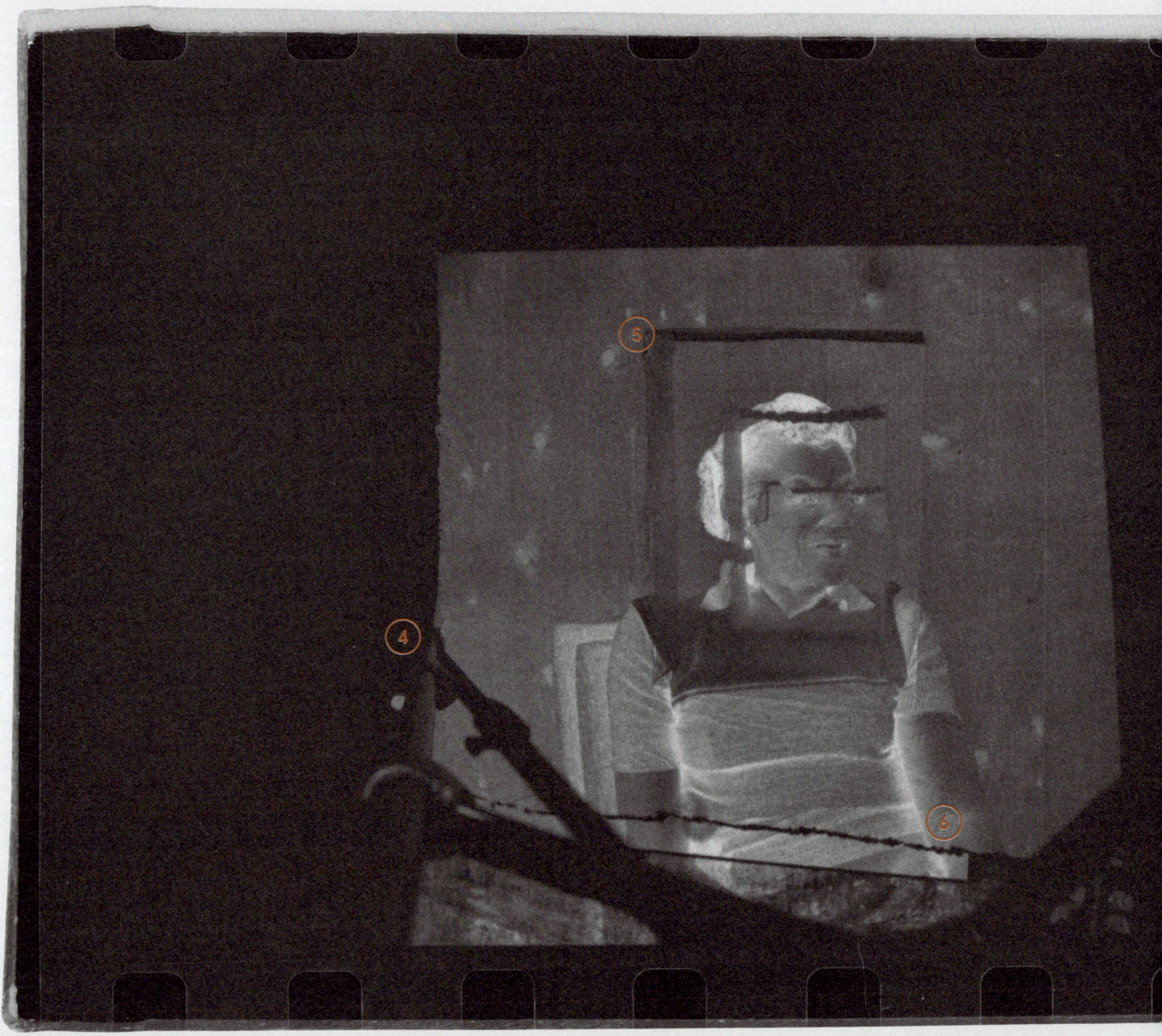

4    The legs of Ellis's tripod are visible, casting a shadow over the projected image. This shadow becomes white when the internegative is printed.

5    Unlike the printed artwork, the shadows here appear black, creating a sense of depth and helping us to see the shape of the geometric relief.

6    The ragged edge of the projection surface casts a shadow on the object beneath it. This ragged line is visible in many of Ellis's photographs.

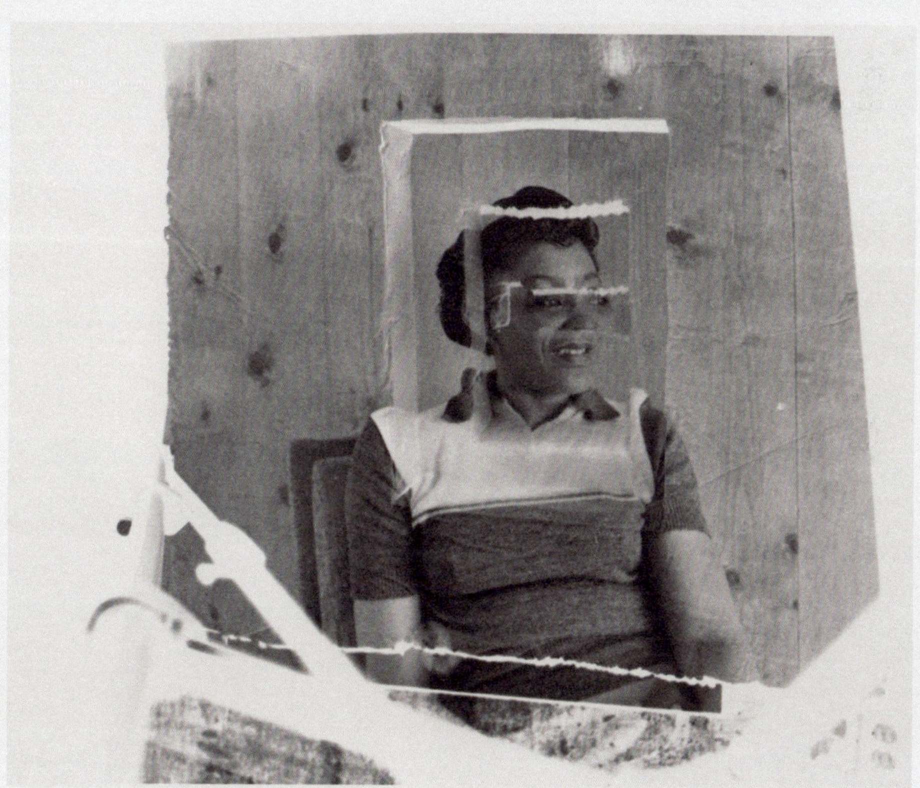

*Untitled* (Grandmother Lillian Ellis)
1989–90
Gelatin silver print
13 × 10 inches

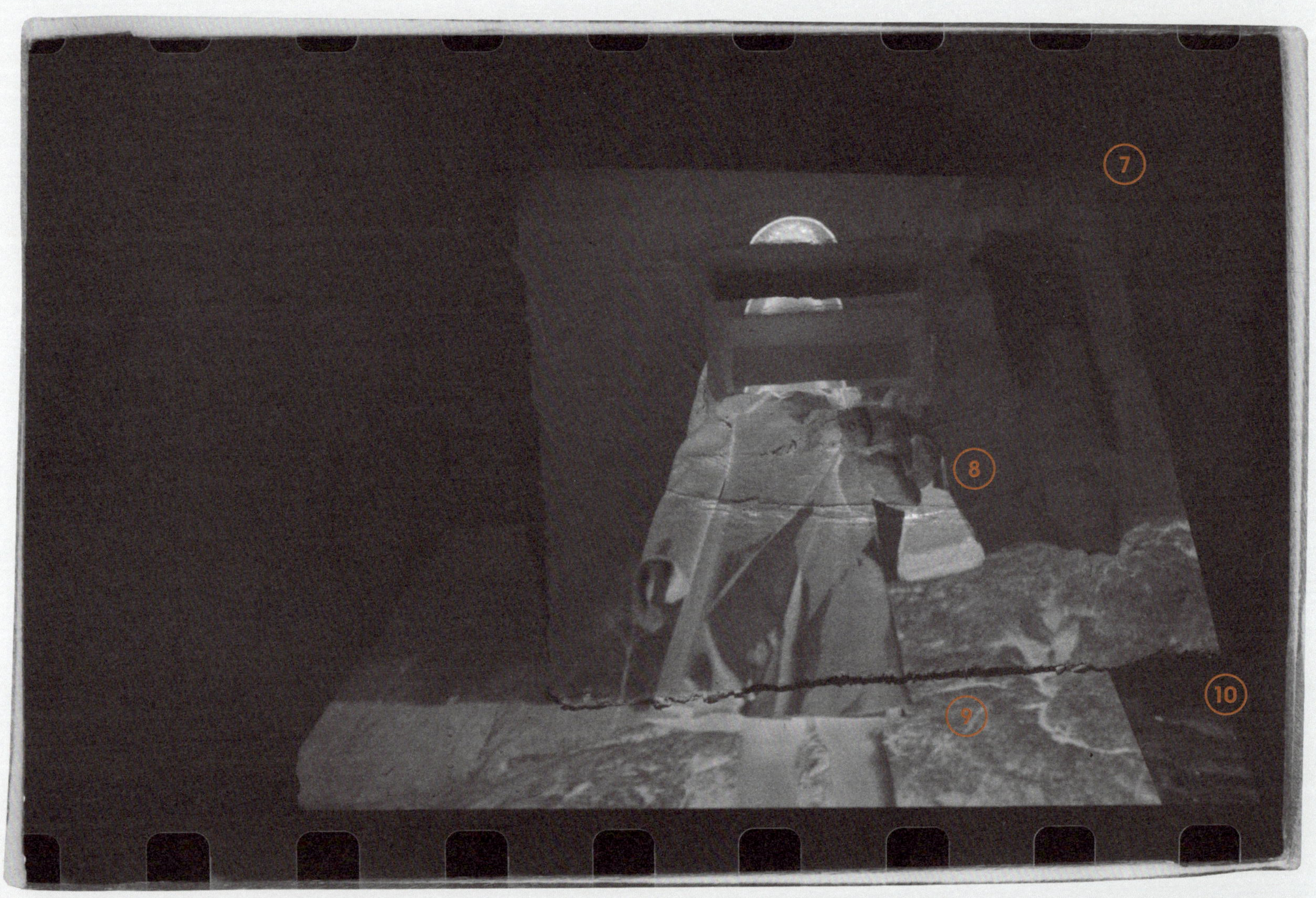

7    In this instance, Ellis tilted the relief to intercept the projected image at an oblique angle.

8    Irregularities in the surface of the relief infuse the projected image with a wrinkled texture.

9    The flat base of the enlarger shows the undistorted projection coming from above.

10   A portion of the projection extends beyond the base, causing this corner to appear more faintly in the printed image.

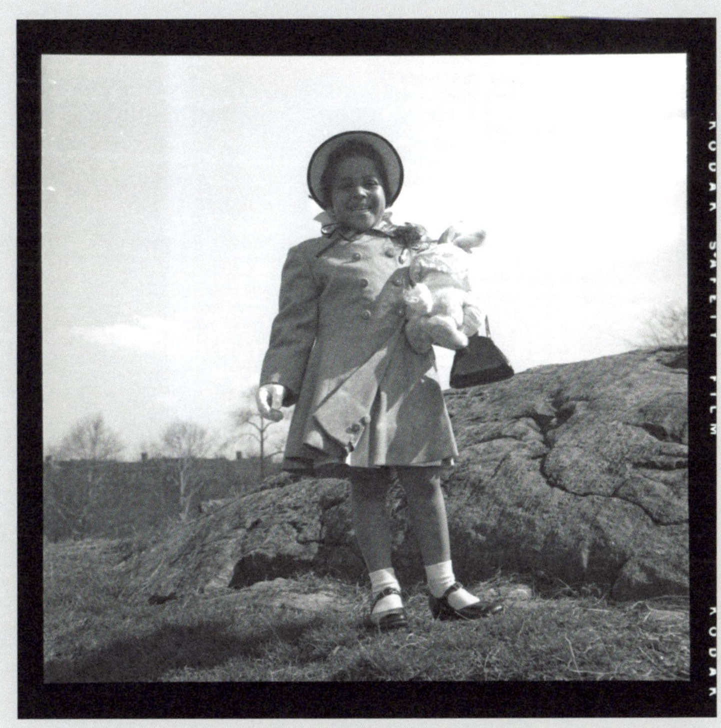

Ellis's sister Laure in Crotona Park on Easter Sunday, ca. 1953. Photograph by Thomas Ellis

# The Case of the Artist's Archive

# Steven G. Fullwood

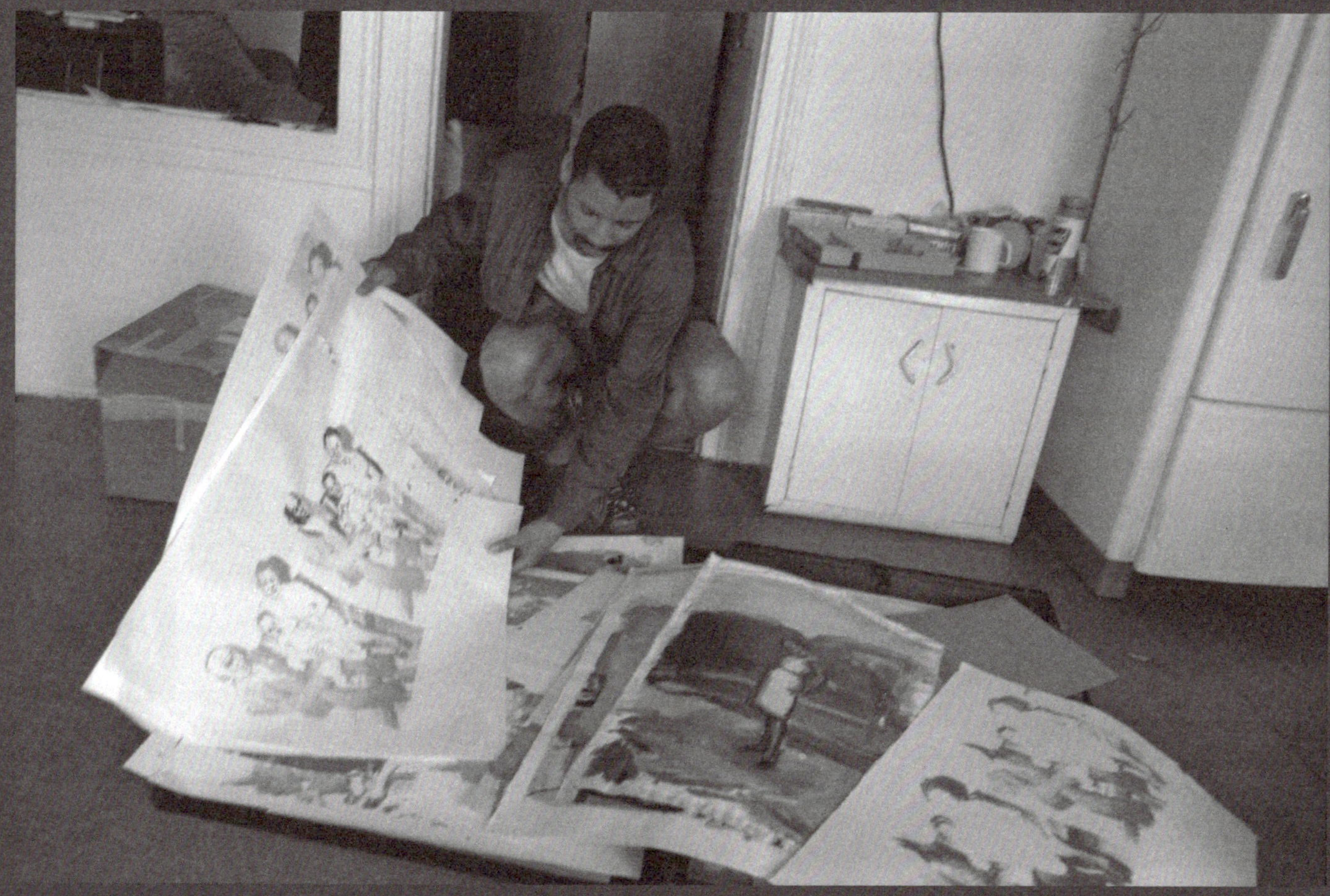

Darrel Ellis with his artwork, 1988. Photo by
Allen Frame

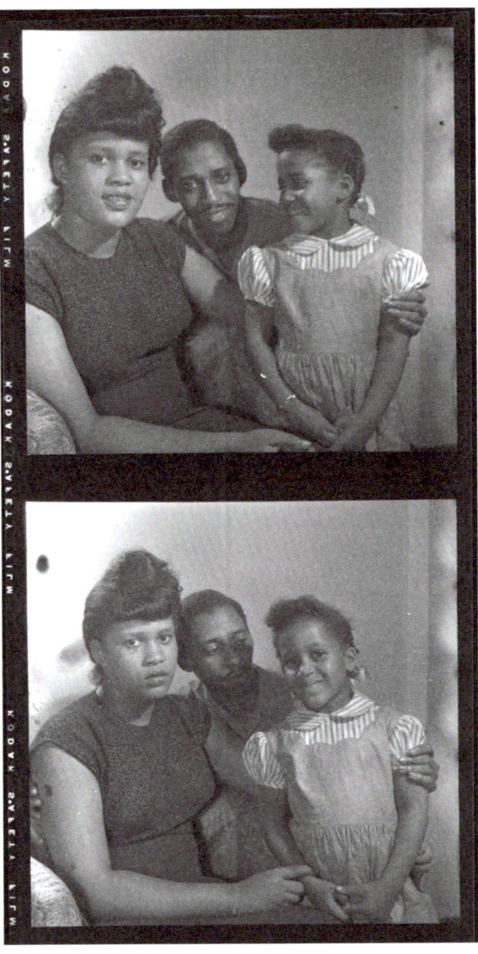



Archives, by default, are exclusive. No one archive has ever collected the entirety of anyone's life—it's impossible. In this way, absences also shape the archive. Archivists note omissions in the collection's guide to alert researchers, as these often point to the precarity of record keeping or the lack thereof. The best of what an archive *can* do in the case of an artist, for example, is to offer a glimpse of the individual behind the art. So how does a collection of art become an archive? For over nineteen years, I was an archivist at the Schomburg Center for Research in Black Culture and responsible for preparing collections for research by the public. Organizing a collection always presents questions: Who created the collection? What is (and isn't) in it? What is its condition? Who cared for it and why?

There's also the possibility that, within any given collection, lies another archive—a subarchive, if you will. For instance, a traditional family photo album can be considered an archive of selected moments chosen for posterity. In this sense, anyone in the family with access to a camera can become, either by chance or desire, the family's documentarian. Photographs gesture toward memories, dreams, genealogies, and possibilities that exist beyond the images' borders. Typically, photo albums are kept by a family for private use, highlighting stories of family milestones, such as birthdays, holidays, reunions, weddings, funerals, and anniversaries. Unlike the private, personal album, the photographs that form what I call a *public family album* circulate beyond the realm of extended family, appearing instead in art museums and galleries, for example.

Such is the case with Darrel Ellis. Born in the Bronx in 1958, Ellis, a mixed-media artist active in the eighties and early nineties, created photographs, drawings, and paintings featuring his family members as his primary subject. As Darrel began pursuing a career as an artist in the early 1980s, his mother shared with him a box of photographs and negatives left behind by his late father, Thomas Ellis. Darrel sampled and remixed his father's photographs in a series of images that would come to define a significant part of his abbreviated legacy. Through artistic distortions, ink washes, and sketches, Darrel explored liminal space, reimagining the lives of his father and family members before he was born. This essay considers Darrel's archive, its history, trajectory, and contents, and includes some meditations on the archival impulses at the heart of Darrel's work.

## What Remains: Darrel's Archive

Twenty-eight years after Darrel's death, I went to Visual AIDS to survey the late artist's archive, currently in care of the estate (stewarded by the artist Allen Frame), and related materials held by the Visual AIDS Archive Project. Collectively, the archive contains sketchbooks, oil paintings, watercolor works, photographs, copies of an artist's book Darrel published through Appearances Press, journals, letters, and programs and flyers from past and recent exhibitions, as well as Thomas Ellis's photographs and negatives. A great deal more art sits in storage.

Also among the materials at Visual AIDS is the only known audio interview with the artist, which divulges his philosophical and spiritual interests, suggesting pathways and context for his engaging, thought-provoking work. The few extant audio clips reveal his warm, impassioned voice. Most exciting are Darrel's journals containing a mélange of his thoughts on photography, sketches, daily tasks, shopping lists, and plans. In other artist collections I've processed, often missing were the artist's own impressions about their work. Pouring over Darrel's journals felt necessary to understanding his essence. He writes in one entry: "I really am torn between what I want to do for pleasure & what I have to do to attain that pleasure."[1] Darrel's journals are filled with moments like these, which reveal aspects of the artist's interior life, his desires and struggles. They are invaluable components of his archival collection and offer future researchers significant reference points for studying his art.

## Allen Frame: The Steward

Shortly after Darrel's death in 1992, his archival legacy was saved by friends and family, and, in particular, the artist Allen Frame, a friend of Darrel's who became the primary custodian of Darrel's archive. Frame's role in securing, maintaining, and promoting Darrel's work is indispensable. Without his effort to preserve the collection by placing it in storage and sharing it with students, gallerists, and curators, it is difficult to imagine what the archive would look like today, or if it would exist at all.

"After Darrel died, several of his friends met with his siblings," Frame told me. "We encouraged the family to let us keep the work together before dispersing it or separating it."[2] When I asked Frame to say more about the collective decision-making involved in this process, he shared, "I guess we all believed deeply in the work and knew there could be significant interest in it."[3] With the family's approval, Frame housed the archive in his studio, and eventually in storage.

Frame's impulse to help preserve Darrel's archive was inspired by studying art history in college; the experience, in his words, "made me very aware of the changing status of artists' bodies of work over time and posthumously. I have that recognition of the value of things beyond their current value. I have that faith that the status of value may change . . . I'm inherently attracted to the underdog, to helping the unseen, the forgotten."

The largest exhibition of Darrel's work to date was a retrospective curated by Frame at Art in General in 1996 that toured the United States until 1998. In the years following, a small selection of Ellis's works appeared in smaller group exhibitions throughout New York, but according to Frame, "No galleries emerged to show interest in representing the estate at that time. So, I was discouraged." For several years, Frame held off on actively pursuing gallery representation. As a result, the bulk of Darrel's work remains unseen by the public.

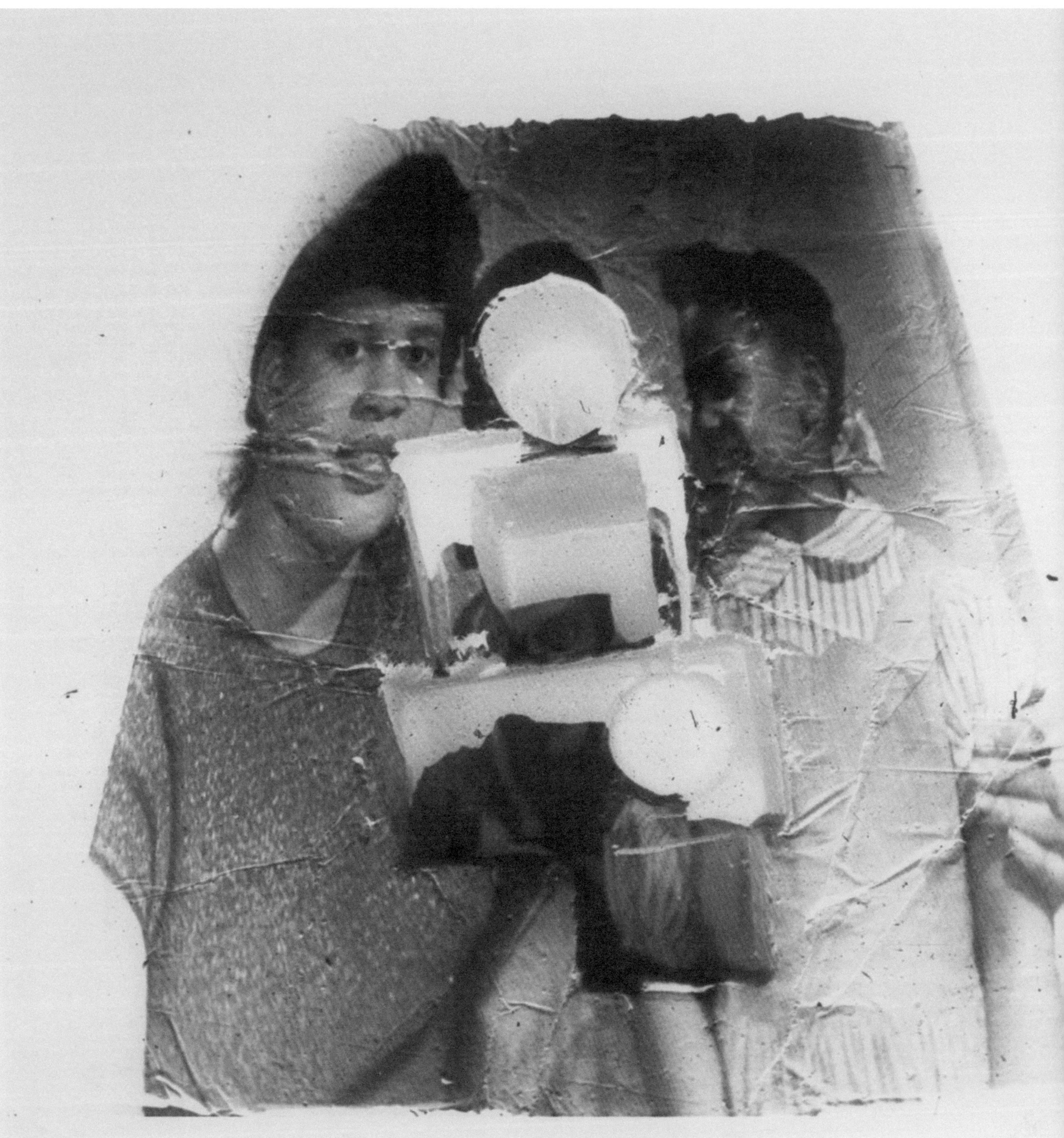

19. *Untitled* (Mother, Father, and Laure)
1990
Gelatin silver print
11 × 14 inches
Brooklyn Museum

### The Family Archive

Darrel's archive not only contains his own works, but those of his father, Thomas Ellis, a photographer who, for a brief time, owned a portrait studio in the Bronx that he ran with his wife, Jean.

In October 1958, Thomas, thirty-three, was murdered by plainclothes policemen. Less than two months after his death, Darrel was born. In the early eighties, Darrel began to revisit the fact of his father's photographs, and examine if there was more to see beyond the framed portraits he became familiar with over the years. The never-before-seen negatives gifted to him by his mother were a revelation—"a treasure trove," as he would later refer to them.[4] Through his artistic explorations, he and his father entered into a conversation beyond space and time that would become foundational for the work Darrel would doggedly explore for over a decade.

The bulk of Thomas's photographs focus on family portraiture and scenes of everyday life. Due to the increased availability of personal cameras in the 1950s, many Black families chronicled their lives with abandon. It was common to find photos of family members on the tables, shelves, mantels, and walls of middle- and working-class homes. Many formal and informal scenes were recorded in photo albums often passed down through generations. Thomas, a professional photographer, used his family as subjects for his budding practice. His family photos are intimate and well-rendered studies archiving the family's earlier years.

When asked to comment on his relation to his father's photographs, Darrel's reverence is clear: "I use images of my family because they affect me so strongly . . . I don't know any life from the forties and fifties with their picnics and their beautiful clothes and everything is so nice and perfect and wholesome. I don't know that little world." As he considers the idyllic time his father's photographs might have suggested, Darrel concedes, "I can't help but have some reaction."[5]

Darrel's manipulation of his father's photographs departs from the originals by imposing expressionistic portals—circles, squares, other shapes—to disrupt the pristine surface captured in Thomas's originals. As scholar Deborah Willis has observed, "In effect, by transforming memory, [Ellis] rewrites family history."[6] In *Untitled (Mother, Father, and Laure)*, 1990 (fig. 19), Thomas, although present, is displaced. He feels *un-there*. One can imagine Darrel and his family might have felt this *un-thereness* after Thomas's murder. A hole in the middle of

what appears to be a "happy" family. Memories for some family members, but for Darrel? His family's recollections were secondhand memories; the photographs, curious images of a man he would never meet.

Darrel recalls that his father was by all accounts "a good man." When he describes Thomas as "optimistic," I understand Darrel to mean his father was aspirational. By contrast, he saw his own work as "sad, dark, and mysterious."[7]

How Darrel used his father's photographs to create new work is provocative. He once intimated that using them "helps me to keep a certain amount of distance and detachment from the reality that I know growing up after my father's death."[8] When it comes to those distorted works, Darrel notes that although the images he uses appear to be damaged, rather than using collage or cut-up as part of his process:

> nothing is destroyed . . . the photos, the negatives . . . the surfaces I use, they're all intact. Everything is intact. It's just that they come together and marry for a while and then they split up . . . The whole thing is ephemeral.[9]

These gestures tug at the boundaries and illuminate faults in the family dynamic. Darrel suspends and challenges the photographs' temporal authority. He queers his father's respectable family portraits by temporarily undoing them, pointing to the elasticity of moments we might assume were static, unmovable. It's a necessary scrutiny. This, too, could be thought of as a yearning. An ongoing, incomplete and unresolvable mourning.

Darrel's siblings, Laure, Thomas Jr., and Katrina, collectively remember their brother's creativity, and his unique sense of style. Laure, Darrel's eldest sister, sometimes charged with caring for her brother, described him as inquisitive, and a wanderer, inclined to go explore by himself. His younger sister, Katrina, posed for Darrel's very first oil painting when she was a preteen, and remembers his hearty laugh.

"We were surprised when his art took another form after he returned from his trip to Europe in the mid-eighties," said Laure. She has described Darrel's interpretations of their father's photographs as "distorted." He was creating from something "he knew nothing about, a family he didn't know," she opined. Although he shared his father's traits, "he looked at those photos, everyone was so happy, but it wasn't real to him."[10]

"I'm really pleased at how his artwork has taken

off, and I wish he were here to see it," remarked Katrina, who has Darrel's artwork in her home. "I carry [him] wherever I go . . . I want for him to have what he couldn't have in life. And have us, his siblings, carry on as much as we can . . . to do right by him."[11]

## The Public Archive

Family photographs have always been part of the public archival record. They confirm a time, a place, the existence of a person or peoples. Print photographs are often preserved in flat files in temperature-controlled environments as collections or serve as components of an individual's papers. The act of a photograph leaving a home to be preserved at an archive for research purposes is rare. In the eyes of the curator, the item has gained historical and research value. It is here that we witness the complexities of the private becoming public.

Consider for a moment another kind of archival experience: Darrel *as* archive, an embodiment of his ancestry and experience. When reflecting upon his creative contribution, Darrel offers: "the photos, they're like regeneration, regenerated . . . from one you get many. And that's like a family."[12] I like to imagine that Darrel was speaking of his future archive. Its trajectory will hopefully encourage artists to plan for their futures with intention. What artists do (and don't do) in order to preserve their archives inevitably impacts the lives of the caretakers of their work. Those caretakers are often family and friends.

Darrel's archive currently lives in a marketplace; its value will in part be subject to the appraisal system upheld by galleries, museums, archives, and nonprofit arts organizations such as Visual AIDS. It is a marketplace disproportionately dominated, managed, and controlled by white actors and agents. What are the implications for Black heirlooms, and, in this case, Black family photographs, being auctioned at, say, Christie's? Imagine what it might be like for Darrel's nieces and nephews to learn about their uncle and his work, not in a family photo album, but in a gallery or university archive. When I worked at the Schomburg, I helped many family members access their parents' or other relatives' records. The question always arises: Who deposited these records here and why? I can sometimes answer the first part, but rarely the second.

My encounter with Darrel's archive was primarily theoretical rather than exhaustive. Nevertheless, the experience left me with these closing thoughts: a very

talented Black man left behind a tremendous collection of materials that will endure thanks to Allen Frame and Darrel's siblings, as well as the curators and writers who engaged with his work while he was alive and posthumously. The best place for his archive to be preserved is a public library, where his work would be as accessible as possible, particularly via an institution whose mission centers Black history and culture, where Black family stories aren't unique or exceptional. Although the work that constitutes Darrel's public family album was only one part of his artistic explorations, it is a significant one. Enough, I believe, to warrant a place among a constellation of Black family archives in an institution where Blackness isn't marginal, it is the universe.


Notes

1    Darrel Ellis, sketchbook (1979), n.p. My thanks to the Visual AIDS Archive Project for providing me with scans of Ellis's sketchbooks and journals, courtesy of the Estate of Darrel Ellis.

2    Allen Frame, conversation with author, November 20, 2020.

3    Allen Frame, email message to author, January 22, 2021.

4    Darrel Ellis, interviewed by Miriam Hernández, October 16, 1990. The Museum of Modern Art Exhibition Records, 1637.12. The Museum of Modern Art Archives, New York.

5    Darrel Ellis, interview by David Hirsh, January 21, 1991, Visual AIDS Archive Project, New York.

6    Deborah Willis, "Darrel Ellis and the Manipulated Family Photograph," in *Darrel Ellis* (New York: Art in General, 1991), 25.

7    Ellis, interview by Hirsh, 1991.

8    Ibid.

9    Ibid.

10    Laure Banks, conversation with author, August 24, 2020.

11    Katrina Stewart, conversation with author, August 24, 2020.

12    Ellis, interview by Hirsh, 1991.

# Chronology

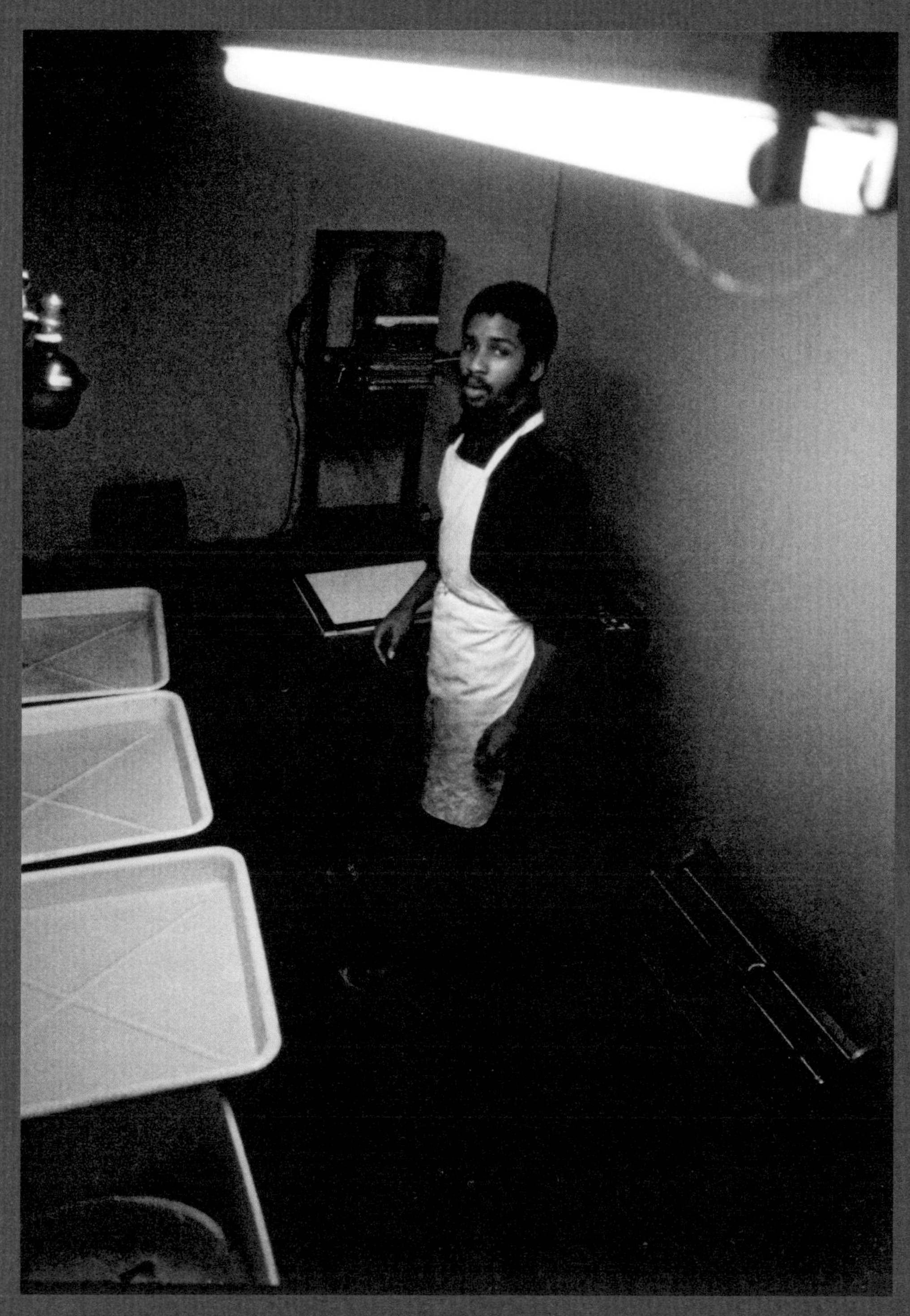

Darrel Ellis in the darkroom at the Whitney
Independent Study Program, 1981. Photo by
Alex Hahn.

# Family History

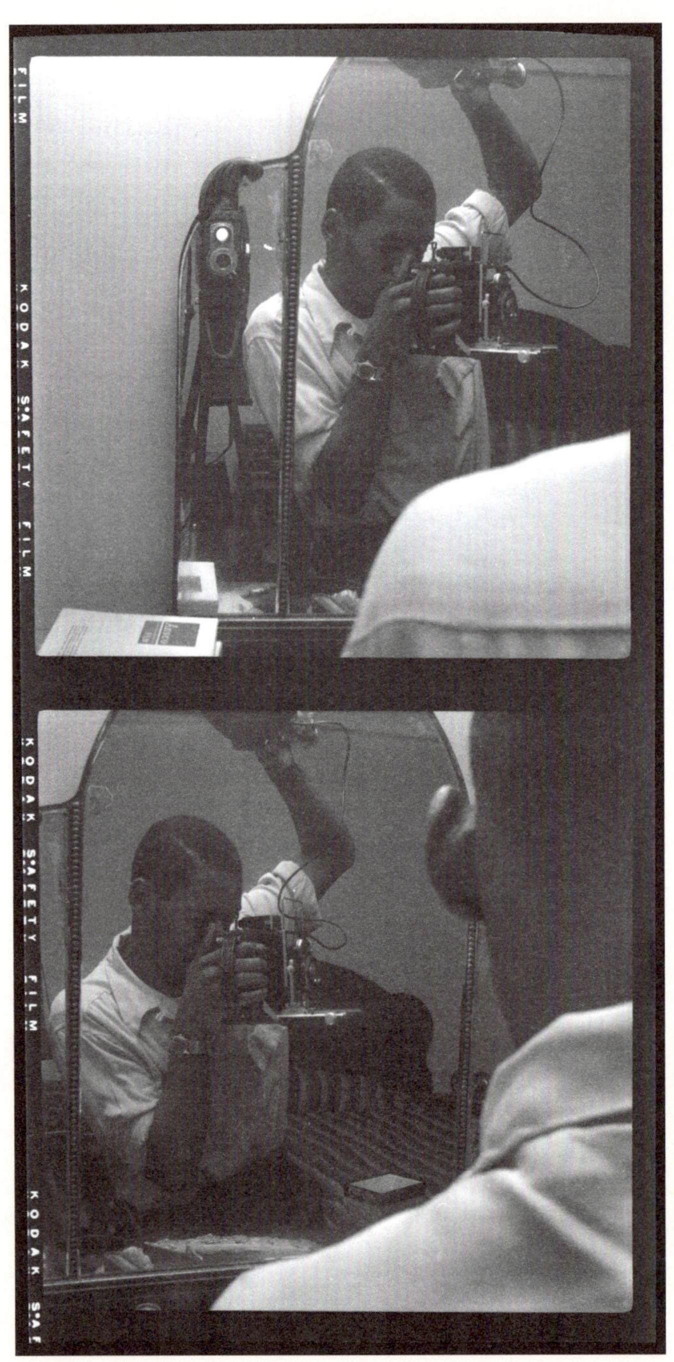

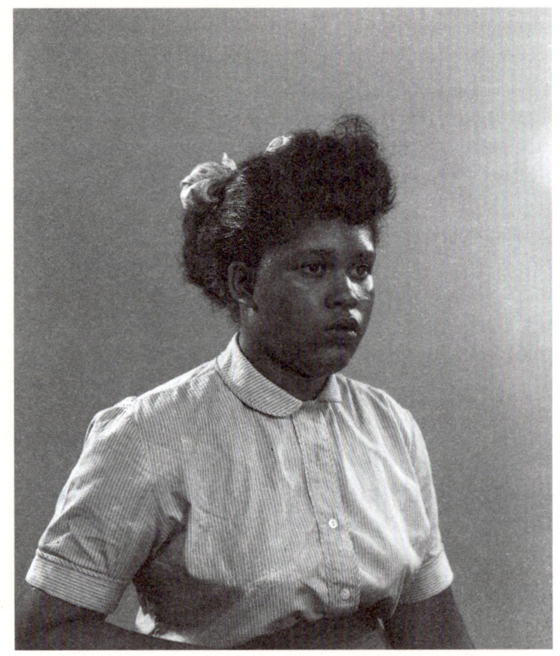

A self-portrait by Thomas Ellis and a studio portrait he took of his wife, Jean, ca. 1950s

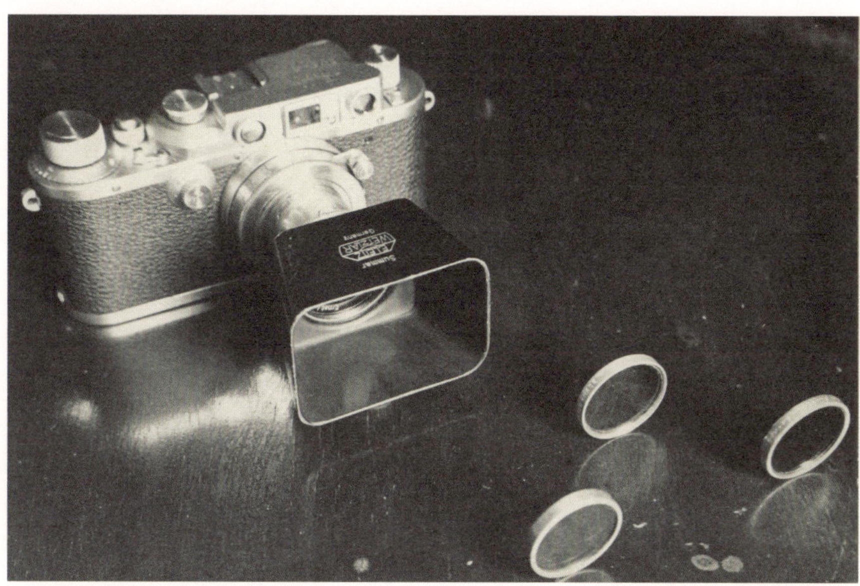



In many ways, the story of Darrel Ellis's life and work begins with his father, Thomas Ellis. Born in New Orleans in 1925 and part of a generation of African Americans who moved north to urban centers like New York City, Thomas Ellis worked as a clerk for the United States Postal Service and was an avid photographer. Thomas met his wife, Jean, in New York City and together they made a home in the Bronx. Thomas's photography ranged from highly composed still lifes to posed and candid portraits of his wife, his children Laure and Thomas Jr., and his extended family. He briefly ran a storefront portrait studio with Jean, and was also a member of the Harlem-based Pine Room Camera Club, a forum for photography enthusiasts to share and exhibit their work.

In 1958, Thomas Ellis was accosted by two plainclothes police officers who had blocked his parked car. The officers arrested him and he was beaten to death on the way to the precinct. Thomas had been studying to become a police officer and it was in the weeks following his death that the family was notified he was eligible to join the police academy. He died at the age of thirty-three, less than two months before his son Darrel was born.

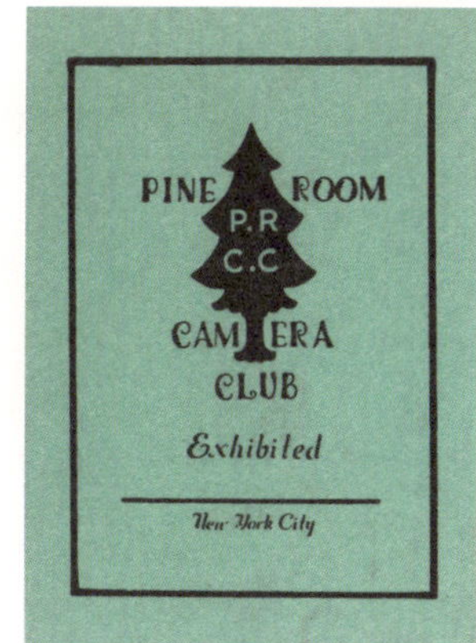

# Early Years

**"Artists and museums were my teachers."**
— Darrel Ellis

Ellis's interest in art developed from an early age; growing up in the Bronx, he loved to draw cars, and later, as an adolescent, write poems. He attended the High School of Fashion Industries in Chelsea from 1972 to 1976, where he honed his draftsmanship in fashion illustration courses, and spent time studying, sketching, and developing his artistic tastes at the Metropolitan Museum of Art. After graduating from high school Ellis committed himself to art, continuing his education through a summer program at Cooper Union and becoming involved in 112 Workshop, an artist-run organization founded by the artists Jeffrey Lew, Alan Saret, and Gordon Matta-Clark.

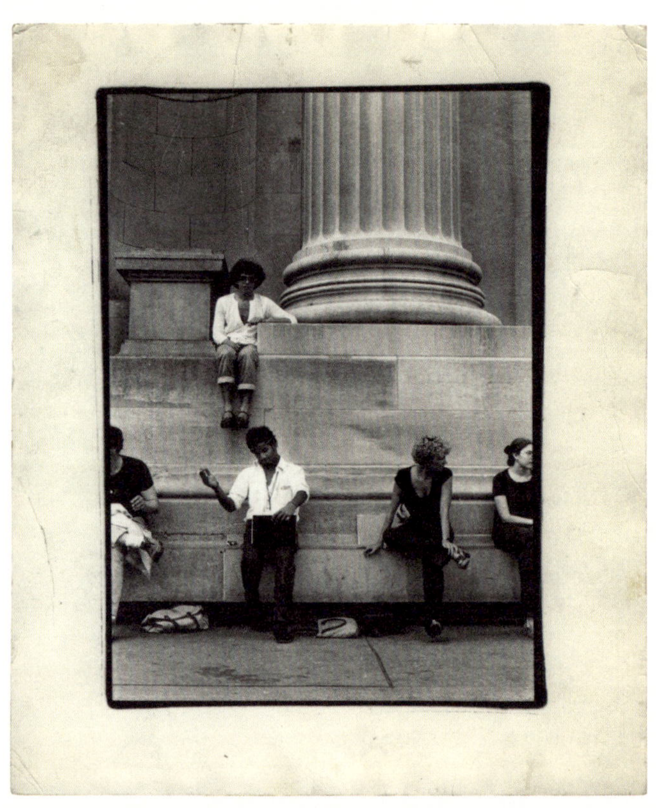

Ellis sketching outside the Metropolitan Museum of Art, ca. mid-1970s

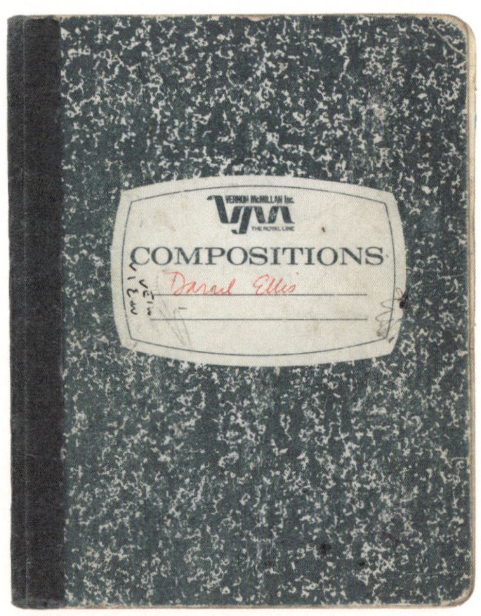

One of Ellis's many notebooks filled with sketches and journal entries

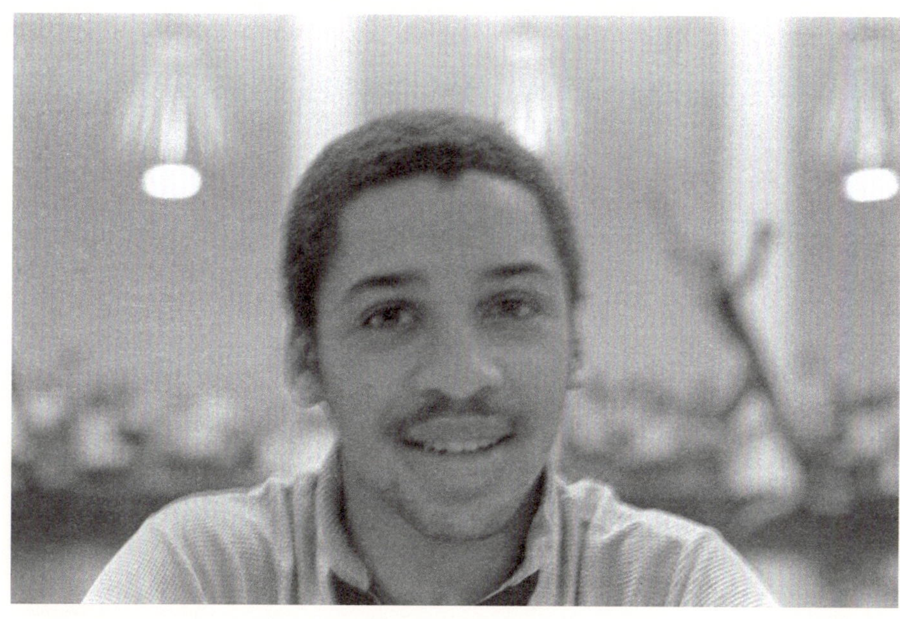

Ellis in the café of the Metropolitan Museum of Art, 1979. Photograph by James Wentzy



A page from Ellis's notebook, 1978

# Experiments in the Darkroom: PS1

**"Darrel was really the first person I met who had set his direction in life as an artist. There was no doubting that was his direction."**
— James Wentzy

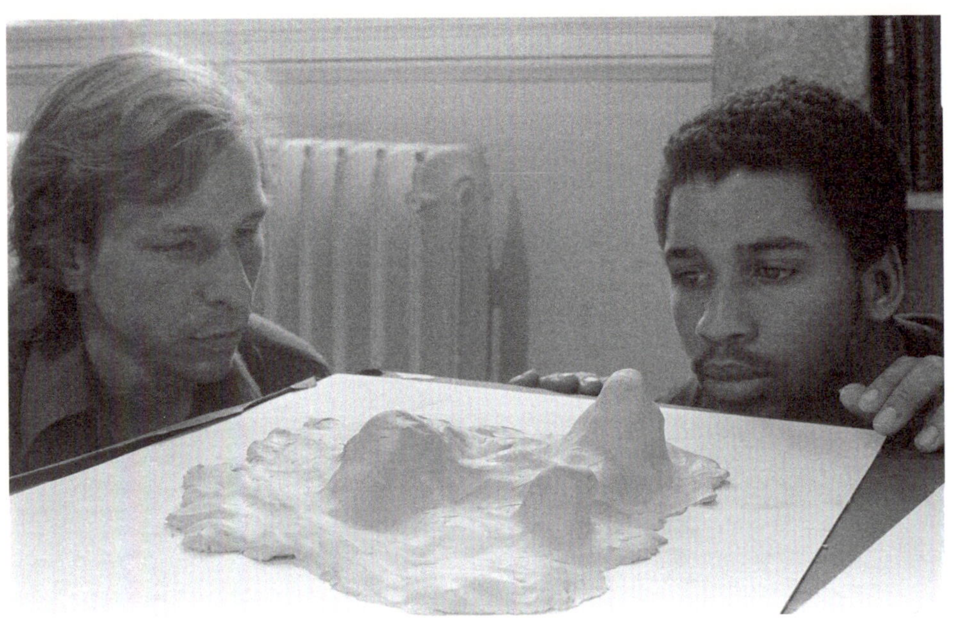

James Wentzy and Darrel Ellis with a plaster projection surface used for their experimental photographs, 1979. Photograph by James Wentzy

In 1979, Ellis met the artist James Wentzy at the Ninth Circle, a West Village gay bar. Together they applied for a studio in the international artist residency program at PS1 in Long Island City, Queens. The two lived together in their shared studio for a year, moving into separate spaces when their residency was renewed in 1980. Wentzy introduced Ellis to the basics of photography, teaching him how to develop and print his own photographs in a darkroom they constructed in an adjoining bathroom. They experimented with using three-dimensional forms to produce distorted photographs with shifted perspectival effects.

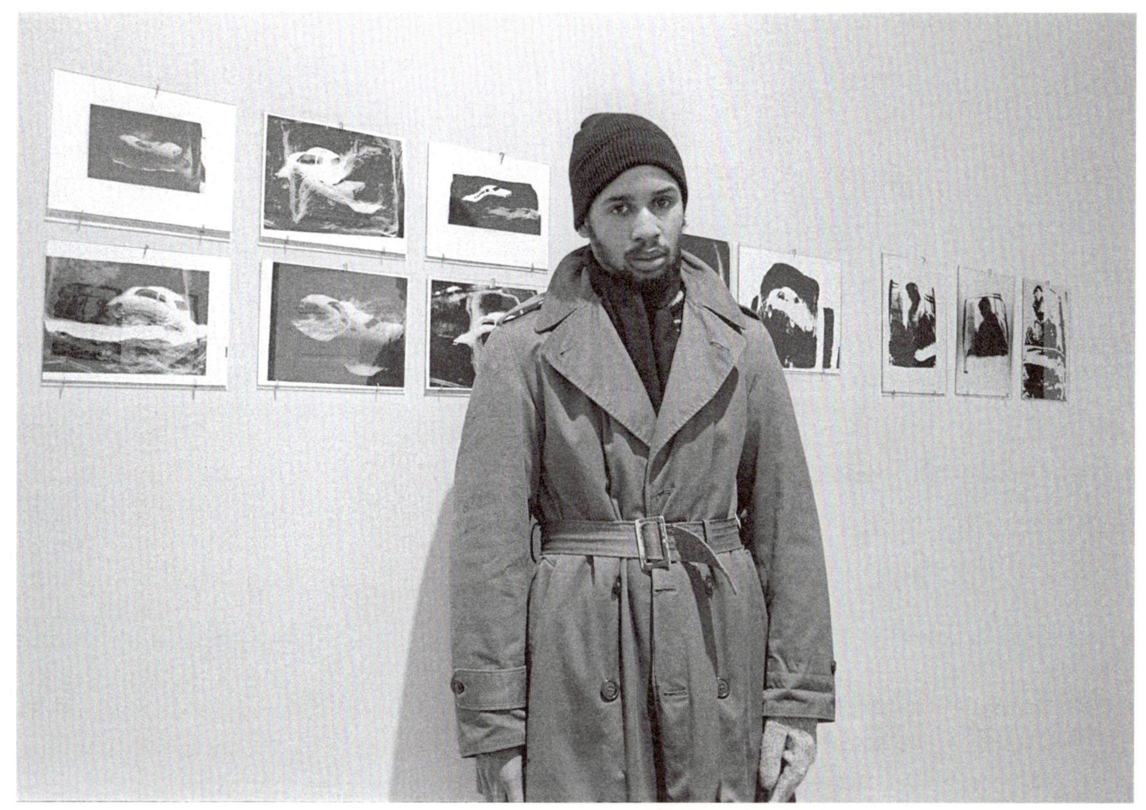

Ellis with his early experimental photographs at PS1, 1981. Wentzy recalls that PS1's coal furnace would only run until 5:00 p.m. to discourage artists from living in their studios after hours, hence the artist's gloves, scarf, and overcoat. Photograph by James Wentzy

WHY ARE YOU INTERESTED IN A STUDIO WORKSPACE AT P.S. 1?
        Because it took such a blessed long time for the construction of a studio
        and darkroom; and for the continuance of the work initiated this last year.

WORKSPACE PREFERENCES:
(Specifications determined by the nature of your work and your work requirements.)
        The same small studio we work in now.  We have constructed
        a darkroom --with running water(no simple task)--in the connecting
        nurses office bathroom and an exibition area for the work of photo-
        graphs and photo-sculpture pieces.

Excerpt from Ellis and Wentzy's application to renew their residency for the 1980–81 season

# The Teaching Artist

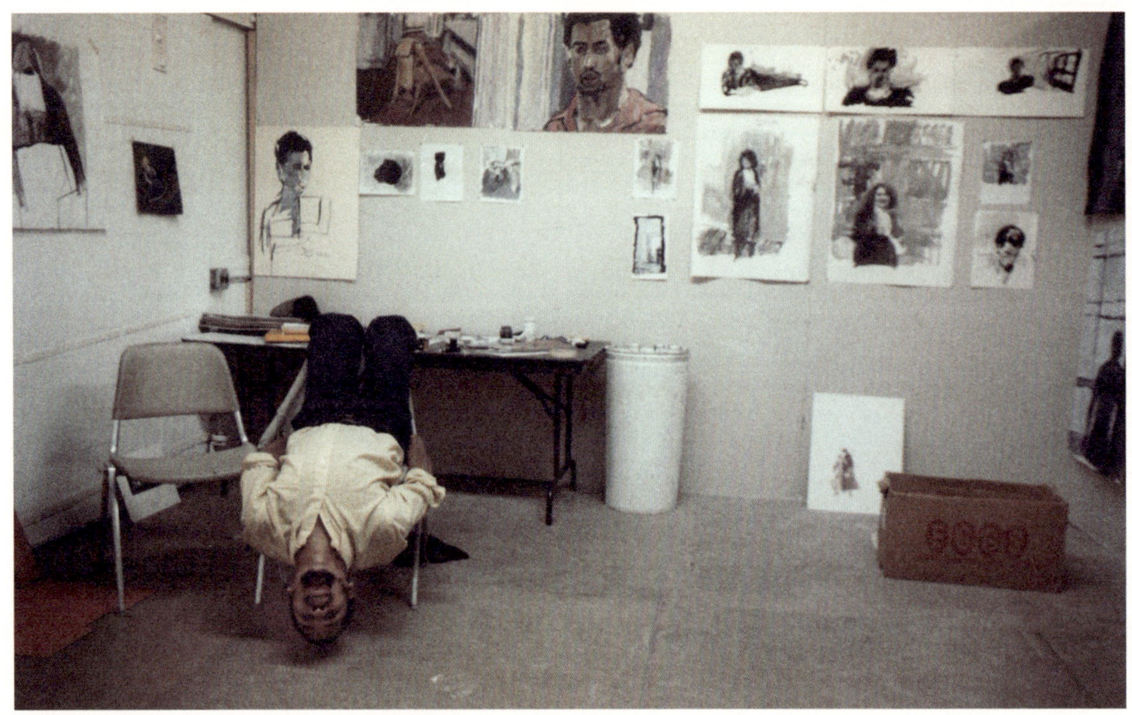

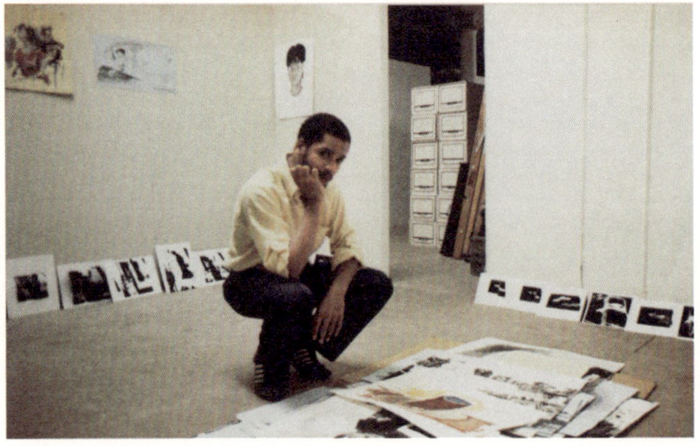

Ellis in his studio at the Whitney Independent Study Program, 1981–82. Photographs by Allen Frame

After his residency at PS1, Ellis was awarded a place in the Whitney Museum of American Art's Independent Study Program (ISP) for 1981–82. The year-long course integrated young artists, art historians, and curators for a series of seminars led by visiting scholars and artists. Artists were given a studio space in a building on lower Broadway, and Ellis had the use of a darkroom where he continued to work with photography.

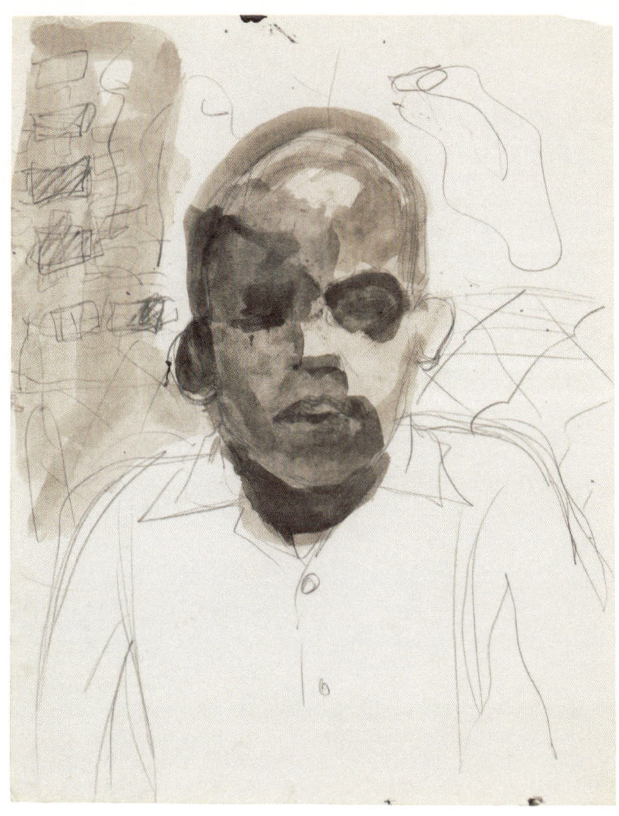

*Untitled* (Child)
ca. 1982
Ink, wash, and graphite on paper
24 × 18 inches

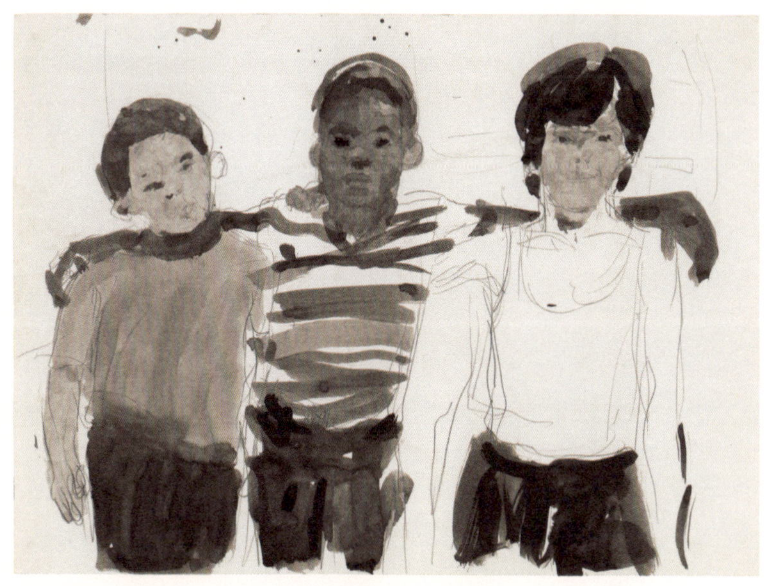

*Untitled* (Children)
ca. 1982
Ink, wash, and graphite on paper
18 × 24 inches

In 1983, Ellis began working as an educator in the Whitney Museum's Artreach program. Artreach sent lecturers to New York City public schools to give slide presentations of works in the museum's collection, followed by a visit to the museum itself. The program gave Ellis an opportunity to work with young students in the Bronx and other boroughs outside Manhattan, and apply his vast self-taught knowledge of art history to "stir up an interest in art," as he puts it in a notebook from the period.

# Downtown Circles

Throughout the early 1980s, Ellis was part of New York's burgeoning downtown arts scene. He lived in the East Village for a time with his boyfriend José Rafael Arango, a member of Charles Ludlam's Ridiculous Theatrical Company, and later stayed with his friend and high school classmate Miguel Ferrando on the Lower East Side. By working as an assistant to artists Not Vital and Malcolm Morley, and frequenting downtown spaces like The Bar on Second Avenue and the Ninth Circle on West 10th Street, Ellis quickly became part of a dense network of artists and participated in numerous group exhibitions.

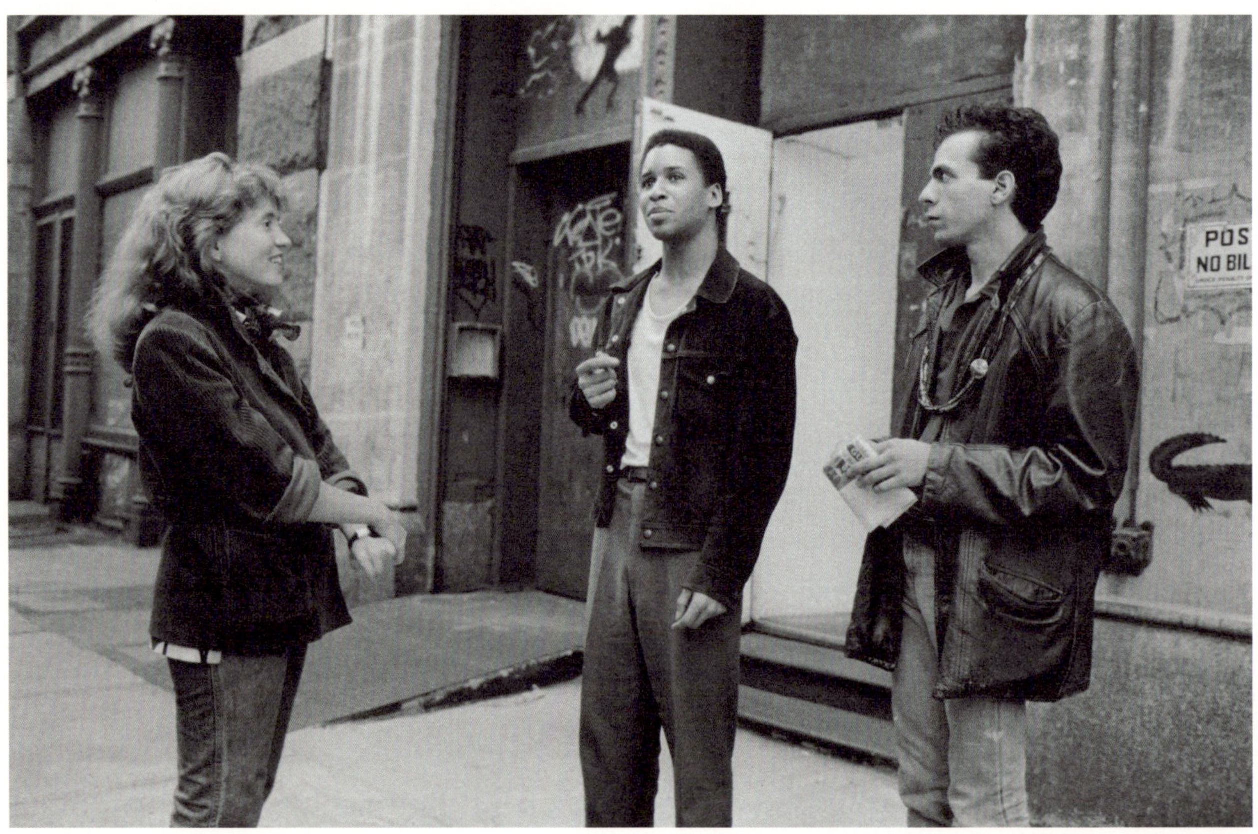



Ellis with the artist Lauren Stringer (left) and his friend Miguel Ferrando (right), outside Patrick Fox Gallery in the East Village in 1984. Photograph by Allen Frame

sal<sup>0</sup><sub>0</sub>n

daile kaplan
chris wool
vince barnes
lynn davis
peter hujar
jacob burckhardt
paul villinski
steven harvey
sophie campbell
peter littlefield
julie wilson
roy fowler
stephen white
michael collins
francie lyshak
barbara ess
dan himmel
joey voitko
steve marrow
bill costa
allen frame
julia hanlon
dieter hall
lona foote
david wojnarowicz
joseph modica
bill crist
anne harvey
bob gober
fritz van orden
ron girard
tony de vito
mark tambella
jane dickson
william morrison
jack millett mosher
gary di pasquale
jack smith
james nares
katie o'looney
dumas
suzanne opton
jason harvey
darrell ellis
gunnars prande
anna reinhardt
andy rutherford
christina schlesinger

opening reception
december 30 6-9pm

bill rice gallery
13 east 3rd street

by appt. thru 1/20
(212) 598-9772

In 1984, Ellis participated in *Salon/Saloon* at Bill Rice Gallery, an expansive group show of downtown artists

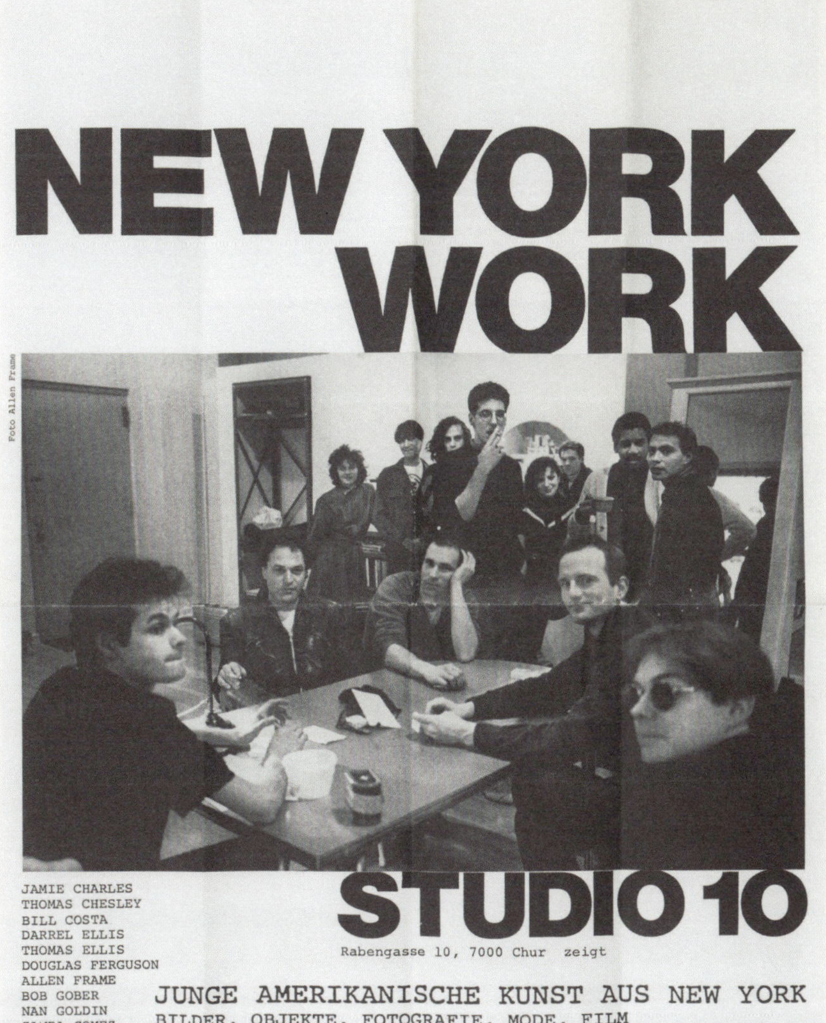


*New York Work: New American Art from New York* (1983), organized by the Swiss artist Not Vital, was Ellis's first opportunity to exhibit his art abroad. His work, as well as a selection of his father's photographs, was shown alongside work by artist friends Allen Frame, Nan Goldin, Frank Moore, and Robert Gober, among others

# Inheritance



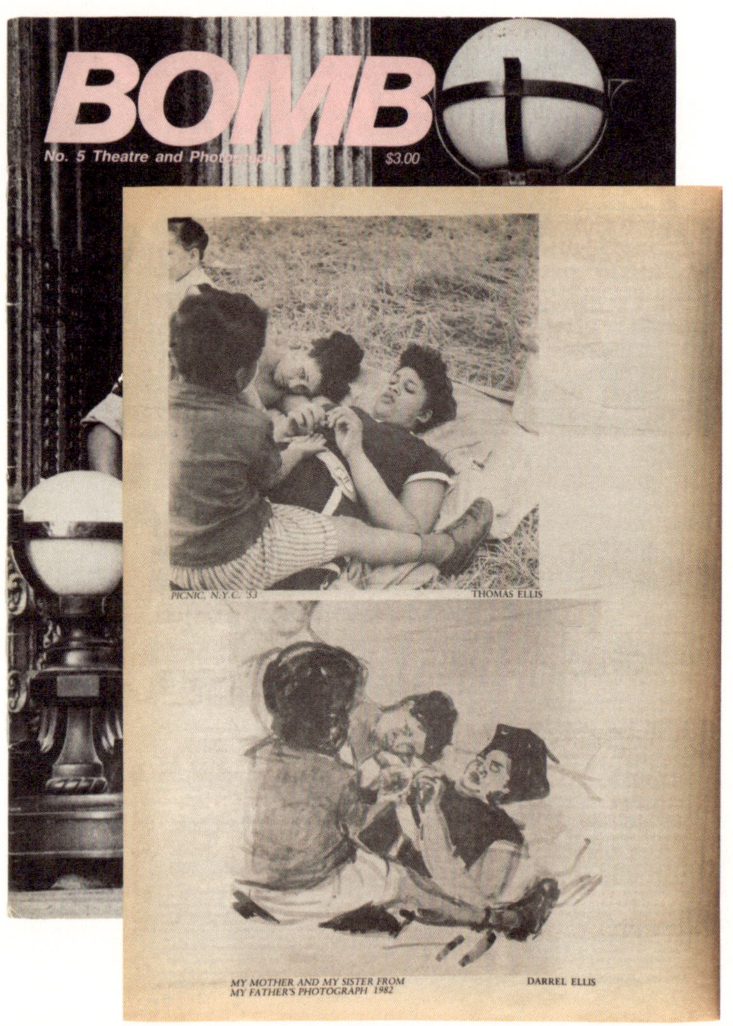

In 1983, Ellis published his drawings based on his father's photographs in two issues of *BOMB* magazine

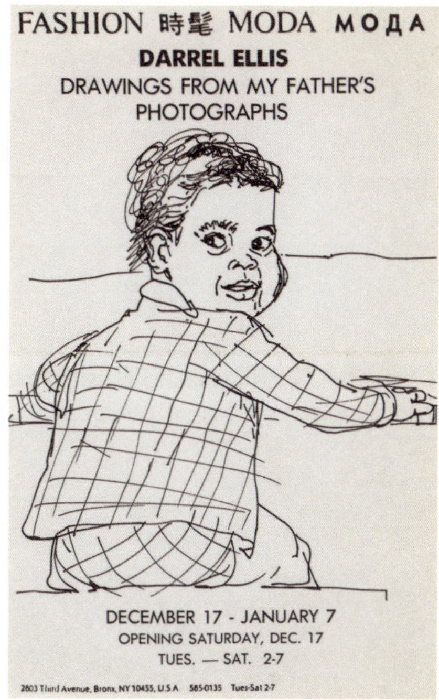


Poster for Ellis's solo exhibition at Fashion
Moda in the Bronx, 1983

In the early 1980s, Ellis began painting and drawing from
a handful of his father's printed photographs. When his
mother saw this work, she gave him a vast collection of his
father's negatives, deepening his interest in working from
photographs and broadening his source material.

In 1983, his first solo exhibition, *Drawings from
My Father's Photographs* at Anichini Gallery on East 20th
Street, showcased these works alongside his father's
photographs. The exhibition opened for a second run
later that year at Fashion Moda, an art space founded in
the South Bronx, close to the neighborhood where Ellis
had grown up.

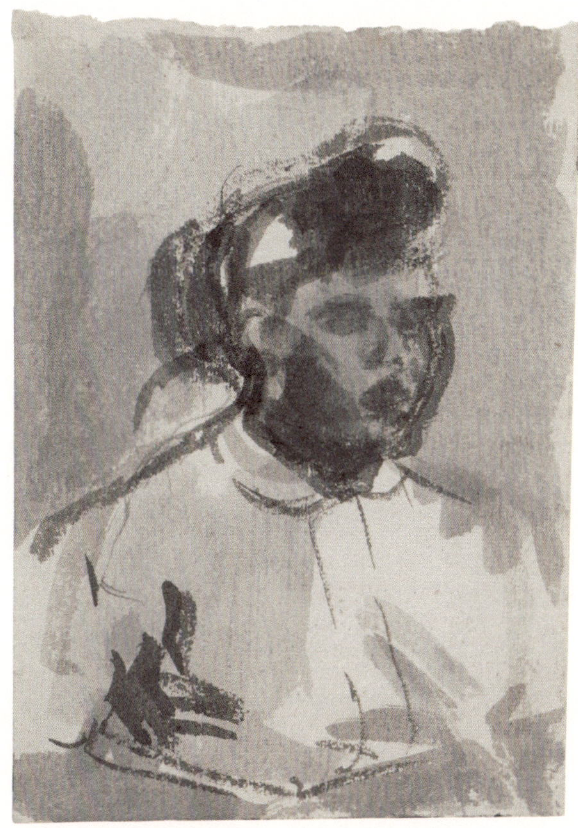

*Untitled* (Mother)
ca. 1989
Ink on paper
11 ¾ × 7 ½ inches

# Life at the Printshop

At Fashion Moda in 1983, Ellis met Susan Spencer Crowe, an artist who was running the Lower East Side Printshop at the time. Crowe invited Ellis to expand his practice into printmaking through participation in the Minority Artist Printmaking Workshop, which offered printmaking education, supplies, and facilities to artists of color. At the LES Printshop, Ellis experimented with reproducing his father's photographs in diptychs that combined screen-printed images with figurative painting.

After living in downtown Manhattan for several years, Ellis returned to the Bronx to live with his mother in the mid-1980s. While there, he made sketches and photographs of his family that would be incorporated into later artworks, including a small self-titled book that Ellis published in 1986 through Joe Lewis's Appearances Press. Lewis, who also grew up in the Bronx, had met Ellis at Fashion Moda, which he helped run in the early eighties.

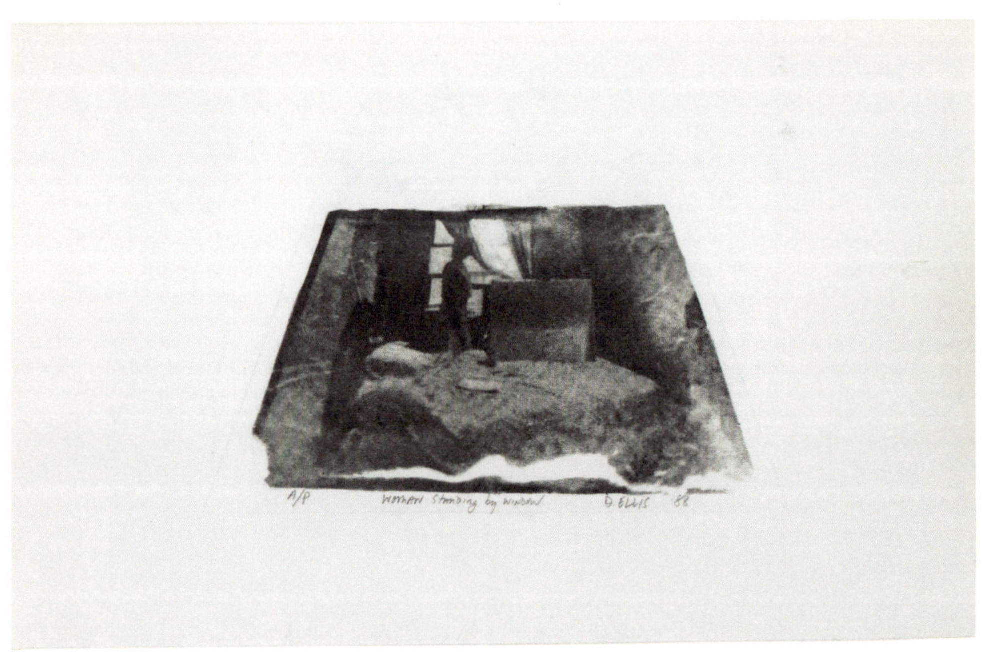

*Woman Standing by Window*
1988
Photolithograph
11 ½ × 17 inches

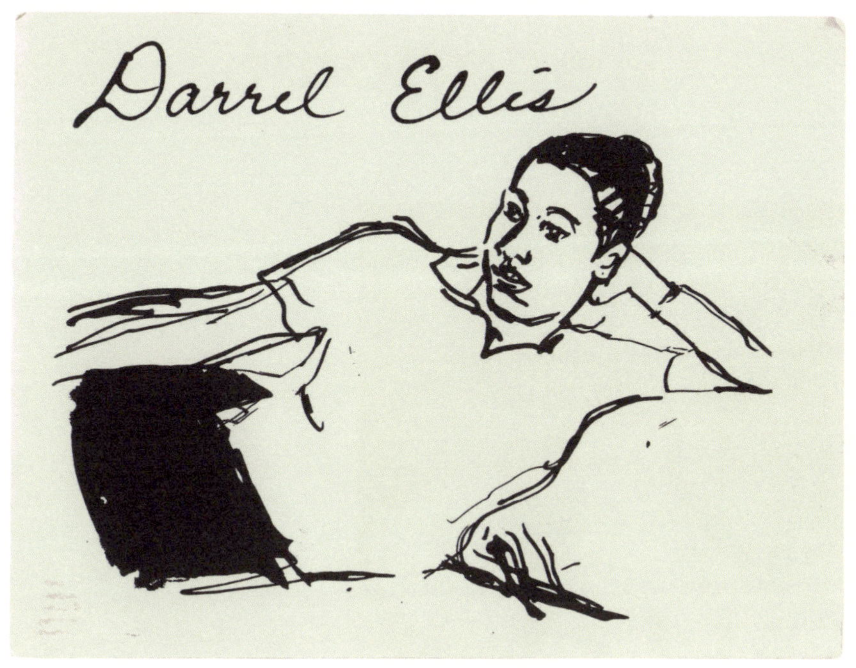

Ellis's 1986 artist's book, published by Joe Lewis's Appearances Press. In addition to Ellis, Lewis invited the graffiti artists Crash (John Matos) and Daze (Chris Ellis), as well as Betty Tompkins, Marilyn Minter, and Christof Kohlhöfer to create silkscreened books

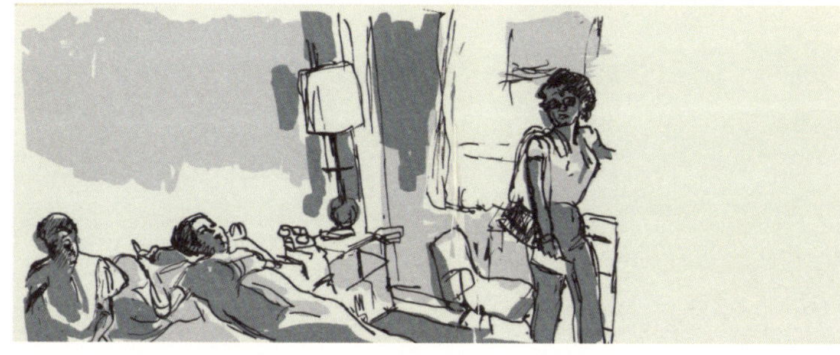

The centerfold of Ellis's artist's book, showing his mother reclining in her bed and his sister, Katrina, to the right

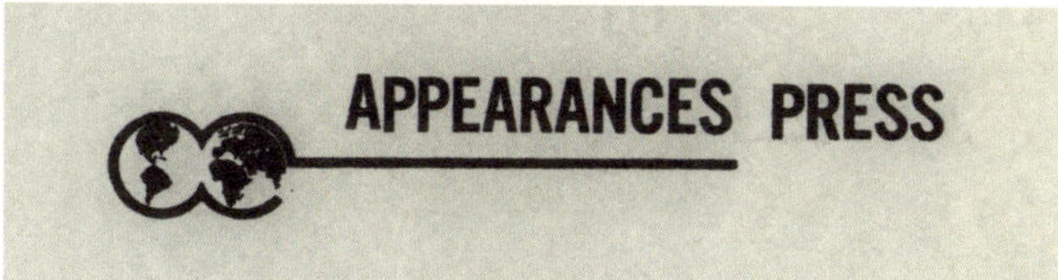



"Darrel was a student of art history. His ideas about composition, the flattening out of the form, the use of grisaille, were all evidence of knowing very classical traditions. His gray scale was a color scale."
— Joe Lewis

# The Move to Greenpoint

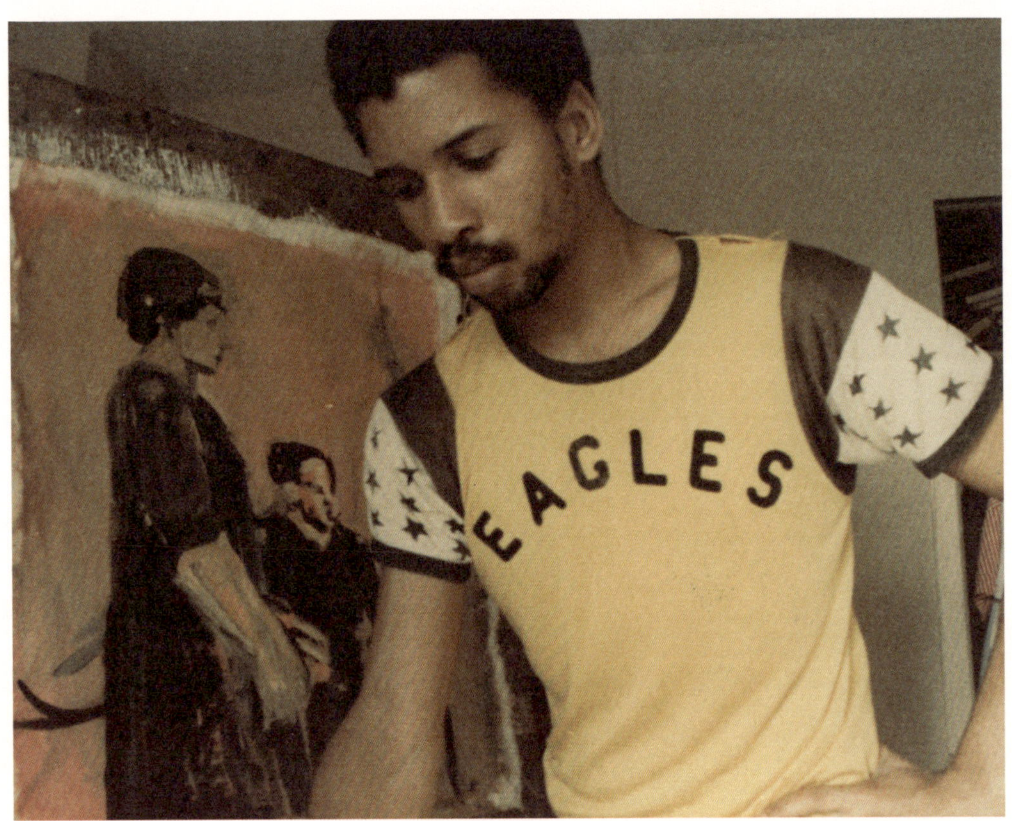

Ellis painting and lounging in his Greenpoint apartment, where he lived for the last five years of his life

In 1987, Ellis moved to Greenpoint, Brooklyn, not far from his friend Susan Spencer Crowe's studio. Crowe recalls: "His apartment on Franklin Street represented a major emotional milestone in his life, in that it marked his first complete break from home and living on his own. At the age of twenty-eight, Darrel was proud of his achievement. This apartment, along with his full-time job as a security guard at the Museum of Modern Art, represented to him a certain sense of financial stability, independence, and wholeness. The responsibility of a job and an apartment absorbed much of his energy in the first months that he lived there while he set himself up to pursue his life as an artist. In the beginning he enjoyed the routines of going to work every day and spending time in the museum's galleries, filled with work by artists he loved: Cézanne, Degas, Picasso, Monet, Klee, and Edvard Munch."

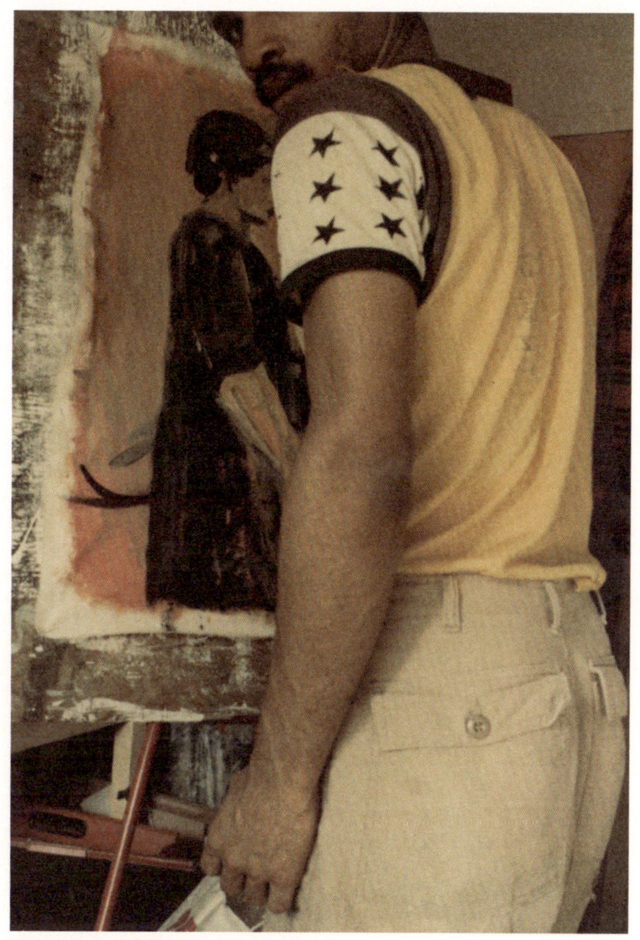

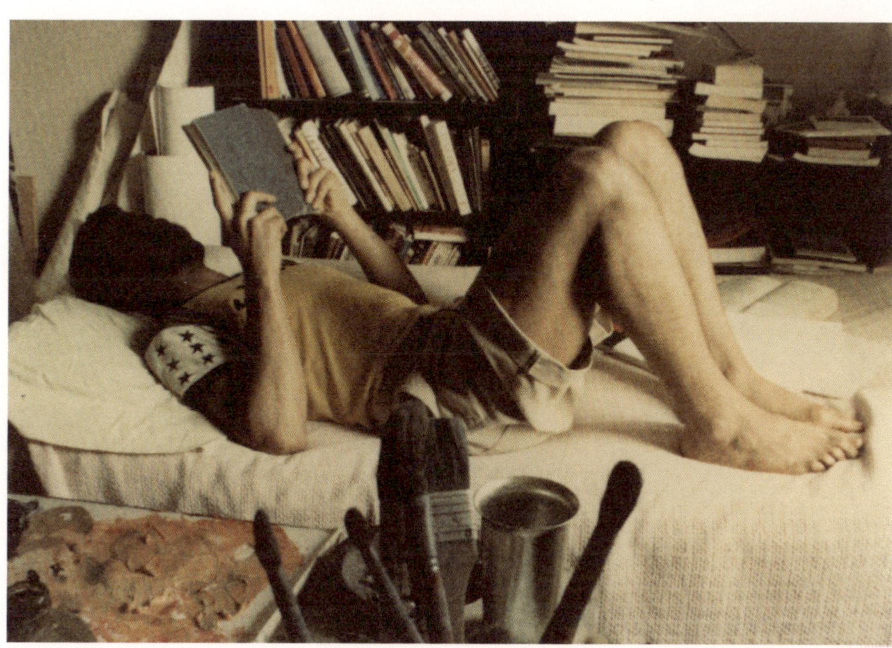

# Controversy at Artists Space

**"I struggle to resist the frozen images of myself taken by Robert Mapplethorpe and Peter Hujar. They haunt me. "**
— Darrel Ellis

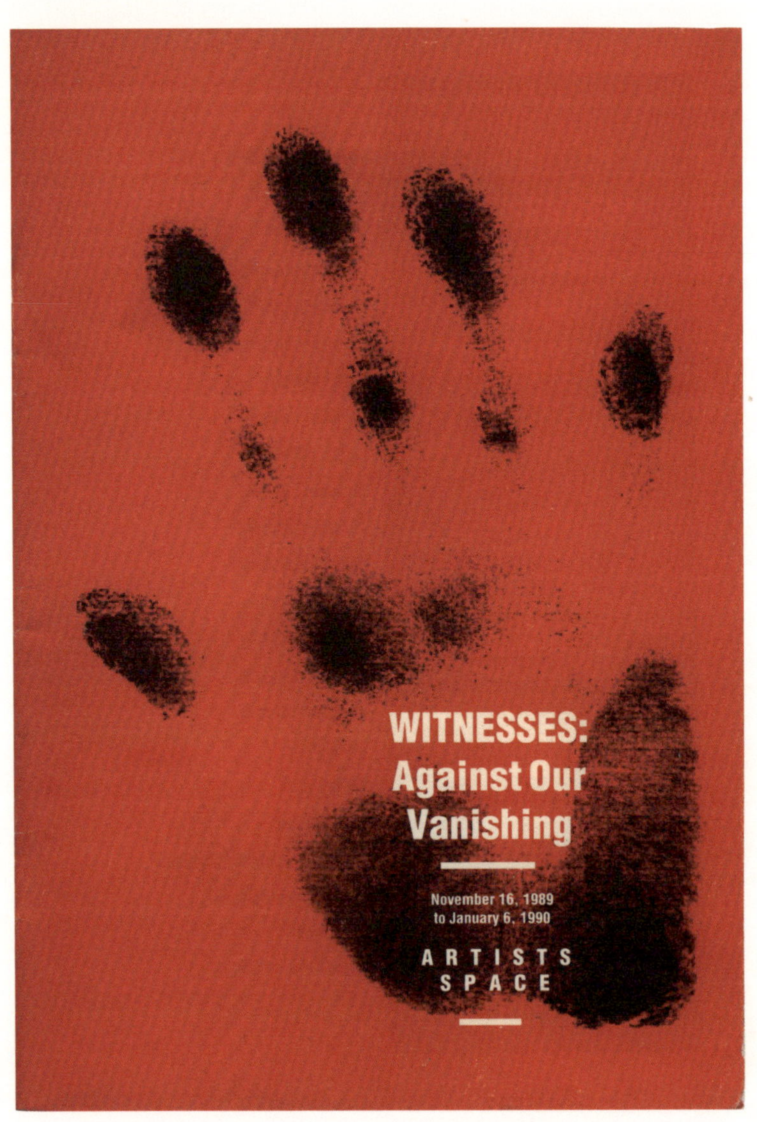

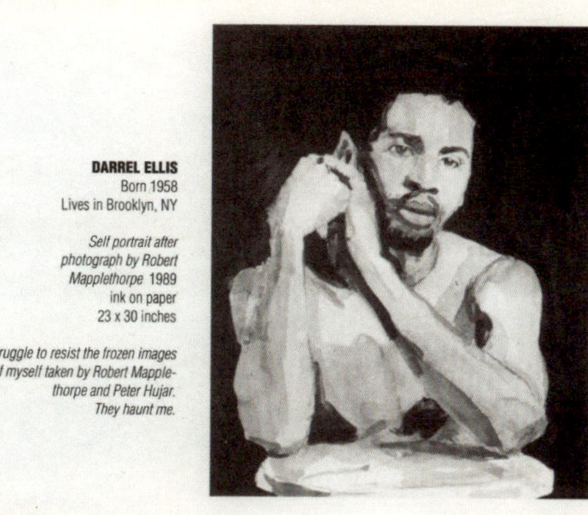


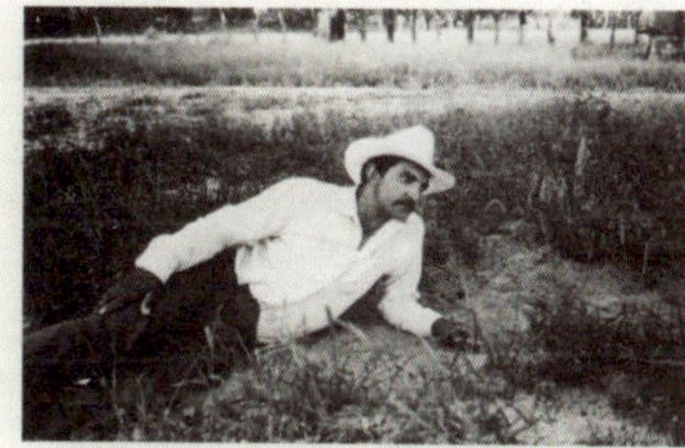


The catalog for *Witnesses: Against Our Vanishing*, curated by Nan Goldin at Artists Space, New York, November 16, 1989–January 6, 1990

In 1989, the photographer Nan Goldin invited Ellis to participate in *Witnesses: Against Our Vanishing*, a group show at Artists Space responding to the intense toll of AIDS on her community of artists. Ellis contributed two paintings to the exhibition, based on photographs that Peter Hujar and Robert Mapplethorpe had taken of him in 1981; the paintings were shown alongside the original photographs. Both Hujar and Mapplethorpe had died of AIDS-related causes, Hujar in 1987, and Mapplethorpe in the spring of 1989.

*Witnesses* became the site of a heated conflict over public funding for the arts when the National Endowment for the Arts (NEA) rescinded a $10,000 grant that was awarded to Artists Space for the project, arguing that "a large portion of the content [was] political rather than artistic in nature." The NEA's actions took place following a summer of controversy over the cancellation of *The Perfect Moment* at the Corcoran Gallery of Art in Washington, DC, a retrospective of Robert Mapplethorpe's work that drew criticism from conservatives for its images of sadomasochism. The NEA controversy brought national press attention to *Witnesses* before the exhibition had even opened. Ellis's *Self-Portrait after Photograph by Robert Mapplethorpe* (1989) became one of the most reproduced images from the show. George Steinberg, Ellis's high school teacher, purchased the painting after reading about it in the *New York Times*.

# In Search of
# New Selves

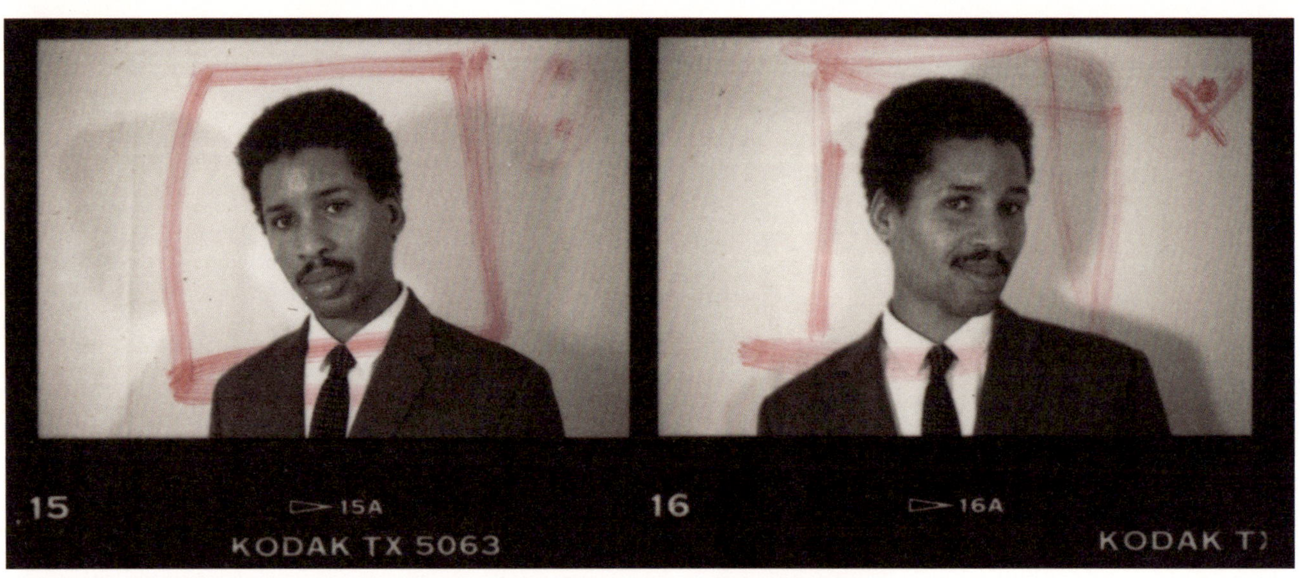

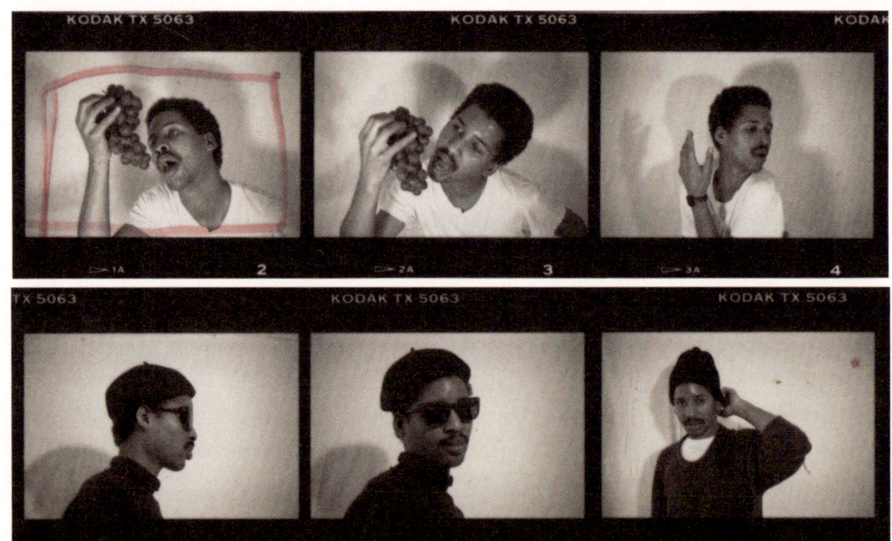

In a series of photographs from 1990–91, Ellis playfully acted out different personae for the camera, exploring his own image through self-portraiture. Some of these photographs became source imagery for later paintings and experimental photographs

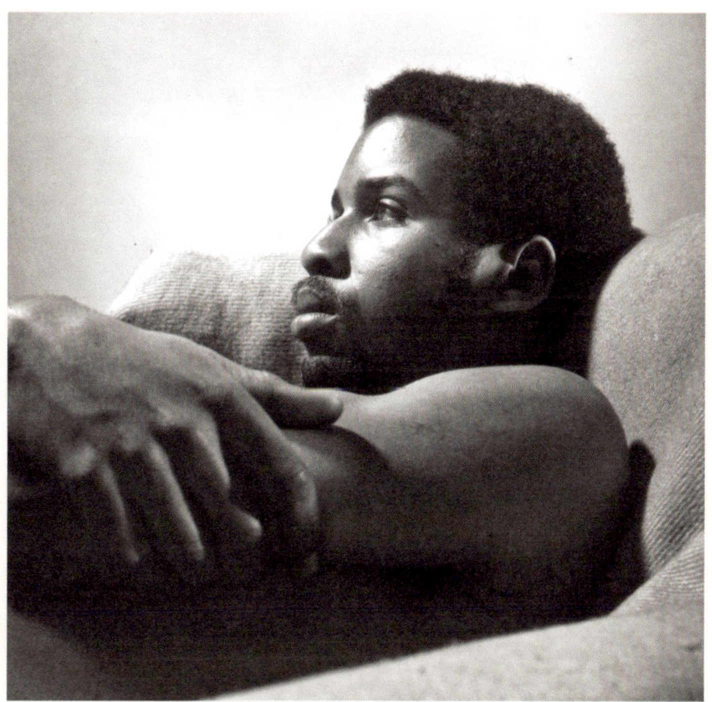

Peter Hujar, *Darrel Ellis (III)*, 1981
Gelatin silver print
10 × 8 inches

Energized by the attention his self-portraits received
in *Witnesses*, Ellis began a series of paintings and
drawings based on photographs of himself, including
portraits taken by Allen Frame. By focusing on his
own image, he sought to further investigate the
tradition of self-portraiture, as he also reconsidered his
relationship as a Black artist to the Old Masters and
the European tradition of painting. His work from this
period demonstrates a developed interest in materiality
and texture, bringing a painterly sensibility to his
photographic source material. The large number of
self-portraits Ellis produced speaks to his desire to
illustrate a plurality of selves, or a "composite being,"
as he wrote in a notebook in 1989.

# Looking Inward

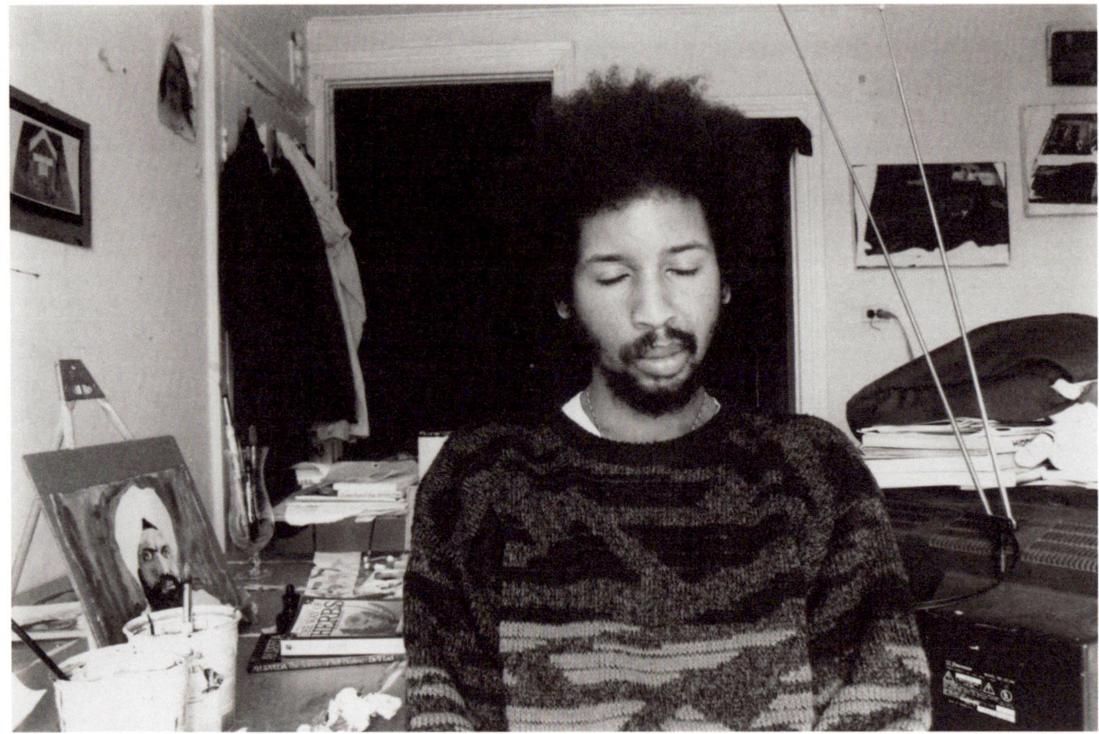

Ellis in his Greenpoint apartment,
ca. 1991–92

"During the last year of his life, Darrel appeared to
have accepted the fragmentary nature of life and
lived each moment to its fullest. He continued to
paint. It was his passion for painting that continued
to fill him with optimism about life."
— Susan Spencer Crowe

In 1991, Ellis presented a solo exhibition at Baron/ Boisanté Editions, a midtown gallery located just blocks away from his job at MoMA. The exhibition was the first major presentation of his reworked family photographs, which he had started making after moving to Greenpoint in 1987. Ellis's friend John Ahearn recalls that the work had "moved up to a different level of appreciation." The show led to Ellis's only published interview, recorded by arts writer David Hirsh, and the inclusion of ten of his photographs in the traveling exhibition *The Surrogate Figure: Intercepted Identities in Contemporary Photography.*

The same year, Ellis was hospitalized with complications from AIDS. He had been diagnosed with HIV several years earlier; however, prior to entering the hospital he had largely kept his status from friends and family. After recovering, Ellis spent much of the last year of his life at his home in Greenpoint, continuing to make work through his final days. Ellis passed away on April 4, 1992.

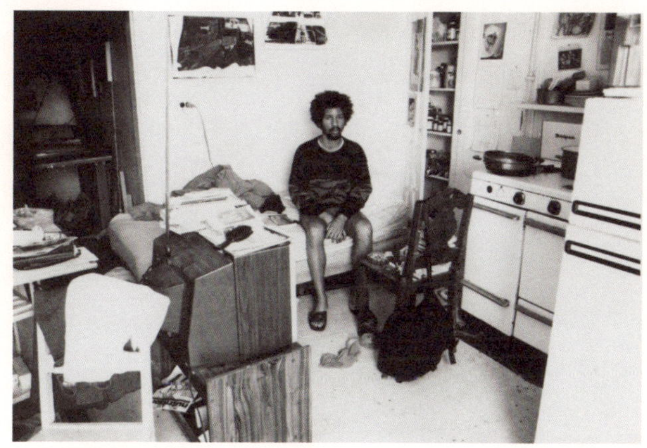

MY MIND IS A PERFECT REFLECTION OF THE UNIVERSE
ITS DIVINE POWERS ARE WITHOUT LIMITS
IT HAS NO BOUNDRIES
IT PROTECTS ME AND FREES ME
MY MIND MIRRORS ALL THAT IS POSSIBLE
I TRUST IT AND KNOW IT WILL BRING ME ONLY GOOD

Printed ephemera from Ellis's archive reflects his interest in spirituality

# Legacy

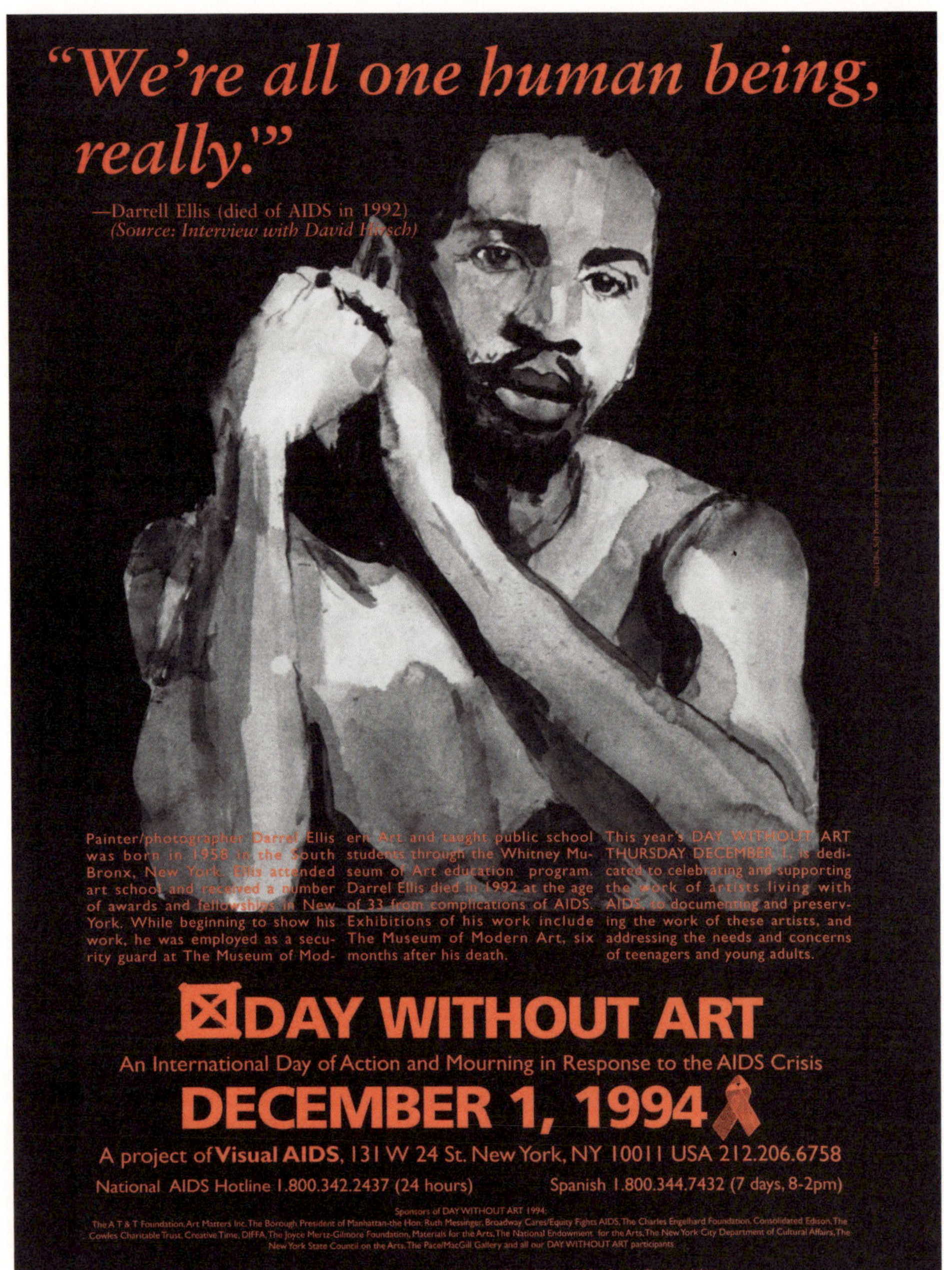


Ellis's *Self-Portrait after Photograph by Robert Mapplethorpe* (1989) was used for Visual AIDS's 1994 Day Without Art poster in a striking design that emphasized the human and artistic losses of the AIDS crisis. The poster was distributed to hundreds of museums, galleries, and schools across the country as part of an annual day of mourning and action.

Just months after Ellis died, his work was exhibited in his former workplace, the Museum of Modern Art, as part of *New Photography 8*. The exhibition was organized by Peter Galassi (MoMA's chief curator of photography), who had met Ellis at the museum and encouraged his work. Galassi later acquired two photographs for the museum's permanent collection.

In the nearly three decades since Ellis's death, Allen Frame has dedicated himself to supporting and exhibiting his friend's artistic accomplishments. Under Frame's care and through his ongoing collaboration with Ellis's siblings, Thomas Ellis Jr., Laure Ellis, Katrina Stewart, and Kim Stewart, Ellis's work continues to find new audiences. In recent years, Ellis's photographs and paintings have been acquired by the Metropolitan Museum of Art, the Brooklyn Museum, the Bronx Museum of the Arts, and the Baltimore Museum of Art.

Ellis's friend and fellow artist Whitfield Lovell reflects: "It would have been very meaningful for him to have known that he was going to be in the MoMA collection. In the Black art community at that time, we did not expect to be shown or considered in mainstream, commercial galleries or museums. We were resigned to the fact that we were not going to be embraced by such venues. Perhaps Bearden and Lawrence were included in the collections of MoMA and the Met, but it was practically an impossible dream for Black artists to aspire to at that time. But you know, once you understood that reality you were knee-deep in it and you couldn't turn back. You had to make the art anyway. Some people give up art and walk away. But real artists have to make art. And that is the kind of artist that Darrel was. He was a genuine, devoted artist. He was going to make his work whether he got mainstream recognition or not."

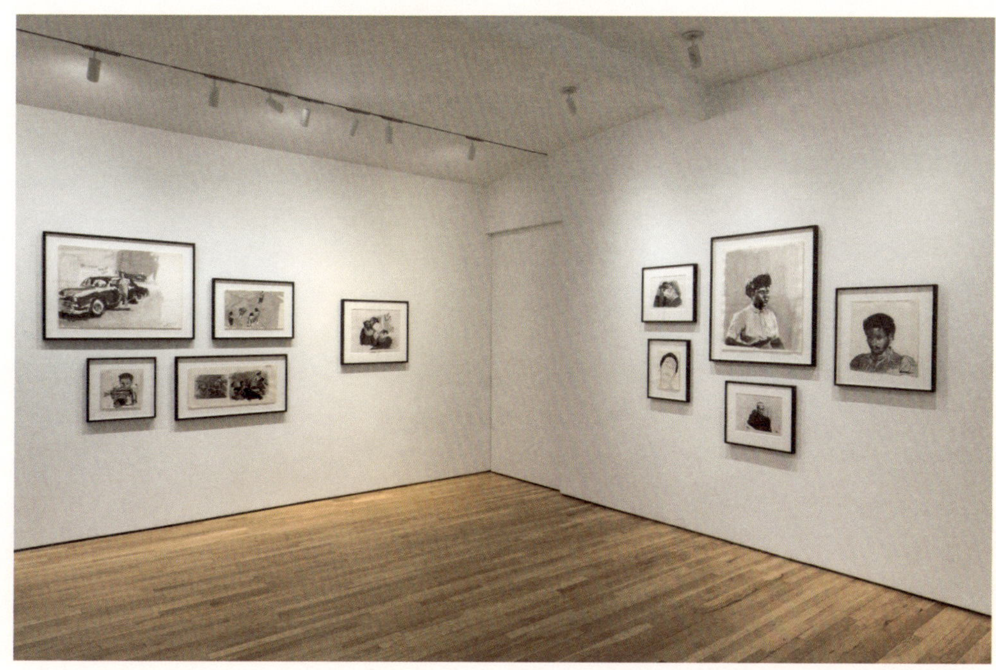

Installation view of *Darrel Ellis: A Composite Being* at Candice Madey, New York, April 17–May 28, 2021

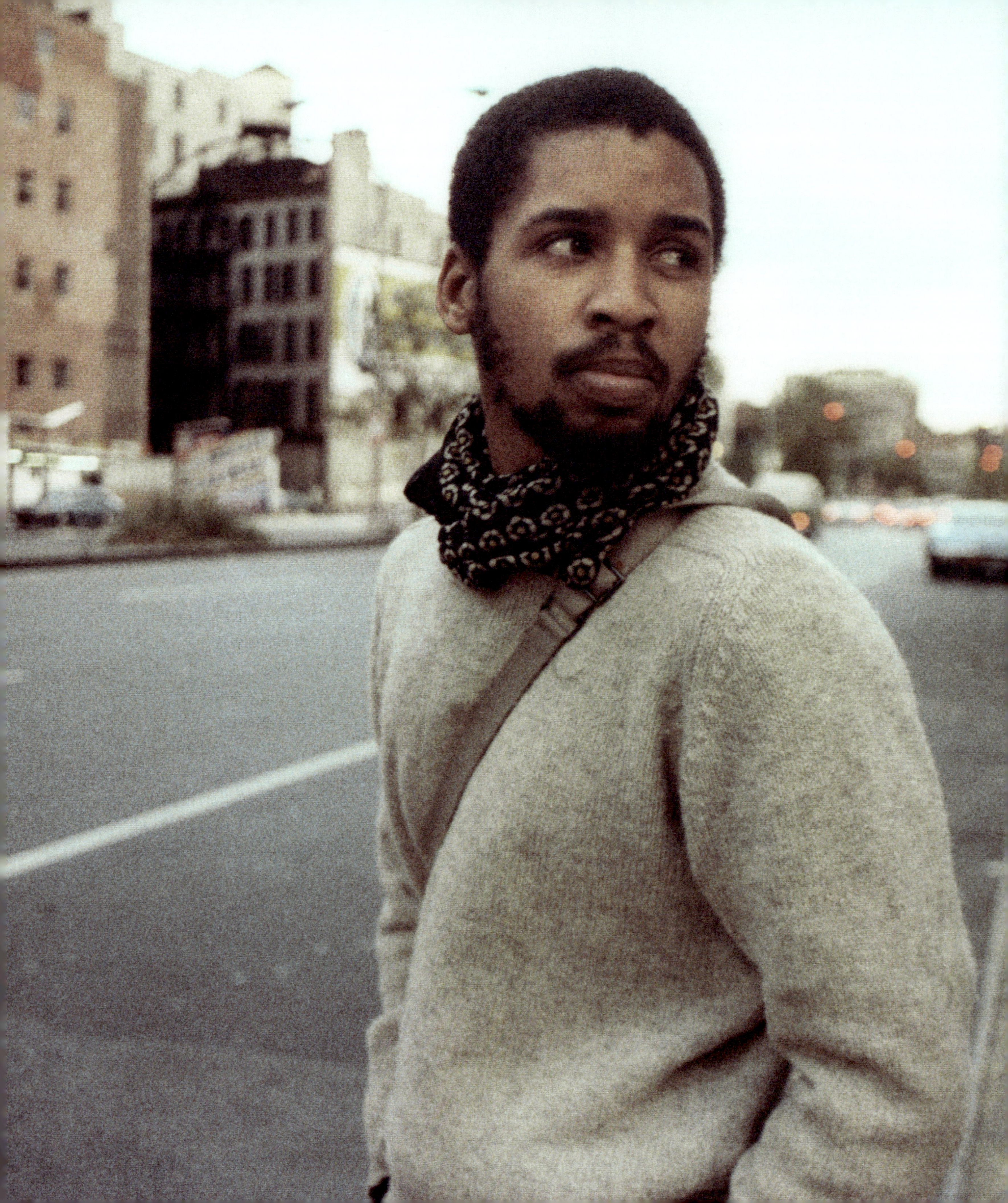

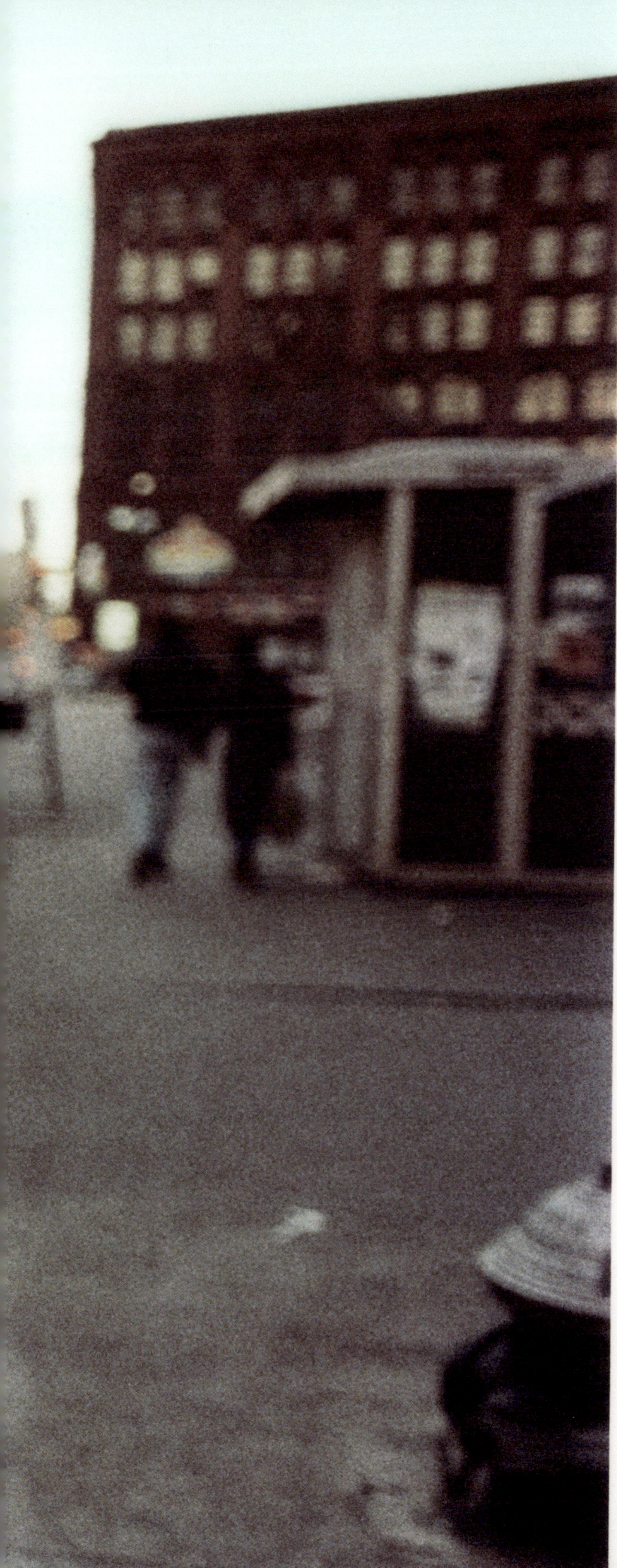

Darrel Ellis in Manhattan, ca. 1981.
Photograph by Allen Frame

# Exhibition History

## Darrel Ellis

Born December 5, 1958, New York, NY
Died April 4, 1992, Brooklyn, NY

## Solo Exhibitions

2021
*Darrel Ellis*, Fundaziun Not Vital, Ardez, Switzerland

*Darrel Ellis: A Composite Being,* Candice Madey, New York

2020
*Darrel Ellis: Matter,* Galerie Crone, Berlin

2019
*Darrel Ellis*, OSMOS, New York

2003
*Darrel Ellis: Family Distortions*, Julie Saul Gallery, New York

1996–98
*Darrel Ellis* (Allen Frame, curator), Art in General, New York; Space One Eleven, Birmingham, AL; Tubman Museum, Macon, GA; Wolfson Galleries at Miami Dade College, Miami, FL; Art Museum of the University of Memphis, Memphis, TN (catalog)

1991
*Darrel Ellis*, Baron/Boisanté Editions, New York (brochure)

1983–84
*Drawings from My Father's Photographs*, Fashion Moda, Bronx, NY

1983
*Drawings from My Father's Photographs*, Anichini Gallery, New York

## 2021

*The Slipstream: Reflection, Resilience, and Resistance in the Art of Our Time* (Eugenie Tsai and Joseph Shaikewitz, curators), Brooklyn Museum, Brooklyn, NY

*Touch* (Augusto Arbizo, curator), Rachel Uffner Gallery, New York

*Pictures, Revisited*, Metropolitan Museum of Art, New York

## 2019

*Altered After* (curated by Conrad Ventur for Visual AIDS), Participant, Inc., New York

## 2012

*Facts, Fictions, and Figures* (Rehema Barber and Jennifer Sargent, curators), Hyde Gallery, Nesin Graduate School, Memphis College of Art and Design, Memphis, TN

## 2005

*Paper*, Nicole Klagsbrun Gallery, New York

## 2002

*Portraits of African-Americans*, Arkansas Arts Center, Little Rock, AR; University of Arkansas - Fort Smith, Fort Smith, AR

## 2001

*The South Bronx Story* (James Fuentes, curator), 1201 Lafayette Ave, Bronx, NY

## 2000

*Reflections in Black: A History of Black Photographers 1840 to the Present*, Anacostia Community Museum, Smithsonian Institution, Washington, DC; Luckman Gallery, California State University, Los Angeles

## 2000

*Family Tales*, Pelham Art Center, Westchester, NY

## 1999

*Urban Mythologies: The Bronx Represented Since the 1960s* (Lydia Yee, curator), Bronx Museum of the Arts, Bronx, NY (catalog)

## 1996

*Arts Communities/AIDS Communities: Realizing the Archive Project* (curated by Geoffrey Hendricks and David Hirsh for Visual AIDS), Boston Center for the Arts, Boston (catalog)

## 1995

*Multiple Exposure: The Group Portrait in Photography* (Leslie Tonkonow, curator), Bruce Museum, Greenwich, CT; Bayly Art Museum, University of Virginia, Charlottesville, VA (catalog)

## 1994–96

*L'amour, la vie, la mort: Photography about AIDS* (Marion Scemama, curator), FNAC Galerie, Paris

## 1993–95

*Disrupted Borders* (Sunil Gupta, curator), INIVA and the Organization for Visual Arts, London; Arnolfini Gallery, Bristol; Ikon Gallery, Birmingham; Photographer's Gallery, London; Canadian Museum of Contemporary Photography, Ottawa; London Regional Art and Historical Museum, London, ON (catalog)

## 1993

*The Black Experience in Photography*, Schmidt Contemporary Art, St. Louis, MO

## 1992

*New Photography 8: Dieter Appelt, Ellen Brooks, Darrel Ellis, Dennis Farber, Robert Flynt, Mary Miss, Gundula Schulze, Toshio Shibata* (Peter Galassi, curator), Museum of Modern Art, New York

1991–92
*The Surrogate Figure: Intercepted Identities in Contemporary Photography* (Julia Ballerini, curator), Center for Photography at Woodstock, NY; Douglas F. Cooley Memorial Art Gallery, Reed College, Portland, OR; Rosa Esman Gallery, New York (catalog)

1991
*Body, Body*, Renee Fotouhi Fine Art West, East Hampton, NY

1989
*Witnesses: Against Our Vanishing* (Nan Goldin, curator), Artists Space, New York (catalog)

*Special Editions from the Lower East Side Printshop*, Henry Street Settlement, New York

1988
*Strange Past*, Longwood Arts Project, Bronx, NY

*Temperaments*, Minor Injury Gallery, Brooklyn, NY

*Afro-America '88: A Dream Deferred?* (Joe Lewis, curator), Robert F. Brush Art Gallery, St. Lawrence University, Canton, NY

1987
*From the Lower East Side Printshop*, Jamaica Arts Center, Queens, NY

*Print Babel: Works from the Lower East Side Printshop*, La MaMa Galleria, New York

1986
*Seventh Heaven: Annual Benefit Exhibition*, New Museum of Contemporary Art, New York

*Skulptur und Fotografie* (organized by Brühler Kunstverein), Orangerie von Schloss Augustusburg, Brühl, Germany

1985
*Mi Casa, Su Casa* (Joe Lewis, curator), Casa du Monde Gallery, New York

*Jules Allen, Darrel Ellis*, Casa du Monde Gallery, New York

*Fashion Moda Benefit Exhibition Sale*, Ronald Feldman Gallery, New York

*Democracy at Work* (Thom Corn, curator, organized with Fashion Moda), Wooster 22 Gallery, New York

*Four Figurative Artists* (Allen Frame, curator), Christminster Gallery, New York

*Hinter Gitter*, Kulturamt der Stadt Köln Unterstützt, Cologne, Germany

1984
*Salon/Saloon*, Bill Rice Gallery, New York

1983
*New York Work* (Not Vital, curator), Galerie Studio 10, Chur, Switzerland

1981
*Studio Workspace Program Exhibition*, Institute for Art and Urban Resources at PS1, Queens, NY

1980
*Studio Workspace Program Exhibition*, Institute for Art and Urban Resources at PS1, Queens, NY

# Bibliography

## Books and Brochures

*Darrel Ellis*. Exh. brochure. Ardez, Switzerland: Fundaziun Not Vital, 2020.

Ellis, Darrel. *Darrel Ellis*. Artist's book. New York: Appearances Press, 1986.

Frame, Allen, Deborah Willis, and Susan Spencer Crowe. *Darrel Ellis*. Exh. cat. New York: Art in General, 1996.

Goldin, Nan, ed. *Witnesses: Against Our Vanishing*. Exh. cat. New York: Artists Space, 1989.

*Hinter Gitter*. Exh. cat. Cologne: Kulturamt der Stadt Köln Unterstützt, 1985.

*New York Work*. Exh. brochure (Not Vital, curator). Chur, Switzerland: Galerie Studio 10, 1983.

*Skulptur und Fotografie*. Exh. cat. Brühl, Germany: Orangerie von Schloss Augustusburg, 1986.

Smith, Joshua P. *Darrel Ellis: Photographs*. Exh. cat. New York: Baron/Boisanté Editions, 1991.

*The Surrogate Figure: Intercepted Identities in Contemporary Photography*. Exh. cat. New York: Center for Photography at Woodstock, 1991.

Willis, Deborah. *Reflections in Black: A History of Black Photographers, 1840 to the Present*, 187. New York: W. W. Norton, 2000.

Yee, Lydia. *Urban Mythologies: The Bronx Represented Since the 1960s*. Exh. cat. Bronx, NY: Bronx Museum of the Arts, 1999.

## Articles

Aletti, Vince. "Photo." *Village Voice*, January 22, 1991, 94.

"An interview with Allen Frame on behalf of Darrel Ellis." *Not Not Awesome*, no. 1 (2013): 44–51.

"A Wider Angle." *New Yorker*, December 7, 1992, 30.

Cotter, Holland. "Art in Review: Darrel Ellis." *New York Times*, November 22, 1996, Section C, 22.

Ellis, Darrel. "Darrel Ellis, Thomas Ellis." *BOMB*, no. 5, Theatre and Photography, 1983, 44.

———. "Family Group at Amityville; The Night My Uncle Went AWOL." *BOMB*, no. 8, 1983, 37.

———. "Photographs." In *New Africa*, edited by Mark Mills, Marpessa Dawn Outlaw, Cathy Taylor, and Joe Woods, 34–35, cover. New York: Portable Lower East Side, 1993.

Frame, Allen. "Altered Images." *Village Voice*, February 2–8, 2005, 12.

Glueck, Grace. "Border Skirmish: Art and Politics." *New York Times*, November 19, 1989, Section 2, 1, 25.

Goldberg, Ariel. "In the Room." *Art in America* 106, no. 4 (April 2018): 56–63.

Goldberg, Vicki. "How to Warm a Post-Modernist's Heart." *New York Times*, February 9, 1992, Section 2, 33.

Goldsby, Jackie. "What It Means To Be Colored Me." *Outlook* 3, no. 1 (Summer 1990): 8–17.

Hagan, Charles. "Scoping Out New Photography at the Modern." *New York Times*, November 15, 1992, 35.

Hirsh, David. "Darrel Ellis: On the Border of Family and Tribe." In *Disrupted Borders: An Intervention in Definitions of Boundaries*, edited by Sunil Gupta, 118–26. London: Rivers Oram Press, 1993.

———. "Family Photos." *New York Native*, February 11, 1991, 50.

King, Sarah S. "Darrel Ellis at Art in General." *Art in America* 85, no. 12 (December 1997): 95–96.

Lewis, Joe. "The Art of Politics: 5 Emerging Artists." *Contemporanea* 1, no. 4 (November/December 1988): 104–6.

Lombardi, D. Dominick. "Works That Reveal Reactions to Family Ties." *New York Times*, April 23, 2000, Section WC, 14.

McCarthy, David. "Darrel Ellis: In the name of the father: Art Museum, The University of Memphis." *Art Papers* 22, no. 4 (July/August 1998): 52.

Montes, Lara Mimosa. "In the Stacks with Lara Mimosa Montes: Darrel Ellis." *Coffee House Press* (blog), August 28, 2019. https://coffeehousepress.org/blogs/chp-in-the-stacks/in-the-stacks-with-lara-mimosa-montes-darrel-ellis.

Nolte, Michaela. "Die Idylle der 50er Jahre transformiert in brutale Gegenwart." *Der Tagesspiegel*, July 31, 2020. https://www.tagesspiegel.de/kultur/ausstellung-in-der-galerie-crone-die-idylle-der-50er-jahre-transformiert-in-brutale-gegenwart/26055718.html.

Raynor, Vivien. "'Election '88,' at Bronx Gallery, Explores Unsolved Problems." *New York Times*, November 13, 1988, Section WC, 34.

Russell, John. "Images of Grief and Rage in Exhibition on AIDS." *New York Times*, November 16, 1989, Section C, 23, 26.

Sawyer, Drew. "Darrel Ellis." *OSMOS*, no. 16 (Fall 2018): 16–27.

Scherer, Sally. "AIDS Day Art, Tubman Hosts Darrel Ellis Retrospective." *Macon Telegraph*, November 28, 1997, 12.

Silas, Susan. "Inspired by Photos Taken by His Murdered Father, an Artist Offers an Eloquent View of Memory and Trauma." *Hyperallergic*, June 26, 2019. https://hyperallergic.com/502187/inspired-by-photos-taken-by-his-murdered-father-an-artist-offers-an-eloquent-view-of-memory-and-trauma/.

Smith, Roberta. "What to See in New York Art Galleries Right Now: Darrel Ellis." *New York Times*, June 28, 2019, Section C, 13.

Strauss, David Levi. "Darrel Ellis." *Artforum* 35, no. 8 (April 1997): 95.

Strenger, Sebastian C. "Das Stottern Der Bilder." *Weltkunst*, October 11, 2020. https://www.weltkunst.de/kunstwissen/2020/10/darrel-ellis-das-stottern-der-bilder.

Williams, Carla. "African-American and African Diaspora Art." In *The Queer Encyclopedia of the Visual Arts*, edited by Claude J. Summers, 10–13. San Francisco: Cleis Press, 2004.

Woeller, Marcus. "Wer schwarz und schwul war, hatte doppelt verloren." *Welt*, July 3, 2020. https://www.welt.de/kultur/kunst/plus210762351/Darrel-Ellis-Wer-schwarz-und-schwul-war-hatte-doppelt-verloren.html.

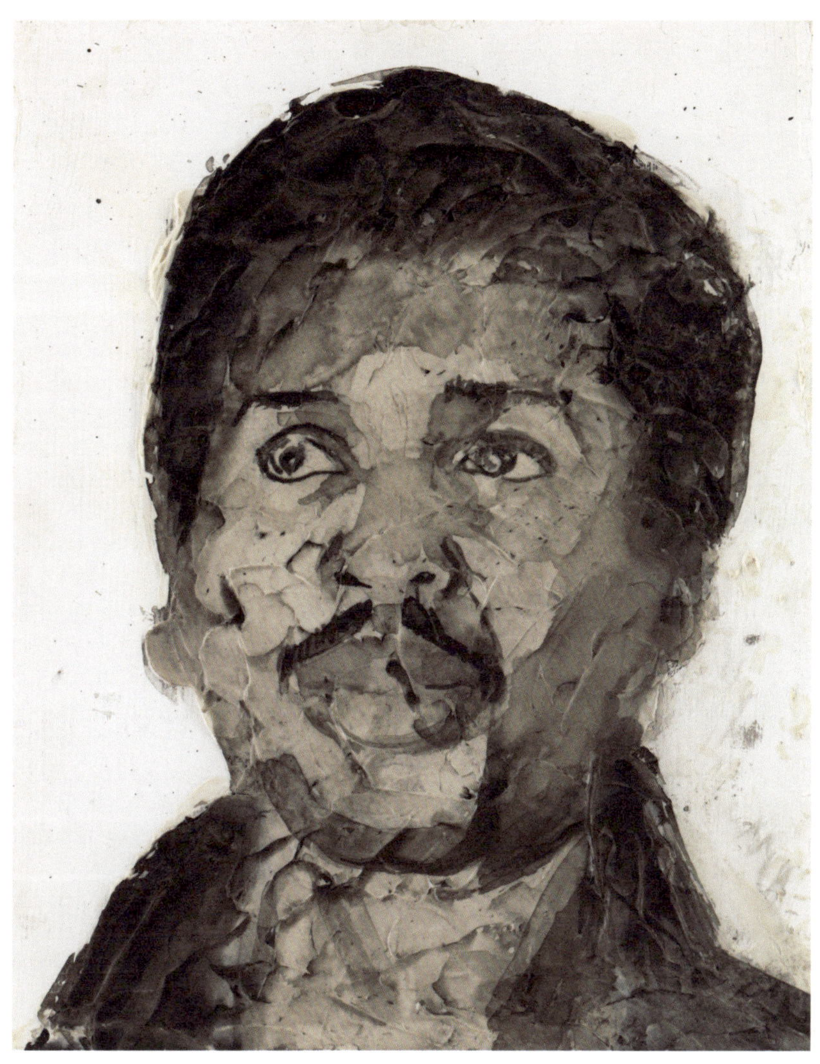

*Untitled* (Self-Portrait)
ca. 1990–92
Ink and wash on panel prepared with
textured ground
15 ½ × 12 ½ inches

# Contributor Biographies

**Sadie Barnette** is from Oakland, CA, and holds a BFA from CalArts and an MFA from the University of California, San Diego. Her artwork reveals quintessential American truths through exploration of her own family history. She has been awarded grants and residencies by the Studio Museum in Harlem, Artadia, Art Matters, Skowhegan School of Painting and Sculpture, and the Headlands Center for the Arts. Her work is in the permanent collections of the Los Angeles County Museum of Art (LACMA); Berkeley Art Museum, CA; Oakland Museum of California, CA; Brooklyn Museum, NY; and the Guggenheim Museum, NY.

**Kyle Croft** is the Programs Director of Visual AIDS. He holds an MA in art history from Hunter College, where his thesis, "Mobilizing Museums Against AIDS: Visual AIDS and Day Without Art, 1988–89," received distinction. His research examines the formative role of AIDS in debates about identity, participation, and social responsibility in the art world. His writing has appeared in *Art in America*, *Bookforum*, *Sleek Magazine*, and *Hyperallergic*.

**Brandon Eng** is an art historian and PhD candidate at New York University's Institute of Fine Arts, where his research considers the relationship between economic crisis and cultural production in the 1970s and 1980s.

**Alanna Fields** is an American mixed-media artist whose work investigates and challenges representations of Black queer identity and history through the lens of photography. Fields's work has been featured at Felix Art Fair, LA, and UNTITLED, ART, Miami Beach, and in exhibitions at MoCADA and Pratt Institute. Fields is a Gordon Parks Foundation Scholar. She received her MFA in photography from Pratt Institute and has given talks at Stanford University, NYU Tisch School of the Arts, Parsons School of Design, and Syracuse University. Fields lives and works in New York City.

**Steven G. Fullwood** is an archivist, writer, and the cofounder of the Nomadic Archivists Project. Fullwood is the former assistant curator of the Manuscripts, Archives & Rare Books Division, Schomburg Center for Research in Black Culture. His books include *Black Gay Genius: Answering Joseph Beam's Call* (2014) and *Carry the Word: A Bibliography of Black LGBTQ Books* (2007). Currently, Fullwood is the cohost of *In the Telling*, a podcast focusing on the global Black family experience, and a regular contributor to *The American Age* podcast.

**Ariel Goldberg's** publications include *The Estrangement Principle* (2016) and *The Photographer* (2015). Goldberg's writing has most recently appeared in *Afterimage*, *e-flux*, *Artforum*, and *Art in America*. Goldberg teaches at CUNY, Bard College, and the New School. Their research and writing has been supported by the New York Public Library, the Franklin Furnace Fund, SOMA in Mexico City, and Smith College. They have been a curator at the Poetry Project, the Leslie-Lohman Museum of Art, and the Jewish History Museum in Tucson, Arizona.

**S*an D. Henry-Smith** is an artist and writer working primarily in poetry, photography, and performance, engaging Black experimentalisms and collaborative practices. They have received awards and fellowships from the Fulbright Program, the Poetry Project, Poets House, and Antenna/Paper Machine, and have read, performed, and exhibited at Basilica Soundscape, Issue Project Room, Brooklyn Museum, the Studio Museum in Harlem, and elsewhere. S*an collaborates with Imani Elizabeth Jackson as mouthfeel; their book *Consider the Tongue* explores histories of aquatic labor and Black food through cooking, poetry, and ephemeral practices. The author of two chapbooks, *Wild Peach* is S*an's first full-length collection.

**David Hirsh** cofounded the Visual AIDS Archive Project in 1994 with artist Frank Moore. He also co-organized a four-week Dance Festival of Lesbian Choreographers, and helped place the Martin Wong Collection of Graffiti Art at the Museum of the City of New York.

**Esther McGowan** is the Executive Director of Visual AIDS, and was Associate Director from 2012 to 2017. She is responsible for overseeing all of the organization's publications, programs, fundraising, and partnerships. She has worked with a variety of arts organizations over three decades, including the Bronx Museum of the Arts, Watermill Center, Arts International, Art Matters, Center for Fiction, Alliance for the Arts, Volunteer Lawyers for the Arts, and Whitney Museum of American Art.

**Lara Mimosa Montes** holds a PhD in English from the Graduate Center, City University of New York. She is a senior editor of *Triple Canopy*. She was born in the Bronx.

**Derek Conrad Murray** is an interdisciplinary theorist specializing in the history, theory, and criticism of contemporary art and visual culture. He works in contemporary aesthetic and cultural theory with a particular attention to technocultural engagements with identity and representation. He is currently a professor of history of art and visual culture at the University of California, Santa Cruz. Murray is the author of *Mapplethorpe and the Flower: Radical Sexuality and the Limits of Control* (2020) and *Queering Post-Black Art: Artists Transforming African-American Identity After Civil Rights* (2016).

**Tiana Reid** is a writer from Toronto. She lives in New York City, where she is a PhD candidate and instructor at Columbia University. Her work has been published in *Art in America*, *Bookforum*, *Canadian Art*, *Frieze*, *The New York Review of Books*, *The Nation*, *The New York Times*, *The Paris Review*, *Teen Vogue*, and *Vulture*, among others. She is a former senior editor at the *New Inquiry* and was a founding editor of *Pinko*, a print magazine of gay communism.

**Paul Mpagi Sepuya** is a Los Angeles–based artist working in photography. His work was featured in recent museum exhibitions at the Guggenheim Museum, the Barbican Centre, and the Getty Museum, and as a project for the 2019 Whitney Biennial. A survey of work from 2008 to 2018 was presented at CAM St. Louis and Blaffer Art Museum, University of Houston, accompanied by a monograph published by CAM St. Louis and Aperture Foundation. He is an acting associate professor in media arts at the University of California, San Diego.

# About Visual AIDS

Visual AIDS is the only contemporary arts organization fully committed to HIV and AIDS awareness through producing and presenting visual art projects. We assist artists living with HIV, preserve the legacies of those we have lost, and celebrate the artistic contributions of the AIDS movement.

Visual AIDS was founded in 1988 to address the devastation of the AIDS crisis on the arts community while impacting change through art, creating initiatives such as Day With(out) Art and the Red Ribbon. Our programs include grants to artists living with HIV, working with estates to preserve artistic legacies, and sharing the work of artists through our Archive Project and online Artist Registry. Visual AIDS strives to represent a diversity of voices within the HIV community by presenting exhibitions, public events, publications, and artist projects that raise awareness and highlight contemporary issues, reminding viewers and audiences that AIDS IS NOT OVER.

**Visual AIDS Staff**

Nancy Chong, Development Associate
Kyle Croft, Programs Director
Tracy Fenix, Archive and Artist Engagement Manager
Esther McGowan, Executive Director
Blake Paskal, Programs Associate

We are grateful to the Andy Warhol Foundation for the Visual Arts for providing a multiyear grant in support of our publications and to Furthermore: a program of the J. M. Kaplan Fund for additional support of this book.

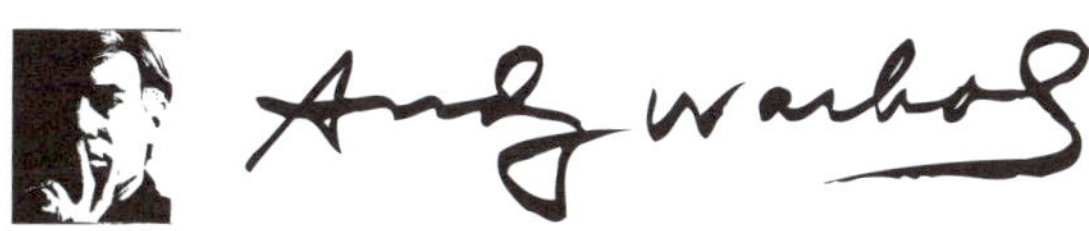

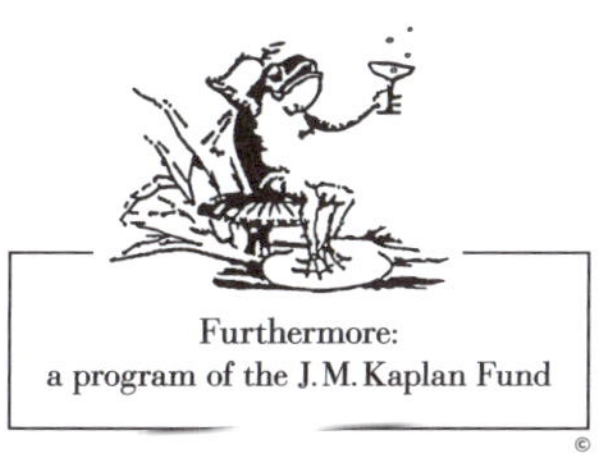


We would like to thank the following funders who support the work and mission of Visual AIDS:

Alphawood Foundation Chicago

Dr. Daniel S. Berger Charitable Giving Fund, a Donor Advised Fund of Renaissance Charitable Foundation

Between Bridges

Broadway Cares/Equity Fights AIDS

Council for Canadian American Relations

The Elizabeth Taylor AIDS Foundation

Gilead Sciences

The Keith Haring Foundation

Marta Heflin Foundation

Humanities NY

Japan Foundation

JW Anderson

Lambent Foundation Fund of Tides Foundation

LOEWE

National Endowment for the Arts

New York Community Trust's DIFFA Fund

New York Gay Pool League

NYU Community Fund

The Shelley and Donald Rubin Foundation

Supreme

Todd Snyder

ViiV Healthcare

Rafael & Diana Viñoly Foundation

and our generous individual donors

Visual AIDS receives support from the Henry Luce Foundation, the Willem de Kooning Foundation, and Teiger Foundation through the Coalition of Small Arts New York. Related programs are supported in part by public funds from the New York City Department of Cultural Affairs in partnership with the City Council. Additional funding is provided by the New York State Council on the Arts with the support of Governor Andrew Cuomo and the New York State Legislature.

**Visual**
**AIDS**

Darrel Ellis

Editors: Lara Mimosa Montes and Kyle Croft
Contributing editor: Brandon Eng
Production: Todd Bradway
Copy editor: Miles Champion

Designers: Brian Johnson, Silas Munro, and
Michelle Lamb, Polymode
Printed and bound by Faenza Group SpA, Italy

Printed on Magno Natural 140 g/m² and 150
g/m² Magno Volume
Typeset in Escalator and Signifier

Published by
Visual AIDS
526 W. 26th Street, #510
New York, NY 10001
www.visualaids.org

Distributed by
ARTBOOK | D.A.P.
75 Broad Street, Suite 630
New York, NY 10004
artbook.com

Publication © 2021, Visual AIDS
All artworks © 2021, the Estate of Darrel Ellis
All texts © 2021, the authors

ISBN 978-1-7326415-5-6
Library of Congress Control Number:
2021912357

Printed in Italy



Unless otherwise indicated, all images
courtesy of the Estate of Darrel Ellis and
photographed by Christopher Burke Studios.

pp. 9, 98, 152: courtesy of OSMOS; pp. 11,
149, 164, 166, 167 (left), 183: courtesy of
Allen Frame; pp. 24, 79–81, 82, 86, 100,
110, 133: courtesy of Galerie Crone, Berlin;
pp. 29, 160, 172, 173, 178, 179: photographer
unknown, courtesy of the Estate of Darrel
Ellis; pp. 32, 54, 120, 181: photo by Adam
Reich, courtesy of Candice Madey; p. 71:
photo by guenzel.rademacher, courtesy of
Sebastian Daub; p. 112: photo by Mitro Hood,
courtesy of The Baltimore Museum of Art;
pp. 134, 177: © 1987 The Peter Hujar Archive
LLC, courtesy The Peter Hujar Archive, Pace
Gallery, New York and Fraenkel Gallery, San
Francisco; p. 156: courtesy of Ron Clark; pp.
161–163: courtesy of James Wentzy; p. 163
(bottom): MoMA PS1 Archives, IV.224. The
Museum of Modern Art Archives, New York;
p. 167 (right): Courtesy of Steven Harvey

Front cover: Darrel Ellis, *Untitled (Mother and
Laure)*, 1990. Detail
Back cover: Darrel Ellis, *Untitled (Self-
Portrait)*, ca. 1990–92
Endpapers: Photographs by Thomas Ellis,
ca. 1950s

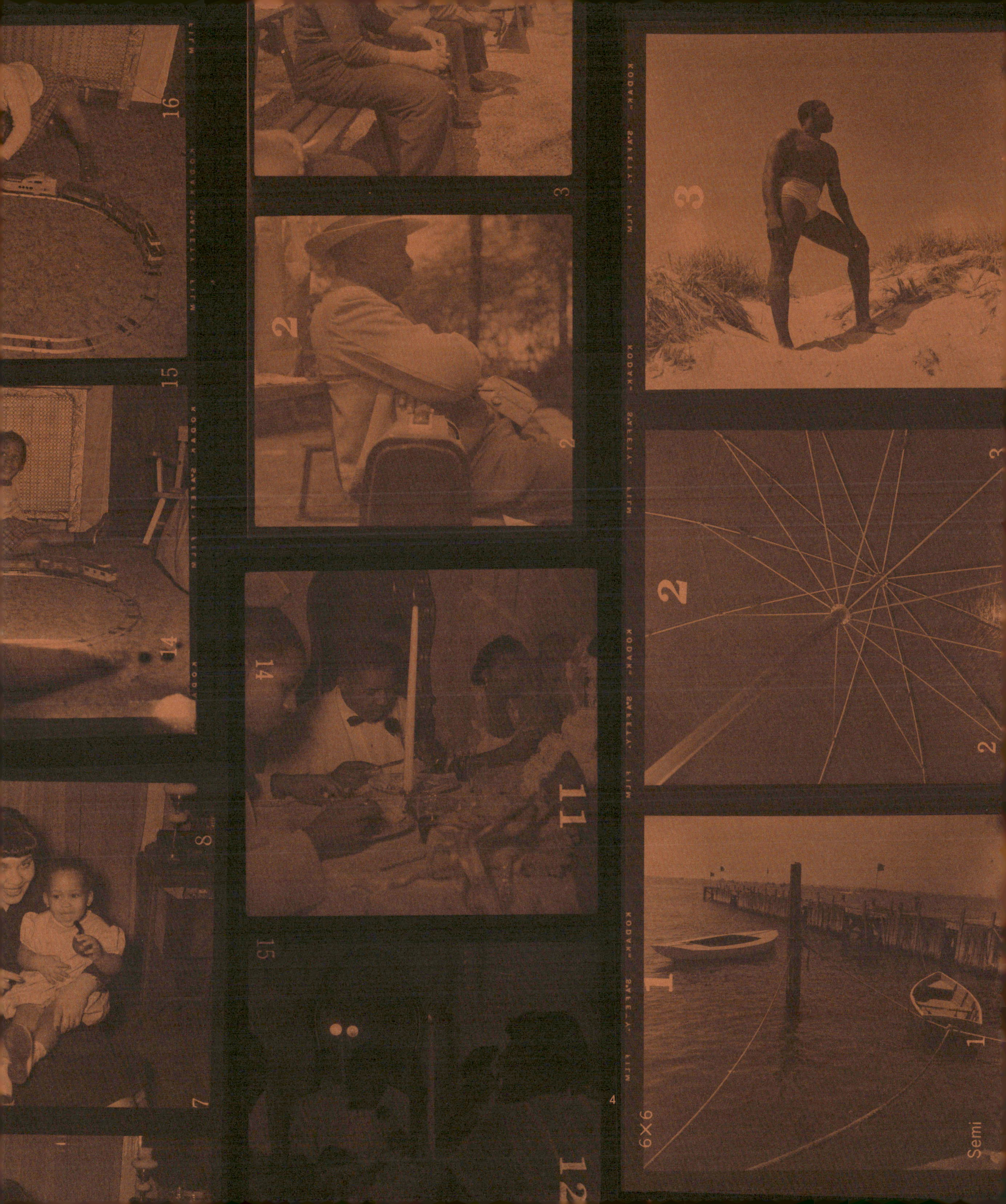

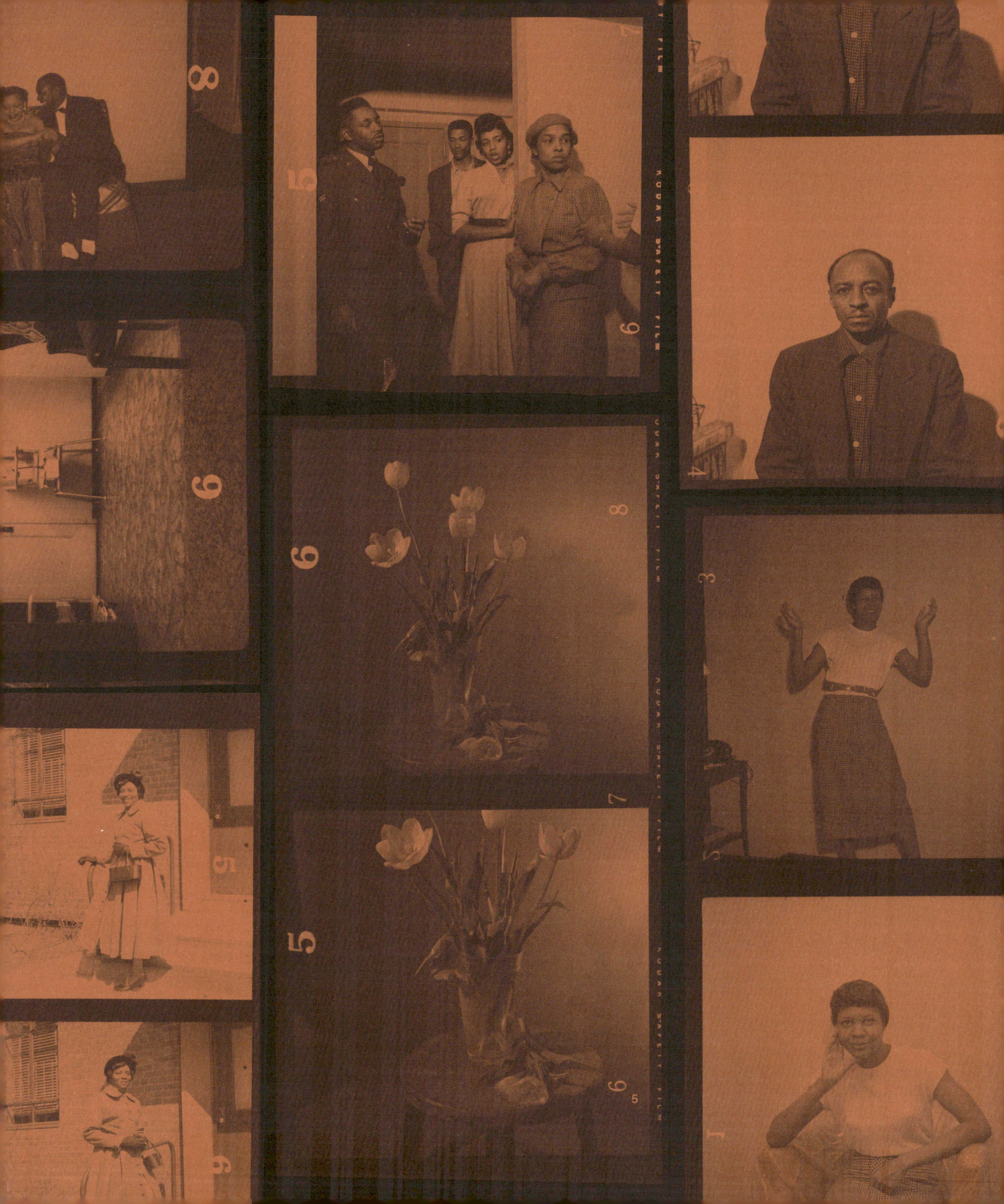